REFRAMING PAUL

Conversations in Grace & Community

Mark Strom

InterVarsity Press
Downers Grove, Illinois

InterVarsity Press
P.O. Box 1400, Downers Grove, IL 60515
World Wide Web: www.ivpress.com
E-mail: mail@ivpress.com

InterVarsity Press® is the book-publishing division of InterVarsity Christian Fellowship/USA®, a student movement active on campus at hundreds of universities, colleges and schools of nursing in the United States of America, and a member movement of the International Fellowship of Evangelical Students. For information about local and regional activities, write Public Relations Dept., InterVarsity Christian Fellowship/USA, 6400 Schroeder Rd., P.O. Box 7895, Madison, WI 53707-7895.

Cover photograph: Victoria & Albert Museum, London/Art Resource, NY

ISBN 0-8308-1570-8

Printed in the United States of America ∞

Library of Congress Cataloging-in-Publication Data

Strom, Mark, 1956-
  Reframing Paul : conversations in grace & community / Mark Strom.
    p. cm.
  Includes bibliograqphical references.
  ISBN 0-8308-1570-8 (pbk. : alk. paper)
    1. Paul, the Apostle, Saint. 2. Bible. N.T. Epistles of Paul—Theology. 3. Philosophy, Ancient—Influence. I. Title.

BS2651 .S86 2000
225.9'2—dc21

00-057541

| 19 | 18 | 17 | 16 | 15 | 14 | 13 | 12 | 11 | 10 | 9 | 8 | 7 | 6 | 5 | 4 | 3 | 2 | 1 |
| 15 | 14 | 13 | 12 | 11 | 10 | 09 | 08 | 07 | 06 | 05 | 04 | 03 | 02 | 01 | 00 | | | |

CONTENTS

Introduction

Around the world, more and more evangelicals are giving up on church. They no longer relate to the sermons and services, systems and cultures that shape church life. Two desires stem from this disillusionment. The first is for grace to subvert the expectations and games of church life. The second is for meaningful and grace-full conversation to replace the irrelevance and harm of much theology, preaching and church life.

Many wonder if they are alone in their suspicion that something is very wrong. Some sense dissonance between the New Testament gatherings and our own conventions of leadership and church. Some ask whether we have misrepresented Paul and his writings. Looking afresh at his anguished relationship with the Corinthians, we may well ask if we have sided with Paul—or with those sophists he derided as "super-apostles."

This book brings together in conversation two worlds: Paul's and our own. My aim is to offer a different view of both worlds as a starting point for grace-full conversation around Christ and everyday life. Doing so will inevitably reopen questions about the nature of church and theology. This is a historical study with a personal twist. The issues have never been merely academic for me; they have persisted through the eras of my life as a goad to experiencing grace and freedom as Jesus intended: from the Jesus movement to mysticism to Reformed theology and beyond; from trucker to theological student to "tentmaking" church planter and university chaplain to corporate strategy and leadership consultant. Searching for grace-full conversation led me to extended research in the ancient sources of Paul's day. If we understand how contemporary ideas and conventions shaped the ways the message of Jesus Christ influenced Paul and his friends, then we find a vantage point for fresh conversation about its significance to us.

Since Paul's gatherings largely consisted of Gentiles in the cities of Asia Minor, Greece and Rome, I have majored on the Graeco-Roman (Greek and Roman) contexts for his life and thought. Paul's background was, of course, Jewish. But our understanding of his dealings with the small groups who embraced his message is most enriched by knowledge of the Graeco-Roman ideas and conventions that shaped their interactions with him.

Many scholars have devoted themselves to identifying formal parallels between biblical authors and their supposed Graeco-Roman counterparts. A virtual industry has developed searching for parallels to Paul among Stoics, Epicureans, Cynics, Hellenistic Jewish scholars, mystics and other tall figures of the ancient past. But as social historian Edwin Judge has argued, it is a waste of time to look for conscious dependence by Paul on classical identities or on specific schools of thought. Paul did not represent any school, yet neither was he isolated from them:

> If one is the kind of independent thinker that Paul is, one is simply building out freely from that, exploiting the material rather than subjecting oneself to it. The ways forward for historical research in this field in my opinion lie along the lines of studying this kind of popular intellectualism. . . . In any community there is a fluid and active field of thought-convention which belongs to every intelligent man and in which he shares.[1]

The significance of this "popular intellectualism" to understanding Paul and his associates depends on where they were placed socially. Older scholarship characterized the Gentile Christians as poor and illiterate masses of dispossessed peasants and slaves—like the crowds in a 1950s B-grade gladiator movie! But it is now clear that Paul moved among "persons of substance, members of a cultivated social elite . . . 'devout and honourable' citizens of the Hellenistic states."[2] More recent scholarship confirms that many members of Paul's groups, especially at Corinth and Thessalonica, were well-connected people with wealth and social influence.

The task before us, then, is (1) to reframe the life and thought of Paul in the light of his Graeco-Roman world; (2) to examine the conventions and systems of evangelicalism in this light; and (3) to reframe church and theology as grace-full conversation.

I wish to thank the supervisors of my original research[3]—Professor David Russell of the University of Western Sydney and Dr. Stuart Piggin of Macquarie Univer-

---

[1]Edwin Judge, "St. Paul and Socrates," *Interchange* 14 (1973): 106–16.
[2]Edwin Judge, "The Early Christians as a Scholastic Community: Part II," *Journal of Religious History* 1 (1960): 125–37.
[3]Mark Strom, "Conversing Across the Ages: A Conversation Around Some Intellectual and Social Paradigms of Graeco-Roman Antiquity, the Apostle Paul and Modern Evangelicalism" (Ph.D. diss., University of Western Sydney, 1997).

sity. I am particularly indebted to Professor Edwin Judge of Macquarie University for his insights into Paul and Graeco-Roman society. Professor Robert Banks of Macquarie Christian Studies Institute and Dr. Chris Forbes of Macquarie University read the original research and offered crucial corrections and encouragement. Many friends continue to share the journey. Our conversations frequently set my thoughts free. You know who you are—thanks, folks.

Most of all, I salute Susan, Miriam, Luke and Hannah. I may have thought of most of it first, but Susan has always been part of the conversation. Thanks for all the talks and the sheer hard work. May Miriam, Luke and Hannah's generation find greater realism and freedom, and richer grace-full conversation, than our own.

Mark Strom

1

REFRAMING OUR CONVERSATION WITH PAUL

ABSTRACTION, IDEALISM AND ELITISM SHAPED THE WORLD OF PAUL. INTELLECTUAL AND social traditions of great antiquity reinforced the priority of abstract and general concepts over the particulars of everyday life. These abstract concepts, such as beauty, goodness and moderation, translated into ideals of true behavior and noble character. These ideals, in turn, maintained a social system in which one was constantly reminded of one's place on the social ladder. The elite must remain elite; the less so must always defer.

Paul fought against the influence of abstraction, idealism and elitism upon his *ekklēsiai*.[1] Ultimately, Paul lost. Only a generation or two after the apostle, the abstract categories of theology had become the model for discussing his God and message. Ideals of Graeco-Roman morality like serenity, moderation and courage shaped the ways believers read and applied Paul's instructions on the life of faith. Church conventions of leadership and authority adapted and reinforced the common marks of rank and status. Similar conventions of abstraction, idealism and

---

[1]I will refer to Paul's groups as *ekklēsia* (singular) or *ekklēsiai* (plural). The word *church* is so heavily laden with tradition gathered through the centuries as to prejudice discussion of what Paul's groups actually were and did. In my experience, this is as true of evangelicalism as of any other Christian tradition. I use the Greek terms for Paul's groups to keep the options open.

elitism have continued to shape Christian thought and practice almost without exception and across all traditions to the present day. Evangelicalism is no exception.[2]

In many ways evangelical thought resembles the categories and methods of classical and Graeco-Roman philosophy and theology. Our interpretive and theological procedures too often abstract the text from its historical and modern settings in order to establish what we regard as undiluted, absolute and objective truth. Ignoring the differences between Paul's words to Corinth, Rome and Ephesus, we reduce the data to supposed common denominators in order to formulate the abstract theological concepts of "Paul's doctrine of church," "Paul's doctrine of leadership" or "the center of Paul's theology." The truth is seen to lie above any historical and cultural setting. This, as we shall see, is Plato, not Paul. Paul's letters are reduced from rich and provocative narratives and improvisations to a data base for systems of theology.

Abstraction, idealism and elitism lay at the heart of the agendas of pride that Paul tried to tear apart. At Corinth that pride fueled the stand-off between the "strong" and the "weak." Both were convinced of the reasonableness and superiority of their respective views. It is not too much of an imposition to put our terms— *biblical* and *unbiblical*—into their mouths. Both groups appeared confident of being demonstrably right. Yet Paul did not adjudicate between them. Instead, he urged a new mindset that was clear of foolish and destructive games about who was more "biblical."

---

[2]It is harder to define evangelicalism than it is to recognize a person or group as evangelical. Most evangelicals define themselves by certain theological distinctives: in particular, Jesus Christ as a real historical person who died for our sins and physically rose from the dead, his centrality to all questions of personal salvation and biblical interpretation, and the complete trustworthiness and authority of the Bible. Evangelicals often distinguish themselves from those they would call fundamentalists, Pentecostals, charismatics, sacramentalists and liberals. Some who go by these other labels also consider themselves to be evangelical. I am happy for the reader to judge whether my sources and sketches fit those groups commonly accepted as evangelical. Many see evangelicalism as only a theological phenomenon. Some refuse any validity to cultural definitions. Don Carson, a widely regarded North American scholar and preacher, argues that evangelicalism is "Christianity at its straightforward best." John Stott, a British evangelical, wrote, "It is the contention of Evangelicals that they are plain Bible Christians, and that in order to be a biblical Christian it is necessary to be an Evangelical Christian" (*Christ the Controversialist* [Leicester: Inter-Varsity Press, 1970], p. 32). The concern is that sociological explanations may misrepresent evangelicalism by ignoring what is central, namely, its theology. There is some validity in this concern. Yet those who voice it may too easily obscure the social realities. My interest is in the ways certain themes from Paul and the Graeco-Roman world continue to shape the experience of evangelical cultural and social patterns. My concern is with what happens in the living experience of evangelical conventions, ideals and beliefs. For historical and sociological analyses of evangelicalism, see James Hunter, *Evangelicalism: The Coming Generation* (Chicago: University of Chicago Press, 1987) and David Bebbington, *Evangelicalism in Modern Britain: A History from the 1730s to the 1980s* (Grand Rapids, Mich.: Baker, 1989).

Paul "reframed" their dispute. His method of reframing brilliantly integrated matters of the heart and matters of the mind. First, he affirmed the position of each group. Both groups saw at least part of the issues correctly. Second, he discredited the position of each group by emphasizing its destructive outcomes. Each group could destroy the other. Third, he reframed the issue in terms of their common identity and purpose. They would destroy the brother for whom Christ had died. Paul did not urge them toward a single correct position. Rather, he called for the death of intellectual and social self-interest: "Knowledge puffs up, but love builds up" (1 Cor 8:1). Fourth, Paul modeled this new disposition of heart and mind in his own refusal of the rights and status of being an apostle: "Though I am free and belong to no man, I make myself a slave to everyone, to win as many as possible" (1 Cor 9:19).

At the heart of Paul's reframing of this dispute was his preoccupation with Christ, who brought coherence to Paul's conversations. Every one of Paul's letters shows him working from the story of Christ to reframe disputes, ideals and expectations in the fledgling *ekklēsiai.* This same preoccupation with Christ is a great strength of evangelical teaching. Theologians and preachers rightly insist on seeing the person and work of Christ as the focal point of the Scriptures. Yet even "the gospel" can become another abstraction. In Paul's thought, neither Christ, nor his dying and rising, nor even his gospel was an idea or category of ideas or ideals removed from relationship. Paul knew and wanted to know the person of Christ, not theological ideas or processes abstracted from him.

Paul offered no set formula for how we are to identify with Christ. He did not blunt the challenge of choosing to die with Christ in order to rise with him as Christ saw fit. Paul's doublets—weakness-strength, poor-rich, slave-free, dishonorable-honorable, suffering-joy—framed the challenges of love and obedience. But they did not settle those choices in advance. Paul was at pains to lift his friends' expectations away from moral codes and to ensure that they did not turn their new freedom into a further set of rules.

Paul would not allow any human system or convention to hedge the communities against the risks of working out what it meant to live by the dying and rising of Christ. Such security would only throw the community back on their own resources, and reinforce individual and communal boasting. The openness of Paul's life and thought to the world around him contrasts with the insularity of parts of evangelicalism. Paul urged believers to remain in the world for the sake of both the gospel and the world; we have frequently retreated into institutional and privatized ghettos. There is a certain irony in this. While evangelicals generally do not warm to the concept of a state church, we have erected what is in effect a Christendom—complete with large organizational structures vying for public influence, educational institutions spanning kindergarten to university, and a vast network of bureaucrats, businesses, tradespeople and professionals. In a further irony, this imitation of "secular" structures has not brought the everyday world within the scope of theology and the gathering. Indeed, it may have deepened the ways we split life into the sacred and the secular.

Paul's gatherings focused on integrating allegiance to Jesus Christ with everyday concerns. The people met to equip one another for the decisions and options they would face outside the gathering. The gathering did not convene for religious worship. They did not gather for a rite. Nor do the sources suggest a meeting structured around the reading and exposition of Scripture following the model of the synagogue. They met to fellowship around their common relationship to one another on account of Christ. Most evangelicals agree that a rite is not central to church; most argue that preaching is central. But rite and preaching share common ground. Both are clergy-centered. Perhaps the reason so many theologians and clergy resist any shift away from the centrality of the sermon lies not only in the fear of subjectivism or heresy, but also in the fear of losing control and prestige.

Professionalism, even elitism, marks the sermon and the service and distinguishes clergy from congregation. Paul faced something similar at Corinth. The strong had transferred to themselves certain social and religious marks of rank and status—education, eloquence, a leader's style, even clothing. They had also come to regard the fruits of Christ's work—the Spirit and the evidences of his presence—as further marks of status, even "spiritual" status. Paul would not tolerate this creation of new rank within the assembly. He urged the Corinthians to see what they had as gifts of grace. They must honor the least honorable. This was not conventional; it was not moral. This was not theology; it was not about words. This was the meaning of grace.

Little in modern Christian experience matches this. Academic, congregational and denominational life functions along clear lines of rank, status and honor. We preach that the gospel has ended elitism, but we rarely allow the implications to go beyond ideas. Paul, however, actually stepped down in the world. His inversions of status were social realities, not intellectualized reforms.

Paul urged leaders to imitate his personal example of how the message of Jesus inverted status. He was at pains to dissociate himself from the sophists, those traveling orator-teacher-lawyers of his day (1 Cor 2:1-5). Though undoubtedly educated and skilled, he did not imitate the sophists' eloquence and persona. In so doing, Paul set himself on a collision course with the contemporary conventions of personal honor—and with his potential patrons. He refused to show favoritism toward individuals or *ekklēsiai*. The gospel offered him rights, but he refused them. Christ was not a means to a career. Yet today the agendas and processes of maintaining and reforming evangelical life and thought remain the domain of professional scholars and clergy. Their ministry is their career.

Dying and rising with Christ meant status reversal. In Paul's case, he deliberately stepped down in the world. We must not romanticize this choice. He felt the shame of it among his peers and potential patrons yet held it as the mark of his sincerity. Moreover, it played a crucial role in the interplay of his life and thought. Tentmaking was critical, even central, to his life and message. His labor and ministry were mutually explanatory. Yet for most of us, "tentmaking" belongs in the realms of missionary journals and far-flung shores. As a model for ministry in the United States, Britain or Australia, it remains as unseemly to most of us as it did to the Corinthians. At best it is second best.

Evangelicalism will not shake its abstraction, idealism and elitism until theologians and clergy are prepared to step down in their worlds. Some might argue that since the world often shows contempt for the pastoral role, then professional ministry is itself a step back. But that is to ignore the more pertinent set of social realities: evangelicalism has its own ranks, careers, financial security, marks of prestige and rewards. Within that world, professional ministry is rank and status.

Ministry as profession feeds the pride that separates the seminary and the pulpit from the congregation. It makes Paul abstract. Theological enterprise becomes self-serving. It entombs its service to the body in inaccessible journals, jargon and symposia. It impoverishes the congregation both by withholding its own contributions from them and by reinforcing the unspoken verdict that so-called lay theology can only ever be second rate. Indeed, the term *lay* itself patronizes and disaffects. Paul's letters sprang from a profound love and desire for God and his Christ, and for their *ekklēsiai*. Exegesis, theology and preaching from any other source must succumb to boasting:

> Pride ruins scholarly endeavor. . . . In Western tradition, this pride goes back especially to Greek philosophy. . . . The Enlightenment exacerbated the problem by bringing in pride at its very core. . . . And now we see almost the whole of the scholarly world conquered by the Enlightenment. . . . It is wiser to admit the truth: the Enlightenment and its fruits have been a vast disaster. . . . We who are Evangelicals like to hear such things. But we have troubles of our own. . . . We take pride in our orthodoxy, our championing of the Bible, our spiritual enlightenment. . . (our) scholarship. . . even in the supposed spirituality of an anti-intellectual fuzziness. . . . We need more than merely technical aids in order to produce right understanding of the Bible. We need the knowledge of God.[3]

Evangelicalism has inherited the concerns of both Paul and his contemporaries. The numerous resemblances between our own cultures and conventions and those

---

[3]Vern Poythress, *The Supremacy of God in Interpretation* (Philadelphia: prepublication manuscript, 1992), pp. 52–57.

of the Graeco-Roman world offer entry points for new conversation. They can allow us to challenge our assumptions to be demonstrably "biblical." Such conversations may suggest new vantage points on what it meant then and means now to gather in community for conversation.

Paul's conversation about God and the affairs of his people did not depend on abstraction or idealism. He did not arbitrate for his *ekklēsiai* according to some rule of rationality or bend his own thoughts toward any criteria of absolute, timeless truths. Every shred of Paul's conversation remained anchored in his wonder at Christ and in the changing circumstances of everyday life. This is not to say that conversation was lost among Paul's contemporaries, as though he (re)discovered the art and joy of conversing about the everyday. It is to say that classical and Graeco-Roman intellectuals often devalued those experiences of everyday life that they sought to understand and shape. Something other than the everyday all too easily assumed greater importance. It is in this sense that Paul's conversations took on much of their distinctiveness.

Paul's conversations were rich in stories. These stories characterized the gathering. The believers came together around Christ and his story. They also came with their own stories. They came to (re)connect their stories to his and to each others' stories. That was the gathering. They taught, prophesied, shared, ate, sang and prayed their stories—their lives—together around Christ. The Spirit made the conversation possible. All the people shared the Spirit through whom they met God and one another face to face. They urged one another in conversation to grow into the full measure of their freedom and dignity.

Recent emphases on community are welcome and helpful.[4] But they may simply lead to more *talk* about change, rather than to *actual* change. We must grapple with how our cultures and conventions systemically and pervasively, even deliberately, gag the most important conversations. The sermon and the service have hijacked conversation. There are conventions for talking and listening, but next to none for true dialogue. Preaching does not allow it. Worship services do not allow it. Theological debate does not allow it. Each has its semblance of conversation. But the rules of each game militate against an open-ended meeting of hearts and minds, free from the controlling agendas of keeping the systems in place.

Am I dismissing evangelicalism? That is not my intent or my disposition. I deeply appreciate much in the traditional emphases of evangelical teachers. I have profited greatly from them. If I must be labeled, then label me an evangelical. But evangelicalism reflects both Paul and the Graeco-Roman world. At our best, we faithfully portray the cutting edge of Paul's remarkable message. I believe this to be

---

[4]See for example, Stanley Grenz, *Revisioning Evangelical Theology: A Fresh Agenda for the 21st Century* (Downers Grove, Ill.: InterVarsity Press, 1993).

true even of sources that I will quote critically in later chapters. At our worst, we have lost the radicalness of grace and freedom championed by Paul.

New conversation requires bringing things to the light. It requires discussing the undiscussable. Conventions of status and control inevitably arise wherever a human system incorporates norms and expectations of authority, order and rectitude. Likewise pride, insecurity and fear are always close at hand. Paul was well aware of the games played by his contemporaries. On at least one memorable occasion he set aside theological accuracy in preference for mutual love and respect grounded in wonder at the impartiality of God's grace. Those of us who long to converse meaningfully with Paul and with each other must wrestle with the wisdom of his choice.

What kinds of new conversation do I envisage? First of all, I visualize not the neutral posturing of traditional exegesis and theology, nor the pseudo-interaction of preaching and church service, but people engaging with one another around concern and desire grounded in their everyday experiences. At heart is a rhythm between ancient narrative and modern story, between insight and healing. The agenda is as broad as life. The mood may be analytical and incisive, light and irreverent, deep and therapeutic. Maybe all, some or none of the above. At its heart are people wrestling with the Spirit and with one another to know the truth, grace and freedom of Christ in all the particulars of who they are and what fills their lives. I think of them as "grace-full" conversations. Conversations marked by grace. Conversations full of grace. Conversations that bring grace.

In the last three chapters I will chronicle my own sense of grace-full conversation lost and regained. But our task now is to enrich our understanding of Paul's world, then of Paul himself, so that we might recover for ourselves more of the vitality of his life and thought. My experience and hope is that in reframing our conversations with Paul we may reframe what it means to live with one another in grace-full conversation.

PART 1

PRIMARY REALITY &
EVERYDAY REALITY

Ancient Frames for a Split World

2

FROM HOMER
TO PLATO

THE PRESUMPTION THAT A PURER REALITY LAY SOMEWHERE OTHER THAN IN EVERYDAY LIFE colored the ideas and social life of Paul's day. Not everyone agreed about just what this purer reality was. Philosophers, poets and teachers put forward widely different, even contradictory descriptions. Yet the basic presumption persisted in literary and nonliterary sources from at least seven hundred years before Paul's lifetime.

This belief was like seeing life split into two realities. To simplify things I have called these *primary reality* and *everyday reality* (see figure 2.1). How the two were understood to relate to each other varied widely. Three things held constant, however. First, the two realities were *connected* in some way. Second, the relationship was *problematic*. Third, each *influenced* the other.

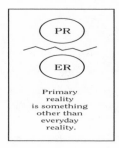 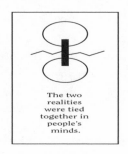 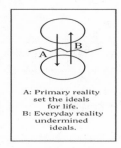

Figure 2.1. The relationship between primary reality and everyday reality

The links between belief in both realities generated deep conflict and ingenious rationalizations. If the everyday world of experience was a smaller version of a greater reality, then the uncertainty and brokenness of everyday life raised hard questions about the elegant models of a perfect reality. But most theorists lived the lifestyle of the local elite. An intellectual living a privileged life could dismiss and rationalize the stinging contradictions of other people's experiences as mere illusion and irrelevance. A professional orator might move an audience to applaud the moral ideal of emotional detachment. Yet that ideal could crumble in the face of a dying child.

We need to see some of the ways this belief in two realities influenced both the people Paul encountered and the ways he lived and framed his message. We particularly need to understand the influence of ideals on everyday life. We will see how common experience upheld these ideals as a vision that gave order and meaning to everyday life, *and* how the harsh realities of life often undermined these same ideals.

In our terms, what do I mean by *primary reality* and *everyday reality?* Think of church. Theologians and preachers largely talk about *the* doctrine of church. But where does this *single* ideal come from? Certainly not from Paul's letters, since he did not standardize the gatherings with which he was associated. A plain look at Paul's letters makes *the* doctrine look rather forced. However, what happens as more people see through these ideals and begin to press for change? Many theologians and churchmen simply convince themselves that they must reinforce the ideals. This is a problem of *primary reality* and *everyday reality*.

But I am getting ahead of myself. Like the fashions of our own time, the Graeco-Roman mood often romanticized and blended the styles of the past. Our search requires us to begin several centuries before Paul.

The Shape of Primary Reality in Early Greek Literature

Homer's character Odysseus sees traces of the gods throughout the world of men.[1] To some, the gods actually appear.[2] When they do appear, they disguise themselves so well that few men ever understand what has happened until after the fact. When they drop the disguises, the gods tower over men, radiating brilliant light, captivating with other-worldly beauty and striking awe with their pounding voices and rapid departures. While the gods may have cared, there was a limit to this familiarity.

---

[1] My use of the masculine is deliberate. Whenever I focus on the ancient world, I refer to *man* and *men*. This is how the ancients uniformly wrote and spoke of humankind as generic and, more often, simply because they discounted women as a worthy audience.

[2] Homer *Odyssey* 14.19-23.

In a bygone age it had been different, and this fragile past survived in Homer's idyllic Phaeacia.

Hesiod's *Theogony* wove together generations of tradition with a new criticism ready to tell the truth about the gods: "We know how to say many lies as if they were true, and when we want, we know how to speak the truth."[3] In his work on the theology of the earliest Greek philosophers, Jaeger argued that Hesiod's epic provided the patterns for later, more systematic and theological thought. Those patterns were

☐ the primacy of chaos

☐ the origin of chaos in some form of generation

☐ the notion of generation as a basic picture of cause and effect

☐ the hint that something existed at the beginning *(archē)* of all becoming without itself coming into being

☐ the subjection of gods and humans to universal law[4]

Hesiod, it seems, was moving to a place where gods and men alike would yield to reason. But in most ancient literature, the gods continued to live somewhere beyond the everyday world of mortals. The encounters of gods and men could not bridge the great gulf between them. Neither could those moments solve that great riddle of destiny, providence and chance: How did a man's will intersect with the greater powers that rule the world?

The poet Aeschylus did nothing to bridge the gulf: "From their high-towering hopes . . . all that is wrought by the powers divine is free from toil."[5] But he also foreshadowed a more systematic treatment of reality. The name of Zeus soon begins to imply more than just another god. It takes on the character of the ultimate justice of Providence, whose designs reconcile the rival claims of men and the powers within an ordered universe. Likewise, the playwright Sophocles moved beyond piety to actively reflect on the universal laws that could explain the actions of both gods and men.

In the amusing argument of Euripides and Aeschylus in Aristophanes' *Frogs,* Euripides shows scant inclination to rely on the old myths to convey his purposes. The time has come to put myth on a diet of reason:

> No hippococks or goatstags, for a start—or any other mythical monsters from Persian tapestries. When I took over Tragedy from you, the poor creature was in a dreadful state. Fatty degeneration of the Art. All swollen up with high-falutin' diction. I soon got her weight down, though: put her on a diet of particles, with a little finely chopped

---

[3]Hesiod *Theogony* 27.
[4]W. Jaeger, *The Theology of the Early Greek Philosophers* (Oxford: Oxford University Press, 1947), pp. 13–15.
[5]Aeschylus *Suppliant Maidens* 100–103.

logic (taken peripatetically), and a special decoction of dialectic, cooked up from books and strained to facilitate digestion.[6]

The Emerging Intellectual Consensus on Primary Reality

This growing sophistication came into its own with the pre-Socratic philosophers.[7] Common ground had emerged. First, an intrinsic principle of order could be discerned in the world and in history. Second, all things could be explained by the one set of principles. Third, any explanation should emphasize simplicity and singularity without pretentious elegance.

A common vocabulary emerged to carry the investigation:

☐ *kosmos* spoke of the totality of things, the ordered and elegant universe

☐ *physis* meant not only nature (those things not made by men, not *technē*) but more importantly, the principle that pervades the natural part of the universe—what makes something what it is and not something else

☐ *archai,* the first principles, the basic stuffs of the universe that make the *kosmos* what it is

☐ *logos,* word or argument or critical thought—an account of the world that one could rationally consider and believe, not the incredible tales of former cosmologies.

This new account opened with the Milesians (Thales, Anaximander and Anaximenes) searching for the *archai,* the stuff that shapes all reality. These *archai* were infinite, imperishable and shaped by the creative tension of opposites. Writing much later, Aristotle looked back with admiration:

> It is with reason that they all make [the infinite] a principle; for it can neither exist to no purpose nor have any power except that of a principle. For everything is either a principle or derived from a principle. But the infinite has no principle—for then it would have a limit. . . . And it is also divine; for it is deathless and unperishing, as Anaximander and most of the natural scientists say.[8]

The creative tension of opposites and the eternal motion of reality allowed the Milesians, as well as Pythagoras and Heraclitus, to grant a place to change within an otherwise fixed reality. For Pythagoras, history was an unwavering, endlessly recurring cycle in which the soul passes through a sequence of incarnations. Likewise for Heraclitus, "the world [is] the same for all, neither any god nor any man made; but it was always and is and will be, fire ever-living, kindling

---

[6]Aristophanes *Frogs* 959.
[7]The summary points in this paragraph and the next come from Jonathon Barnes, *Early Greek Philosophy* (London: Penguin, 1987), pp. 9–24.
[8]Aristotle *Physics* 203b6–11.

in measures and being extinguished in measures."[9]

Change was therefore part and parcel of the *kosmos* and must therefore be a basic principle of any underlying reality. But the Eleatics (Parmenides, Melissus and Zeno) started at the other end. Change was too obviously linked to imperfection and decay. Our senses show us change, but true being, the essential reality behind all things, must be perfect. However, whatever is perfect must not change (or so the argument went). Now the argument really starts to get heady. If reality is perfect, and perfection doesn't leave room for change, then what we see as change is only a surface view of things, an illusion. Reason shows us we are being tricked. True being cannot involve change. Being, or reality, is pure, single and unchanging: "Being . . . is infinite . . . unique . . . changeless . . . always homogenous with itself . . . can neither perish nor grow nor change its arrangement nor suffer pain nor suffer anguish . . . [nor] move."[10]

Empedocles preserved Parmenides' and Melissus's arguments that nothing comes into existence or ceases to exist.[11] But he also revived the earlier idea of a creative tension between opposite principles. Motion and change are possible, since the eternal stuffs (earth, air, fire, water) can move and change places according to the opposing powers of Love and Strife working via chance and necessity. Several centuries after Paul, Simplicius looked back on Empedocles' insight this way:

> [Empedocles] also hints at a double world—one intelligible and the other perceptible, one divine and the other mortal, one containing things as paradigms and the other as copies. He showed this when he said that not only generated and perishable things are composed of these but so too are the gods. . . . In the following verses too you might think he is hinting at a double world: "For they are all in union with their own parts— Sun and Earth and Heaven and Sea—which have been separated from them and grown in mortal things."[12]

The idea of twin realities or opposing forces raised the question of balance. If two powers or realities shape the cosmos, then perfect reality would hold these in perfect balance. Now apply this idea to people and watch how it becomes an ideal. If each person is a microcosm of the whole, then balance must be the key virtue of a truly harmonious life. According to Plutarch, a contemporary of Paul's, another pre-Socratic named Alcmaeon had anticipated this response: "Alcmaeon says that health is conserved by egalitarianism among the powers—wet and dry, cold and

---

[9]Heraclitus *Fragment* B30.
[10]Melissus, in Simplicius *Commentary on the Physics* 103.13–104.15.
[11]We depend heavily for our understanding of these pre-Socratics on a commentary by Simplicius (sixth century A.D.). There is an obvious question as to how well Simplicius retained what the pre-Socratics intended.
[12]Simplicius *Commentary on the Physics* 160.8–161.1.

hot, bitter and sweet and the rest—[illness] comes by an excess . . . [or] from a sur-feit . . . health is the proportionate blending of the qualities."[13]

In a bold new move, Anaxagoras dismissed both the Eleatics and Empedocles, and argued that every substance or stuff is eternal—there are no "basic" elements or stuffs. Moreover, no stuff is ever entirely separate from the others (i.e., there are no pure stuffs); each stuff has a bit of all the others. So there is no purest or small-est piece of reality.

It sounds like Anaxagoras has contradicted our theme of a split view of reality. But there's more. Behind the cosmos is mind, pervading everything and responsi-ble for everything. Later philosophers saw a designer here, but for Anaxagoras this mind was probably an impersonal force:

> Mind is something infinite and self-controlling, and it has been mixed with no thing but is alone itself by itself. . . . For it is the finest of all things and the purest, and it possesses all knowledge about everything, and it has the greatest strength. And mind controls all those things, both great and small, which possess soul. . . . All mind, both great and small, is alike. . . . Mind is where all the other things also are.[14]

The atomists, Leucippus and Democritus, offered a further picture of reality. Rather than appeal to contrary forces or to an all-embracing One, they concluded that the universe consisted of an infinite number of bodies in an infinitely extended void. These bodies have primary qualities (size, shape, hardness, etc.) and combine in an infinite number of substances.[15]

What are we to make of all these theories?

First, there was no single "pre-Socratic" explanation of reality. Some put for-ward alternate proposals for first principles. Some emphasized the creative interac-tions of eternally opposing principles. Some looked to an all-embracing One. Some thought of "simple" stuffs shaped by pervasive mind. Others argued for atomism. What was incredible to one pre-Socratic was irrefutable to another.

Second, each theory presumed a greater reality behind the world we know. The key task was to peel back the everyday in order to uncover the essence of true real-ity. This concept held good throughout classical and Graeco-Roman times and even down to our own day. We can see its traces in the ways theologians and preachers today peel back the text of Scripture in search of its "essential truth."

Third, the investigation challenged tradition and convention. Xenophanes ridi-culed the immoral behavior of the gods in Homer and the poets, and dismissed cus-tomary religious beliefs as groundless. The gods must yield to the categories of a

---

[13]Plutarch *On the Scientific Beliefs of the Philosophers* 911A.
[14]Anaxagoras in Simplicius *Commentary on the Physics* 155.21–157.24.
[15]The theory may sound familiar to those who remember older style high school physics.

rational theology: moral, motionless, all-knowing and all-powerful. Slowly but surely, in the minds of intellectuals, an abstract force was replacing the dubious personalities of the gods (though the old gods were far from dead in popular belief):

> Xenophanes . . . supposed that the first principle, or existing universe, was one and neither finite nor infinite, neither changing nor changeless. . . . Xenophanes said that this one universe was god. . . . "Always he remains in the same state, changing not at all, nor is it fitting for him to move now here now there . . . but far from toil he governs everything with his mind."[16]

Fourth, the investigation gave new prominence to reason. Whatever the final picture, it was the job of reason to provide a comprehensive, systematic understanding of the cosmos. Whatever the precise character of primary reality, reason said it had to be something other than the simple appearance of things. If our senses disagree, then this only confirms that the senses are corrupt and unreliable, and not to be trusted. Reason and reality were now intertwined:

> Now these things do not agree with one another. For we said that there are many eternal things with forms and strength of their own, but they all seem to us to alter and to change from what they were each time they were seen. So it is clear that we do not see correctly, and that those many things do not correctly seem to exist, for they would not change if they were true.[17]

The last pre-Socratics faced a dilemma: what value should be placed on the senses? The Eleatics had dismissed the senses along with change, and there seemed no going back. Yet devaluing the senses threatened scientific pursuit. Slowly a new respect for sense perception began to assert itself. Plutarch, the contemporary of Paul, looked back approvingly on Philolaus's choice of reason as the path to a knowledge of primary reality: "All the so-called mathematical sciences are like smooth flat mirrors in which traces and images of intelligible truth are reflected. But it is above all geometry which, according to Philolaus, being the origin and native city of the others, turns and elevates the mind which is purified and gently released from perception."[18]

Democritus's answer was that most of what we take for the fixed laws of nature is simple convention: "By convention hot, by convention cold: in reality atoms and void. . . . In reality we know nothing—for truth is in the depths."[19] "That in reality we do not know how each thing is or is not has been shown in many ways. . . . And

---

[16]Xenophanes, in Simplicius *Commentary on the Physics* 22.26–23.20.
[17]Melissus, in Simplicius *Commentary on the Heavens* 558.17–559.13.
[18]Plutarch *Table Talk* 718E.
[19]Democritus, in Diogenes Laertius *Lives of Eminent Philosophers* 9.72.

a man must recognize by this rule that he is removed from reality."[20]

The pre-Socratics grew confident in the power of reason to peel away everyday phenomena and reveal the essence of reality. Confidence had shifted from the observable phenomena to reason as the surer guide for explaining life.

Plato Sets the Pattern for Primary Reality

The various theories of primary reality and its relation to everyday reality were bound to provoke a range of responses. Plato's initial direction was to make self-knowledge the basis of understanding.[21] In the *Charmides*, however, the argument ran out of puff. By the time he wrote the slave boy passage of the *Meno*, he had Socrates implying that all knowledge is a recollection of what our souls already knew.[22] By identifying reason as an activity of the soul, Plato sharply separated it from any empirical or "bodily" means of knowledge. The stage was set: reason is the key to knowing things as they really are, whereas the senses are unreliable because they are linked to the body, not the soul.

In the *Phaedo*, Plato separated soul from body, reason from nonreason, even more radically. The *Republic* pushed this further yet. Years of mathematical training, he argued, prepare the soul for its quest to grasp the higher levels of knowledge. This dichotomy between body and soul inevitably made everyday life inferior to a reality that could only be grasped by the mind. Yet Plato wanted the primary to influence the everyday. In works from his most mature period, the *Statesman, Critias* and *Laws,* Plato appears to take history more seriously and to shift from the ideal to the workable. But in the *Critias* the ideal for Athens remained the mythical Atlantis.

Plato began his account (in the voice of Timaeus) of the creation and of the character of reality by making a huge concession: real reality is beyond our everyday experience and understanding:[23]

> We must, in my opinion, begin by distinguishing between that which always is and never becomes from that which is always becoming but never is. The one is apprehensible by intelligence with the aid of reasoning, being eternally the same, the other is the object of opinion and irrational sensation, coming to be and ceasing to be, but never fully real. (*Tim* 27D–28A)

---

[20]Democritus, in Sextus Empiricus *Against the Mathematicians* 5.2.135-40.

[21]Plato *First Alcibiades* 132, and *Lovers* 138b.

[22]Plato *Meno* 82b–86c.

[23]The translation of Plato's *Timaeus* is from Desmond Lee, *Plato: Timaeus and Critias* (London: Penguin, 1971). Textual citations are to this edition. I have focused on the *Timaeus* for Plato's characterization of primary reality and his relegation of the everyday. The theme can be discerned throughout his works, but the *Timaeus* is unique in its cosmology and explicit comparisons of the two realities.

We may need a little help to make sense of this and what follows from Plato. The terms *being* and *becoming* are key to his picture of primary reality. But they are notoriously difficult to grasp when first reading ancient philosophers (modern philosophers are even worse).

It helps to begin at the beginning: *being* is simply a form of the verb "to be." It is the way we say that something is or was or will be or must be or can't be. It became a technical term as philosophers tried to find ways to talk about "what *always* is." In other words, they wanted "something" to serve as the foundation for explaining "everything." They began to speak about "pure being." The philosophers used *becoming* to speak of things as they exist in a form somehow different from (usually less than) pure being. Plato ends up saying that things in the process of change, "becoming," don't really share in "being" as such, they just share some of its qualities. This is because he had bought the old pre-Socratic line that what is perfect is beyond change.

There is a simple implication in all this for our enquiry into Paul and faith today. The philosophers' searches ended up putting more weight on abstract ideas than on everyday life. We will soon see how these abstract ideas become ideals that people must live up to. Later we will consider ways in which evangelical theology and preaching has also emphasized abstract ideas and ideals over the changing circumstances of everyday life.

Coming back to Plato's *Timaeus,* we learn from the outset that there are two types of reality.

The fully real	The less real
eternal	perishing, changing
perfect "being"	imperfect "becoming"
known by intelligence through reason	never known beyond mere opinion and irrational sensation

For Plato, the two realities require two methods of knowing, each with its own level of certainty:

> We must lay it down that the words in which likeness and pattern are described will be of the same order as that which they describe. Thus a description of what is changeless, fixed and clearly intelligible will be changeless and fixed—will be, that is, as irrefutable and uncontrovertible as a description in words can be; but analogously a description of a likeness of the changeless, being a description of a mere likeness will

be merely likely; for being has to becoming the same relation as truth to belief. (*Tim* 29BC)

Since the fully real doesn't change, our descriptions of it can be certain. The less real, however, is only a poor copy of the truly real. Our descriptions of it only point to changing appearances, so our knowledge is uncertain. So what do we know of the fully real?

Plato had established the basic parameters of perfect reality. It is, first of all, eternal, unchanging, ordered and complete. Not that different from what many of the pre-Socratics had said. Perfection, for Plato, consisted of a symmetrically ordered hierarchy, evidenced in harmony and order of geometry, mathematical sequences and musical scales.

Yet Plato knew the reality of failure. He sensed how life deviates from the intelligent design. The soul's fight to control the "sensations" of the body is like the universal struggle of reason over necessity. As the soul comes into union with the body, the results are less than perfect:

[The gods] took the immortal principle of the creature and . . . borrowed from the world portions of fire and earth, water, and air . . . and welded together [a body] . . . subject to the flow of growth [into which] they fastened the orbits of the immortal soul. Plunged into this strong stream, the orbits were unable to control it, nor were they controlled by it, and because of the consequent violent conflict the motions of the whole creature were irregular, fortuitous, and irrational . . . but still greater was the disturbance caused by the properties of objects which it encountered. . . . The motions caused by all these were transmitted through the body and impinged on the soul, and for that reason were later called, as they still are, "sensations." (*Tim* 42D–43C)

The soul's struggle to achieve harmony, order and gentle rhythm becomes a pattern for understanding everyday realities, particularly individual and social development. Since a child depends upon outside help, the orbits of its soul are irregular and behavior is irrational. But as "the stream of growth and nourishment flows less strongly, the soul's orbits take advantage of the calm and, as time passes, steady down in their proper courses, and the movement of the circles at last regains its correct natural form, and they can name the [underlying patterns of life] correctly and render their possessor rational" (*Tim* 44B).

The image of the perfect man as unchanging and unmoved and as having mastery over sensation was not new. Although arguing from a novel place, Plato simply reinforced conventional ideals for the wise man and leading citizen. We will keep returning to this theme of how the ideas of intellectuals largely reflected common convention and social experience.

Plato continued the *Timaeus* with an account of the origins and purposes of the human body. Note the role he gave to reason: (1) reason alone explains each part—

there is no need for clinical observation; (2) reason (seated in the head) is primary—the significance of the other parts depends on their relation to the head; and (3) each part serves the head:

> [The gods] copied the shape of the universe and fastened the two divine orbits of the soul into a spherical body, which we now call the head, the divinest part of us which controls all the rest . . . they then put together the body as a whole to serve the head. . . . And to prevent the head from rolling about on the earth . . . they provided that the body should act as a convenient vehicle . . . carrying on top of it the seat of our divinest and holiest part. That is the reason we all have arms and legs. (*Tim* 44D)

A similar line of argument explains the role of the eyes. Their principle function is to aid understanding and inner calm:

> The first organs they fashioned were those that gave us light. . . . The pure fire within us that is akin [to gentle nonburning fire] they caused to flow through the eyes, making the whole eye-ball . . . smooth and close-textured so that it would keep in anything of coarser nature, and filter through only this pure fire. . . . When the eyelids . . . are shut, they confine the activity of fire within, and this smoothes and diffuses the internal motions, and produces a calm. . . . [The cause and purpose of sight] was that we should see the revolutions of intelligence in the heavens and use their untroubled course to guide the troubled revolutions of our own understanding . . . [to] correct the disorder of our own revolutions by the standard of the invariability of those of god . . . and all musical sound is . . . a heaven-sent ally in reducing to order and harmony any disharmony in the revolutions within us. (*Tim* 44D–47D)

Until now, Plato has looked at the creation from "above," from the designs and intelligence of what he called the Demiurge and the world-soul. Now he views the universe from "below," from the chaos and abyss that confronted the Maker. So far the process of creation reads mostly like a steady unfolding of unhindered intelligence. Now he seeks to relate reason to necessity, to bring a reality check into his system:

> For this world came into being from a mixture and combination of necessity and intelligence. Intelligence controlled necessity by persuading it for the most part to bring about the best result . . . [but] to give a true account of how it came to be on these principles, one must bring in the indeterminate [or errant] cause so far as its nature permits. (*Tim* 48A)

"Errant" necessity mixes with reason, and the influence is not good. Plato now becomes clearer about the extent of reality in the world we experience. What we can see or touch is not fully real:

> Whenever we see anything in process of change, for example fire, we should speak of it not as being a thing but as having a quality . . . in general we should never speak as if

any of the things we suppose we can indicate by pointing and using the expressions "this thing" or "that thing" have any permanent reality: for they have no stability and elude the designation "this" or "that" or any other that expresses permanence. (*Tim* 49CE)

Plato returned here to his initial distinction between being and becoming, and the resulting levels of reality. But there is a problem lurking. If the perfect and the imperfect mix, the perfect will no longer be perfect. According to Plato, this cannot and therefore did not happen. The perfect remained perfect. So how does the imperfect bear some resemblance to the perfect? Plato introduced a third element: between being and becoming is the *receptacle,* the "nurse of all becoming and change" (*Tim* 49C). This receptacle "never alters its characteristics. For it continues to receive all things, and never itself takes a permanent impress from any of the things which enter it . . . and the things which pass in and out of it are copies of the eternal realities" (*Tim* 50BC).

Plato used the metaphor of birth: the model is the father, the receptacle is the mother, and the resulting things are their children. Those who can remember it might think of a type of carbon paper. The receptacle must not hinder the pure imprint of being on becoming. Thus, "so as to receive in itself every kind of character," the receptacle itself must be "devoid of all character . . . invisible and formless, all-embracing, possessed in a most puzzling way of intelligibility, yet very hard to grasp" (*Tim* 50E–51B).

Plato was at least right about that—it is very hard to grasp! The specific characteristics of the receptacle remain shadowy. One thing is clear, however: the receptacle must lie on the being side of the being-becoming equation. It is unchanged, untainted and passive. But what is the model, the original eternal reality? Plato is ready to introduce his "forms."

Unlike his accounts in the *Phaedo, Parmenides, Republic,* and *Sophist,* Plato did not expound this "unchanging form, uncreated and indestructible, admitting no modification and entering no combination, imperceptible to sight or the other senses, the object of thought" (*Tim* 52A) at any length in the *Timaeus.* Instead, he pinned his proof of the forms on what he regarded as the self-evident distinction between intelligence and true opinion. Some things hold true no matter what, and we all know it. Other things come and go and ultimately are not as important. Plato believed that few people ever get to the heart of this:

If intelligence and true opinion are different in kind, then these "things-in-themselves" certainly exist, forms imperceptible to our senses, but apprehended by thought; but if, as some think, there is no difference between true opinion and intelligence, what we perceive through our physical senses must be taken as the most certain reality. Now there is no doubt that the two are different, because they differ in origin and nature. One is produced by teaching, the other by persuasion; one always involves truth and rational argument, the other is irrational; one cannot be moved by persuasion, the other can; true opinion is a faculty shared, it must be admitted, by all men, intelligence by the gods and only a small number of men. (*Tim* 51DE)

Plato saw in this a reflection of how things really are on the biggest scale. His forms are notoriously difficult to define precisely. It seems he never intended to provide a single system of thought but used the language of "forms" quite fluidly. Yet although there is no definitive picture of the forms, they do stand as "something other," a truer reality beyond the corruption and change of experience.

An illustration might help (though it runs the risk of oversimplifying Plato). If I say "tree," we will all think of something similar enough to allow for shared meaning. But there are thousands of species of trees and millions upon millions of actual trees. So how can we all think of "tree" in a way that allows us to converse intelligently about trees? Is there something basic and essential behind all the individual trees? Is there some bottom line form of the tree? Is there one true tree of which all our thoughts and perceptions are dull copies? These are the kinds of questions that prompted Plato and the philosophers before and after him, the problem of the "One and the Many."

All of this leads us to the tough question of how being and thought are related. The question holds practical implications for our quest to understand Paul and faith today. At the risk of oversimplifying again, if we can think of the ideas of "goodness" or "beauty" or "justice" (or many other attributes) and see them in different ways in life, then they must exist (i.e., have "being") in some perfect form somewhere—or so the argument roughly went. The point for us is that Plato reinforced the priority of abstract thought as the way to grasp higher reality and thus set the scene for ideas to take on a life of their own.

The last major section of the *Timaeus* begins again with the divine purpose[24] making the best it can out of the materials of the universe and their physical processes. The personal faculties and attributes that make up everyday experience are some kind of necessary evil. They enable our mortal life but get in the way of anything higher:

[The gods built onto the soul] another mortal part, containing terrible and necessary feelings: pleasure, the chief incitement to wrong, pain, which frightens us from good, confidence and fear, two foolish counsellors, obstinate passion and credulous hope. To this mixture they added irrational sensation and desire which shrinks from nothing, and so gave the mortal element its indispensable equipment. (*Tim* 69CD)

---

[24]Plato's references to god(s), God, Demiurge and divine purposes do not appear to follow any one pattern.

Plato now assumes the threefold model of the soul that he had made in the *Republic* (435–44): reason, emotion and appetite. These three aspects struggle for supremacy, order and balance. Like his earlier remarks on the body existing for the head, the struggles of reason, emotion and appetite explain the roles of the bodily organs. In a charming section, Plato deliberates on why we have a neck and why it is relatively short and narrow (questions I'm sure we have all asked ourselves). As at least one wag has noted to me, Plato's answer may unwittingly help explain the absence of neck in many football players:

> Since (the gods) shrank from polluting the divine element with these mortal feelings more than was absolutely necessary, they located the mortal element in a separate part of the body, and constructed the neck as a kind of isthmus and boundary between head and breast to keep them apart . . . the seat of courage, passion, and ambition . . . nearer the head . . . well-placed to listen to the commands of reason . . . the heart . . . in the guardroom, in order that when passions were aroused to boiling point . . . commands and threats should circulate quickly . . . they secured appetite (in the belly) like a wild beast . . . to feed at its stall, but be as far as possible from the seat of deliberation . . . and wound the bowels round in coils, thus preventing the quick passage of food, which would otherwise compel the body to want more and make its appetite insatiable, so rendering our species incapable through gluttony of philosophy and culture, and unwilling to listen to the divinest element in us. (*Tim* 69DE–73A)

The universe is a mixture of the intelligible and sensible, of the orderly and chaotic. Now if the person is a microcosm of this same stability and instability, then disease is the absence of balance, and health is its restoration. Tranquillity should be preferred to disruption, and inner impulse rather than external influence:

> The good . . . is always beautiful, and the beautiful never lacks proportion. A living creature that is to have either quality must therefore be well-proportioned. . . . For health and sickness, virtue and vice, the proportion or disproportion between soul and body is far the most important factor. (*Tim* 87B, D)

> Among movements, the best is that we produce in ourselves of ourselves—for it is most nearly akin to the movement of thought and of the universe; next is movement produced in us by another; worst of all is movement caused by outside agents in parts of the body while the body itself remains passive and inert. (*Tim* 89A)

This emphasis on balance is entirely predictable. Plato's moral and social conservatism has been leading us here all along. The *Timaeus* has opened up to us the character of the ideal and the perfect. The reasoned life turns toward the tranquil apprehension and expression of purest reality. After all, our home is not here: "We should think of the most authoritative part of our soul as a guardian spirit given by god, living in the summit of the body, which can properly be said to lift us from the earth toward our home in heaven; for we are creatures not of earth but of heaven, where the soul was first born" (*Tim* 90A). Furthermore, he continues:

> The motions in us that are akin to the divine are the thoughts and revolutions of the universe. We should each therefore attend to these motions and by learning about the harmonious circuits of the universe repair the damage done at birth to the circuits in our head, and so restore understanding and what is understood to their original likeness to each other. When that is done we shall have achieved the goal set us by the gods, the life that is best for this present time and for all time to come. (*Tim* 90D)

Although there were many other influential thinkers in classical times, the basic patterns of Plato's thought largely set the debate throughout antiquity. Not all agreed with him. In many cases, later writers had not even read him. The key to his influence is more social than intellectual: his ideas reinforced common social ideals and expectations. At this level we will find broad agreement across the centuries between philosophers.

So which came first—Plato's philosophical hierarchy of reality or his everyday experience as a privileged man in a society structured by rank and status? What was it about the social structures of antiquity that made Plato's perspectives so acceptable, adaptable, and durable? This question takes us to Aristotle, the next great expositor of primary reality in Greek antiquity, then to the everyday experiences of fate, rank and status. From that vantage point, we will turn our attention to Paul.

3

FROM ARISTOTLE
TO SENECA

IT MIGHT IN MANY WAYS SEEM MORE ACCURATE TO PICTURE ARISTOTLE RESCUING PHILOS-
ophy from abstraction and relocating reality in the everyday, rather than as a key
player in the move to abstraction. The son of a physician, Aristotle is credited as the
first biologist, amassing and classifying large collections of natural specimens. His
philosophical methods generally were sensitive to the social context of inquiry.
Whereas his teacher Plato had based his political theory on the abstract forms and an
idealized mythology of Athens and Atlantis, Aristotle drew on hard data gathered from
the constitutions of over one hundred and fifty city-states. In the *Nicomachean Ethics*, he sought a realistic account of everyday experience and practical reasoning. He
rejected abstract concepts wherever these cut him off from the world of experience,
reframing Plato's forms and locating them squarely within the functions of the mind.

Yet although Aristotle was more outward-looking than Plato, we do not look far
before encountering similar presumptions of a primary reality:

> Of substances constituted by nature, some are ungenerated, imperishable, and eternal,
> while others are subject to generation and decay. The former are excellent and divine,
> but less accessible to knowledge. The evidence that might throw light on them, and on
> the problem which we long to solve respecting them, is furnished but scantily by sen-
> sation. . . . The scanty conceptions to which we can attain of celestial things give us . . .
> more pleasure than all our knowledge of the world in which we live.[1]

---

[1]Aristotle *Parts of Animals* 1.5.

Aristotle on Abstraction as the Key to Primary Reality

Primary reality shifts ground somewhat in Aristotle. Plato had largely followed the pre-Socratics' lead and focused on the "stuff" basic to all apparent reality. Aristotle was not as concerned with this "stuff" as with its inner *logos*, or reason. At times his approach to *logos* was entirely traditional: "The universal is known by logos, and the particulars by sense-perception."[2] In other places, the "inner" logos took him toward mysticism. In two difficult passages, *On the Soul* 3 and *Nicomachean Ethics* 10, he presents abstract thinking as the pinnacle of human achievement. The highest goal is to lift our thought beyond all topics or objects to thinking about thought itself.

Classical scholar Raoul Mortley has argued that "the general thrust of the notion [of *logos* in Greek tradition] is that mind is identical with the 'essential,' or most intelligible part of reality."[3] We have seen this already in Plato. Aristotle accepted that in some sense the mind already possesses the object of its inquiry. But he did not go down Plato's path of knowledge as recollection of what we already know. Instead, Aristotle began to reify *logos*, to turn *logos* into something with its own independent existence. The *logos* of a thing is not an idea external to it but is something like the rational element within it. Thinking comes from first principles, *archai*, or form, *eidos*.[4] The thinking process is basically "receptive of the form of an object [which is] potentially of the same nature, though not identical with it."[5]

So what is the form? It is that "intellectual" aspect of a thing that the mind can grasp. Aristotle's forms are not "out there" like Plato's. To Aristotle, they are *within* the object. But "within" is far from simple: "Therefore mind thinks itself, if it is that which is best; and its thinking is a thinking of thinking."[6]

Heady stuff! What are we to make of all this? The key to the riddle seems to lie in Aristotle's aversion to matter. This is entirely traditional. He wanted to restrict thought to whatever in an object is like thought itself—in other words, whatever is without matter. Purity of being and of thought are only maintained by being separate from matter and change.

For all his aversion to Plato's forms, Aristotle remained caught in the same web of

---

[2]Aristotle *Physics* 189a.
[3]Raoul Mortley, *From Word to Silence*, vol. 1, *The Rise and Fall of Logos*, Beitrage zur Religions und Kirchengeschichte des Altertums 30 (Bonn: Hanstein, 1986), p. 160. See also *From Word to Silence*, vol. 2, *The Way of Negation, Christian and Greek*, Beitrage zur Religions und Kirchenge-schichte des Altertums 31 (Bonn: Hanstein, 1986). My summary of Aristotle's understanding of mind and reality draws on Mortley's superb analysis of the shift in Greek philosophy from reason to silence as the means of grasping ultimate reality.
[4]Aristotle *Metaphysics* 1032b15.
[5]Aristotle *On the Soul* 429a15.
[6]Aristotle *Metaphysics* 1074b35.

"otherness." Like so many before him, he located pure reality away from what he too regarded as the imperfections of the material world. And like Plato, ironically his presumption of two realities was most stark when he sought to be most practical: the life of virtue is about finding balance between the material and the intellectual:

> Consequently when one of these elements, the material or the intellectual, is active it is acting in opposition to the nature of the other. When they are exactly balanced the result is something which is not felt as either painful or pleasurable. . . . For there is an activity not only of movement but of immobility, like that of thought, and there is in rest a more real pleasure than in motion. Yet, as the poet says, "in all things change is sweet." It is sweet to us because of some badness in us. For a nature that needs change is bad, just as a changeable person is bad.[7]

Aristotle's verdict on change and character—"a changeable person is bad"—was entirely conventional. This held true in Paul's day and is part of the background that explains why his relationships with the Corinthians, Thessalonians and others were so vexed. Why did so many discredit him? Why was he forced to defend himself? Why did the Corinthians prefer the sophistic "super-apostles"? The answers in large part center on Paul's seeming fickleness. He was neither balanced, serene nor detached. From the perspective of conventional Graeco-Roman morality, Paul was given to excess and passion. He was an embarrassment to them and he knew it, yet he refused to conform to their entirely conventional and reasonable expectations.

Aristotle's search for the perfect led him to abstraction as the key methodology for higher thought. We might call it the onion principle. Since reality is many-layered, or at least the form of an object is not identical to the object itself, reason must peel back the layers, stripping away what is only matter, until the essence is reached. When this method is applied to grasping purest reality, it is only a short step to the idea so tantalizing to later philosophers that the highest truth and being are only known by saying what they are not, or by falling into silence. As Raoul Mortley put it:

> Abstraction, then, leads towards a negative state, and so grasps non-existence, but it grasps it as a cause. It will therefore reach an apprehension of non-existence, which it can place in a causal context, that of generating the superstructure of physical reality. Abstraction is the science of removing the layers with a view to finding the first principle, and so it is directed towards the discovery of causes. The layering of reality secretes a causal connection, as well as an originating principle, and abstraction follows this trail: ironically, it may pursue it to the point where the mere absence of reality is left as the cause.[8]

---

[7]Aristotle *Nicomachean Ethics* 7.14.
[8]Mortley, *Word to Silence*, 1:149.

Our study of Plato ended with the speculation that his experience of social privilege had shaped his theories about primary reality. Aristotle's preference for abstraction was similarly grounded in his own social position. The noblest human activity was that least active of activities, the pure intellectualism of contemplating thought and reality. We must not romanticize philosophy at this point. Who could afford the luxury of spending time reflecting rather than working? Only the privileged had the means and self-sufficiency to indulge in philosophy:

> For "contemplation" is the highest form of activity, since the intellect is the highest thing in us and the objects which come within its range are the highest that can be known. . . . At all events it is thought that philosophy ["the pursuit of wisdom"] has pleasures marvelous in purity and duration, and it stands to reason that those who have knowledge pass their time more pleasantly than those who are engaged in its pursuit. Again, self-sufficiency will be found to belong in an exceptional degree to the exercise of the speculative intellect.[9]

There are some vital links between abstraction and evangelical life and thought. Abstraction has always been the key tool of theology. Soon after Paul, Christians began amalgamating his teachings with the frameworks, categories and methods of theology. Evangelicalism continues this tradition. For the moment, note the broad similarities in one evangelical hermeneutic to Aristotle's method. According to Old Testament scholar Walter Kaiser, the end of analyzing a text is to " 'principlize'. . . the author's propositions, arguments, narrations, and illustrations in timeless abiding truths . . . [that constitute] the essential substance . . . the permanent, abiding, and doctrinal part of the passage."[10] The methods of many evangelical theologians are fundamentally those of the classical Greek tradition: so-called irrelevant bits of text and history are stripped away to reveal the "real essence" of passages and things.

Hellenistic Philosophy and the Framing of Primary Reality as Moral Idealism

The Hellenistic period[11] was an age for practical action, not idle speculation. Aristotle's Lyceum had virtually folded by the second century B.C., while Plato's Academy

---

[9]Aristotle *Nicomachean Ethics* 10.7.

[10]Walter Kaiser, *Toward an Exegetical Theology: Biblical Exegesis for Preaching and Teaching* (Grand Rapids, Mich.: Baker, 1981), pp. 152, 161, 209.

[11]There are no hard and fast lines between the classical, Hellenistic and Graeco-Roman periods. The classical period is roughly the time of Homer to Plato and Aristotle. The Hellenistic is the next few centuries in which the influence of Greek thought and culture spread throughout the Mediterranean and Middle Eastern worlds. The Graeco-Roman period is commonly identified with the spread of Roman rule across the Hellenized world, roughly the last century B.C. and first two A.D. The Hellenistic and Graeco-Roman periods are commonly lumped together as Hellenistic. Likewise, the classical and Hellenistic periods are often simply called classical. References to the imperial age roughly equal the Graeco-Roman period.

had begun to decline even earlier. Aristotelianism was still an influence, but as a distinct school it was now a relic. Platonism had lost its way too. Philosophers increasingly confined themselves to the art of living. An intense traditionalism emerged. Schools formerly opposed to each other formed a united front. Antiochus of Ascalon believed that the teachings of the Old Academy, Peripatetic, and Stoa were basically the same. Panaetius and Posidonius incorporated Platonism and Aristotelianism into Stoicism. A century apart, Cicero and Seneca followed suit in Rome. The Stoic Seneca reflects this mood in the way he frequently and approvingly quotes Epicurus to his friends while throwing in the odd jibe about Epicureans.

The split between primary reality and everyday reality survived this reshaping of the schools and tasks of philosophy. The art of living needed a secure foundation. The philosophical schools maintained their interest in nature as the basis and guide of the reasoned life and the quest for moral perfection. No schools pursued this method more than the Stoics and Epicureans. At first glance both schools seem disinterested or even opposed to any idea of a primary reality. A second look, however, shows the theme alive and well.

The Stoics were strict materialists, but not atomists. There is no "other" level of reality. This world is the best of all possible worlds under the benevolent providence of Zeus or of Nature. The ideal differs from the everyday only in scale. The universe is governed by reason and providence and therefore is intelligent and has purpose. We perceive evil because we see only part of the grand design of Nature. A chain of cause and effect, frequently identified with Fate, shapes all. But Fate sits uneasily with individual freedom, a point that both Epicurean and Skeptic critics did not miss. In defense, Chrysippus, a Stoic of the third century schooled in the skepticism of the Academy, had developed elaborate classifications of causes to sidestep the charge of believing everything was determined.

The heart of the Epicurean system, on the other hand, reduced everything to matter and to natural processes and causes. There is no overall purpose. There are no gods to fear. The study of nature produces tranquillity by showing that our fears of another reality are groundless. Epicurus dismissed the now-traditional model of reason rising beyond matter to contemplate purest being. Sense perception was the one and only basis of knowledge. But two centuries later, Lucretius (IBC), ironically, had to deal with accusations similar to those leveled at the Stoics: the Epicurean "system" also led to determinism. Lucretius countered with the novel argument that atoms *swerved*. There is no Providence here, just a random and dangerous world in which strict materialism rules. On the face of it then, atomism, whether pre-Socratic or Epicurean, seems the major exception to our portrait of two realities.

Yet if we focus on the differences between Stoics and Epicureans over their understanding of nature, and on their pedantic debates about the value of the emotions, we will obscure the stronger common ground. The moral ideals of both schools were entirely conventional. Epicureans seemed somewhat more socially radical than their Stoic cousins, but their nonconformity rarely took them beyond what was socially acceptable to the affluent. Grant's summary of the goal of Epicurus applies equally well in this respect to Stoicism: "Happiness was *ataraxia*, or freedom from disturbance: renunciation, independence, imperturbability."[12] Well beyond the time of Paul and down into late antiquity, these schools continued to hold sway in spelling out the moral perfection that set men apart from the everyday.

Platonist Revivals of Transcendent Reality

The Hellenistic spirit of rationalism brought about great scientific and technological advances. Yet there were also clear longings for immortality and a more inward route to perfection. In this context, Platonism was revived and became the leading intellectual force for centuries to come, absorbing Aristotelian tradition and outliving Stoicism and Epicureanism. But why Platonism?

Although scholarly Platonism kept its distance from religion, the tradition could provide an intellectual platform for religious experiences of another reality. Intellectuals found what they needed in such tantalizing phrases as Plato's oft-quoted remark that the Supreme Being lived completely "outside the realm of being."[13] The obvious impression this gives is of a reality tiered like a pyramid: the changing, perishing and imperfect at the bottom; the unchanging, eternal and perfect at the top. Albrecht Dihle captured the mood: "Only from this peak far above sensual experience in the realm of the intelligible could one hope to come to a proper understanding of the structure of both reality and human consciousness . . . [that knowledge basic] for a moral and happy life."[14] Philosophers increasingly arrived at a very similar place: they began to speak of the summit as the "One."

But here lay the Achilles heel: if the pinnacle was beyond being, then how could philosophy lay hold of it? The One that was above all being and change could not be fully known by reason alone. The mind could only get as close as a profound grasp

---

[12]M. Grant, *The World of Rome* (New York: World, 1960), p. 217.

[13]Plato *Republic* 508B/509A.

[14]Albrecht Dihle, *The Theory of Will in Classical Antiquity* (Berkeley: University of California Press, 1982), p. 10. There are parallels between Dihle's work and my own focus. Dihle notes that it took a long time for a clear and positive theory of will to emerge in the intellectual world of antiquity. His thesis is that rationalism tended to preclude and devalue will as a determinative aspect of human behavior. Putting my concerns in his terms, Greek rationalism dismissed the relational and the everyday in preference for a reality undiluted by experience. It thus shied away from the immediacy and open-endedness of the will.

of the difference between being and nonbeing. Aristotle had said as much when he guessed that the Supreme Being might be either mind or something beyond mind. Unlike the new mood, however, Aristotle sought to open up this summit to full rational inquiry via an elaborate scheme of ideas about potentiality and motion.

But for all his brilliance, the system didn't work. As Dihle puts it: "Ideas such as indirect knowledge of the Supreme Being [and] intellectual contact with the One as distinguished from its intellectual cognition . . . did not make much sense."[15] Whatever way Aristotle saw it, the One could only be spoken about negatively and "known" irrationally. Plato had stopped in a similar place: on the verge of the summit, needing "sudden illumination" and "revelation" to complete the climb. Reason could take him only so far.

The idea that the pinnacle of reality was beyond the reach of reason gained new currency in the Graeco-Roman period. Pseudo-Pythagorean fragments dating from the first centuries picture the One as beyond both being and thought.[16] It is neither supreme intellect, nor can it be known intellectually. The question loomed: how does one "know" something beyond being? This could threaten the principle of an ordered rational universe, a principle to which most seekers were still committed. After all, what is to stop the One that is beyond being and thought from fiddling with the system? If we allow the pinnacle to be *anything* and to be beyond reason, then what is to stop the One from "proving" that all our reasoning has been wrong?

This quest and its links to Platonism have considerable significance for understanding the popular intellectualism of Paul's day—so long as we keep several qualifications in mind. Platonism as a formal school was not prominent in this time. Indeed, there was never a single body of Middle or Neo-Platonism, nor any clear dependence between thinkers. Yet there was a general ill-defined allegiance to Plato's ideas. While people sensed the deep gulf between primary reality and everyday reality, they remained nonetheless committed to both.

The materialism of the dominant schools, Stoicism and Epicureanism, was somewhat out of touch with the growing fascination for immortality and the transcendent. Two nearly identical first-century inscriptions to the Platonist Laetus, one in Athens and one in Ephesus—"Plato lives again"—indicate that Stoics and Epicureans were probably not having it all their own way.[17] In this sense, the mood and themes of Neo-Platonism that show up in the second and third centuries were

---

[15]Ibid., p. 170.

[16]Stobaeus *Anthology* 1.

[17]*I.Eph.* VII, 2.3901 and *IG* II, 3816, cf. Acts 17:18. For translations of the inscriptions, see Greg Horsley, ed., *New Documents Illustrating Early Christianity* (Sydney: Macquarie University Press, 1987), 4:70.

already finding a home among the educated of Paul's day.

By the second century, many educated people were finding the knowledge and experience they sought through the elaborate philosophical-religious hybrids of the Hermetics, Gnostics and so-called Chaldaeans. The genius of these systems lay in a blend of intellectualism and an appeal to a divine revelation that surpassed reason. Each stressed an act of will rather than of intellect as the way to gain access to the Absolute. Purist Platonists fought hard to keep philosophy from this kind of religious synthesis. But the new mood was prevailing. In the second-century work *Life of Apollonius*, Philostratus has his hero conquer the old-fashioned Stoic Euphrates. The moral? Philosophy only comes after divine revelation. But what happens to ethics? Greek philosophy in all ages had always based virtue and happiness on conformity to nature through reason. Divine revelation was revealing new codes to be accepted apart from reason. Reason would continue to spell out the shape of perfection, but the act of acceptance was becoming prior and primary.

This move from intellect to will resonated with the Jewish philosopher, Philo. The Jewish Scriptures had grounded ethics in a covenant relationship to God. The will to act and the substance of the action both stemmed from the same root: the compassionate rule of God over his chosen people. What was unthinkable to Graeco-Romans—surrender of the intellect to the revelation of God's will—was the height of piety and wisdom to Jews. For the Graeco-Roman, reason opened the way to wisdom; for the Jew, obedience to God was the wellspring of wisdom.

Philo saw himself bridging these two worlds: the grace of God and the perfect rationality of a Supreme Being and nature. His system was clearly hierarchical: at top, the first God and Father of all, incomprehensible and eternal (often described in familiar Platonic terms); next, a second God or Logos, the mind of God, the first-born, the agent of creation; at bottom, the world of the senses.[18] Yet Philo did not completely identify God with impersonal being. Frequently his explicit doctrine was very un-Platonic: God gave the law because of his sheer mercy and friendliness; he simply wanted to communicate with his people; it is entirely due to the mercy of God if some people come nearer to him than others; he goes to greet those whom he wants.[19] The same two-sided approach appeared in Philo's anthropology and ethics. As a Platonist, he spoke of the irrational affections drawing men away from their spiritual selves and from the rational appreciation of nature toward the enslavement of their material bodies. As a Jew, he put

---

[18]See Philo *On the Creation of the World* 3; *On the Decalogue* 11; *On the Sacrifices of Abel and Cain* 18; *On the Life of Moses* 1.51; *Allegories of the Law* 1.5.
[19]See Philo *On Drunkenness* 145; *On the Virtues* 185; *On the Migration of Abraham* 79; *On the Life of Moses* 2.189.

the matter plainly in terms of disobedience to God.[20]

Returning to the Platonist dilemma, Philo agreed that intelligence *(phronesis)* was the consummation of all virtues and the basis of freedom. But the Old Testament emphasized obedience, not intellectual mastery. Revelation bridged the gap. The intellect takes one so far, then God completes this knowledge with the revelation of his will and intellect *(logos)*. This new knowledge surpasses the limitations of normal knowledge and is beyond intellectual dispute. But how could a man acquire this knowledge? The means, according to Dihle, were familiar:

> The psychological mechanism, as foreseen in philosophical theory, remains unchanged. But now it is the divine spirit and no longer human reason that controls affections and emotions. Perfection in human life can be brought about by the supranatural gift of the divine Logos or Nous that provides the superior knowledge and restores man's nature as the image of God *(Conf.* 145f, *det.* 138f) . . . [such perfection results from the] unswaying knowledge, granted by revelation or the divine spirit, that God is imperceptible to the human intellect.[21]

Much the same mechanism served the Gnostics well. The everyday world is a regrettable intermingling of matter and spirit. Particles of the light of the purer world lie trapped in human souls and bodies unaware of their loftier home. But the Supreme One has sent messengers to confer knowledge and freedom. The messenger brings knowledge of the soul's home and opens a way to return to the Father. This knowledge does not conform to the rules of reason. The soul must free itself through a series of acts of apprehending what lies beyond. Picking and choosing among the teachings of Christians, philosophers and cults, the Gnostics relocated the interaction of God and man from history to the realm of pure spirituality. As Dihle notes, "This fitted the general tendency, from the first century B.C. onward, to locate man's salvation beyond the limits of time and space."[22]

The complexities and subtleties of social and religious experience precluded any simple single set of ideas. There was no agreed upon formulation of the two realities, nor of how the perfect could be "known" or experienced. Plato had looked for his forms "out there": a realm of being over against becoming. Aristotle located the essence of reality "inside," embedded in the categories of mind. Hellenized Jewish scholars talked of two spirits or of an ethical dualism of good and evil. Later Platonists became more explicit in the contrast of intellect and matter or spirit and matter. Christians added the novel social dimension of the separation of the sacred and the secular.

---

[20]See Philo *Allegories of the Law* 3.113; *On the Migration of Abraham* 128.
[21]Dihle, *Theory of Will*, pp. 94–95.
[22]Ibid., p. 102.

Since at least classical times, people have made distinctions between "higher" and "lower" forms of life. Variously described as spiritual-physical, sacred-secular, higher-lower, inner-outer and many other dichotomies, these distinctions have had a profound impact on beliefs and lifestyles. Paul, however, did not think or act this way. As we will note later, his language of spirit-flesh does not fit this pattern. Yet the tendency to split life was so influential in Paul's gatherings that he took the time to fight it. Paul lost, however. Christianity continued to reinforce this split, and evangelicalism is no exception.

Think for a moment of those conventions that reinforce the sense of certain things, events or people being somehow closer to God. Think of architecture, meetings, ordination, the Lord's Supper, clothing, vocations and the sundry methods for a "deeper, closer walk with God." Think of the ideals and expectations that shape church-related experiences. Think beyond what theologians, churchmen and congregations *say* to what actually *happens* for people and between people. The split between primary and everyday reality remains alive and well in our own backyard.

The differences in how the Greek philosophers gave voice to this split reality should not mask its common soil: ideas do not simply grow out of other ideas; they grow from everyday personal and social experiences. The patterns of Plato, Aristotle and the rest were not merely the stuff of philosophical speculation; they carried the ideals of a society gripped by the contradictions of rank and ambition. We move now to enrich our understanding of these contradictions that were so formative in Paul's day.

4

THE INADEQUACY
OF IDEALS

CONFIDENCE IN THE HOUSE OF REASON PERSISTED DESPITE A GROWING MYSTICISM ABOUT ultimate reality. Although some philosophers and theologians spoke of an irrational last step for those trying to reach the One, their speculation could not displace reason as the chief guide to the moral life. This house was still standing in Paul's day. The order of nature stood, and its laws were sovereign over all: "Not even for God are all things possible. . . . He cannot bestow eternity on mortals . . . he cannot cause twice ten not to be twenty or do other things along similar lines, and these facts unquestionably demonstrate the power of nature."[1]

The Inadequacy of Primary Reality

Moral idealism was built on the same foundations of nature and reason. A man's lack of moral progress came from his failure to judge what he could and could not control. The remedy was to correct one's judgment and to gain control of the mind. In his study on the theory of will in antiquity, Albrecht Dihle sums up the ways philosophical reflection about nature interacted with moral ideals and teachings: "When Greek philosophy turned to social and moral problems . . . its main task was to find standards of moral conduct that were as rational and generally applicable as the rules of the cosmic order . . . there was hardly ever disagreement about the principle that only rational understanding

---

[1]Pliny the Elder *Natural History* 2.27.

of reality leads to a good life or moral perfection."[2]

The intellect must control the passions. But theory and practice did not always match. The experience of failure was too obvious and could undermine confidence in reason. To Plato the answer had been clear: "Nobody fails on purpose," "Nobody chooses to sin."[3] A choice may later prove to have been bad, but the person did not see it that way at the time. He was ignorant of the outcomes. As a *rational* being, he could not have deliberately chosen to be irrational. It was fear or anger that led him unwittingly against reason.

What Plato seems to have meant by "Nobody fails on purpose" is that a man always intends to accomplish "the good," but sometimes he has the wrong idea of what is good.[4] Something interferes with his rational processes. In the *Republic*, Plato appealed to a simple dualism: failure comes from matter interfering with reason (which seems to include the will). In the *Timaeus*, however, the will belongs to the immaterial part of the soul. So the soul must have some involvement in failure. But how? Plato's solution was to posit two souls in the universe and the person: the first causes regular motion; the second causes irregular motion, and thus evil.

One of the key issues here is that Plato (and the generations who followed him) almost exclusively emphasized what happens internally for the person. The game is won or lost without reference to any actual context or relationship. Dihle again:

> Only the human mind participates in the intelligible, only the intelligible is entirely real. The world that we experience through our senses is perishable, disorderly, irrational in many respects, unpredictable as to its further development, and has, therefore, only a small share in reality. Knowledge, however, which the intellect acquires, can only refer to reality, to that which is lasting, unchanging, and structured by reason. So knowledge which leads to action cannot be tested by any results this action may cause in the empirical world. Moral quality can only be ascertained by examining the state of mind, the consciousness of the human being who produced action.[5]

These are critical points for understanding the world in which Paul lived and for clarifying what he meant by a transformation of mind and behavior.[6] It will become clear that in the matter of making moral choices, Paul radically parted company with the following entirely conventional framework for moral reasoning:

☐ Our experience reflects the two realities; we must rise above the material to the rational.

---

[2] Albrecht Dihle, *The Theory of Will in Classical Antiquity* (Berkeley: University of California Press, 1982), pp. 36–37.
[3] *oudeis ekōn hamartanei;* Plato *Gorgias* 467C.
[4] Ibid.
[5] Dihle, *Theory of Will*, p. 40.
[6] E.g., Romans 12:1-2.

☐ Any particular act and its context are secondary to the ideal of harmony between intellect and action and to the personal goal of moral perfection; perfection is the real issue at hand, not the merits of the individual action or its consequences.

☐ The moral life is about taking care of one's own soul.

This is fine in theory. But what was a man to do with his own sense of failure? What was he to do with the sense of intellectual frailty, moral weakness and fallibility so powerfully captured in tragic poetry and drama? Moral knowledge needed more than intellectual profundity. A man had to face his own inadequacy. Indeed, the realization of personal imperfection might be the essential first step on the path to freedom of moral choice. The great ones had always acknowledged this, even if indirectly. Socrates claimed he could only know his own ignorance and deficiency in relation to a particular context: he could not know lack of the fear of death except in the face of his impending execution. Knowledge of ignorance thus actually brings about knowledge of something definite. But this can only be tested in concrete experience. The moralists can not be free to do anything; they must show *sophrosyne*, that curious classical hybrid of self-control and sound judgment.

An abstract "good" could not adequately shape moral knowledge. Nor could it tell a man what he ought to believe about himself. He needed concrete contexts and specific instances to gauge his progress. But this need for context and particulars ran contrary to the tenor of tradition. The contemplative intellect had always been honored as the only guardian of moral freedom. Cracks, old cracks, were appearing in the house of reason.

The intellectual traditions could not deliver freedom of choice in the changing fortunes of everyday life. They presumed that intellect was sufficient to discern and evaluate the means and ends of action. Without particulars, without the subjectivity of others' affairs and the chaos of everyday relationships, the ideals of freedom of thought and choice seemed hollow and illusory.

Yet the priority of purest reality held. Aristotle's answer had been to create two categories of intellect, the theoretical and the practical (theory was naturally superior). Orthodox Stoics and Epicureans did not want to drive a wedge between the orders of nature and human affairs. Yet they tended to side with Plato, for whom theory held far more dignity than practice, given its link to the world of the senses. Matter, after all, was the realm of fate or chance, and the philosopher sought "to go beyond fate." If man felt helplessly bound to the relentless march of cosmic processes, then that only showed that his experience was imperfect and his senses unreliable. The ideals of order, balance, harmony and self-sufficiency remained beyond question. Notions of primary reality would remain so long as men felt the weight and authority of these ideals.

So much for the house of reason. But primary reality always had another house too, a darker dwelling where some forces loomed larger than reason.

Fate, Fortune and Everyday Uncertainties

Stoicism and Epicureanism enjoyed an Indian summer throughout the heady days of the third and second centuries B.C. Stoicism was to remain a vital force for several centuries to come. Confidence in nature and reason was buoyed by remarkable scientific advance. The tensions between order, fate and freedom were no longer a problem for the man who had achieved philosophical enlightenment. As Epicurus had put it: "Fortune but seldom interferes with the wise man; his greatest and highest interests have been, are, and will be, directed by reason throughout the course of his life."[7] Or so a tiny handful of intellectuals believed.

Intellectuals, of course, were in fact split over Fate. Epicurus had stated his preference for an enslavement to the old gods rather than to the Fate of the philosophers. Cicero attributed Fate to natural causes and to ignorance. Virgil couldn't make up his mind, Tacitus was similarly uncertain, and Lucian parodied Fate. Some Stoics, like Manilius and Fuscus, argued strongly for Fate as an essential part of the mechanism of nature. Even the educated elite sensed that Fate and Fortune were fickle and indiscriminate:

> Fortune, like some poetess, creates roles of every kind: the shipwrecked man, the poor man, the exile, the man of repute, the man without repute.[8]

> Fortune, exulting in her cruel work, and stubborn to pursue her wanton sport, shifts her fickle favors, kind now to me, now to some other.[9]

Seneca, a near-contemporary of Paul, complained of a widespread feeling of pointlessness and tedium in his time. If Pliny the Elder is any guide, the grand achievements of Hellenistic rationalism could not hold back this darkness encroaching on the soul:

> Throughout the whole world, at every place and hour, by every voice, Fortune alone is invoked and her name spoken: she is the one defendant, the one culprit, the one thought in men's minds, the one object of praise, the one cause. She is worshipped with insults, counted as fickle and often as blind, wandering, inconsistent, elusive, changeful and friend of the unworthy. . . . We are so much at the mercy of chance that Chance is our god.[10]

---

[7]Epicurus, in Diogenes Laertius *Lives of Eminent Philosophers* 10.144.

[8]Teles *On Circumstances* 6.52.2-3.

[9]Horace *Odes* 3.39.49-52.

[10]Pliny the Elder *Natural History* 2.22. Fortune (Tyche) figured prominently throughout the empire. Copies of her famous statue at Antioch by Eutychides (290 B.C.) proliferated so that virtually every community and family had a Fortune of their own. The coins of emperors ("Fortune of Augustus") bore the same message and ideal.

Even the most privileged could feel the dark presence. A funeral oration in the late first century B.C. for a Roman lady[11] offers a fascinating insight into the world of the elite—her husband has no doubt been a magistrate. We learn from the inscription that she had been cruelly orphaned on the eve of her marriage, had arranged revenge with her sister, orchestrated her husband's escape from enemies, negotiated with Caesar for his return from exile, vigilantly kept him out of further scrapes, whisked him away to safety again, defied the insults and abuses of his colleague while she resolutely stuck fast to Caesar's pardon for her husband, and offered to divorce him so that her (!) infertility would not prevent him from siring heirs. No wonder he missed her! As in the Jewish book of Esther, the omission of any direct reference to the favorable hand of the gods only seems to make them more present. But it is bitter Fate that consumes this nobleman's attention as he seeks solace for life's caprice:

> It would have been more just for me to have yielded to fate, since I was older than you. . . . I should confess, however, that on this occasion I suffered one of the bitterest experiences of my life, in the fate that befell you. . . . We longed for children, which an envious fate denied us for some time. If Fortune had let herself smile on us in the normal way, what would have been lacking to complete our happiness? . . . But fate decreed that your life ended before mine. You left me the grief, the longing for you, and the sad fate of living alone. . . . I pray that your Manes [protective spirits] may assure and protect your rest.[12]

Nearer the other end of the social scale is a gladiator's epitaph from Amasia in the imperial period. While hopes of immortality revived somewhat during this period, there continued to be strong denials of anything beyond the grave. The first line of this epitaph to a rough-and-ready man shows this plainly:

> I did not exist, I was born; I existed, I do not exist; so much [for that]. If anyone says anything different he will be lying; I shall not exist. Greetings, if you are a just person.[13]

The two verdicts appear again and again. Note the contrast between a matter-of-fact epitaph for a dead infant (first text below) and another expressing hope for a young child recently deceased (second text):

> When I had just tasted life fate snatched me, an infant, and I did not see my father's pattern; but I died after enjoying the light of eleven months, then I returned it. I lie in

---

[11]The so-called *Laudatio Turiae* inscription. See Greg Horsley, ed., *New Documents Illustrating Early Christianity* (Sydney: Macquarie University Press, 1983), 3:33–36.

[12]Ibid.

[13]Inscription at Rome from the imperial period, *IG* XIV (1890) 1201. See Horsley, *New Documents*, 4:42.

the tomb forever, no longer seeing the light; but you, stranger, read this and weep as you come upon the tomb of Eunoe.[14]

This tomb encloses a beautiful body which—alas!—[suffered] a violent fate. For Kore, wife of Ploutos, led you to Hades when you were six years old or a little more. But the blessed gods taking pity did not abandon your soul to sink into Hades' dwelling, and in the air it is in flight in the sky.[15]

From Smyrna in the second century A.D. comes a moralizing poem found on an epitaph near an image of a bearded man with his staff resting on a skull. Horsley thinks the figure is likely to represent a philosopher:

This is a human being; consider who you are and what awaits you. As you look at this image reflect upon your end and do not treat life as though you had forever to live, nor as though you are short-lived, with the result that many will scourge you verbally when you have become old and are afflicted with poverty.[16]

What are we to make of the author's response to life's brevity and uncertainty? One thing seems sure: death's imminence has brought him to the bottom line. No rarefied metaphysics or theology or moral idealism here. The message is simple: Your turn will come too—so make of life what you can now.

Life for most remained caught between a mysterious, awesome and frightening "other" and a pressing world of everyday concerns and opportunities—between the unseen powers and the puny efforts of men:

Magic without doctrine; devils without priests; prayers unintelligible; worship home-less; and ignominious realms of rule over a single house, a single field, cow, racehorse, gladiator, rival in love or adversary to one's career or party—all, together, constituted the broad underpart of the world above this one, the part which mortals felt them-selves to be most in contact.[17]

No wonder many looked for ways to predict and manipulate these forces and to shield themselves from their power.

The Everyday Manipulation of Primary Reality

The philosophers had a hard time refuting belief in the stars. Not only did astrology enjoy great popularity, but unwittingly or otherwise, philosophy had given it an intellectual framework. The basis lay in common cosmological assumptions: the order, unity and harmony of the universe; the interdependence of all its parts; and

---

[14]Inscription at Rome from the imperial period, *IG* XIV (1890) 1607 + 2171. See Horsley, *New Documents,* 4:40.

[15]Inscription *BE* 440. See Horsley, *New Documents,* 2:51–52.

[16]Inscription Pfuhl/Möbius I.847. See Horsley, *New Documents,* 4:43–44.

[17]R. MacMullen, *Paganism in the Roman Empire* (New Haven: Yale University Press, 1981), p. 83.

the general conviction that affairs on earth were a microcosm of the heavenly relationships. There had always been a deep curiosity to find a place for man in this system. Somewhat unwittingly, Plato's cosmology had fueled the occult. Astrology was proof that the universe was ordered. It could fit easily with Stoic acceptance of the divinity of the heavenly bodies, and it even received support from no less a figure than Posidonius. The doctrine seemed neat, complete and indisputable.

But astrology never depended on intellectual appeal. It was essentially religious: it dealt with the heavenly bodies and powers and with hope in immortality. It was practical: it offered a way to beat the cosmic system. It was eclectic: it drew together a deified Time, the ritual significance of seasons, and the movements of the divine heavenly bodies. And it could not be dismissed as the foolishness of the uneducated: even emperors believed in astrology.

Astrology belonged with other "manipulative" techniques in this period. It found a ready clientele for the same reasons that attracted faith in magic, prophecy, charms and oracles. Wherever people were disturbed by the sense of greater realities manipulating their lives, they found ways to make the greater reality work in their favor. So how could one calm the gods and keep in favor with them?

An introspective emperor only needed piety and platitudes: "Walk with the gods. And he does walk with the gods who lets them see his soul invariably satisfied with its lot."[18] Many intellectuals preferred to keep a low profile, like this Roman "theologian" of the third or fourth century whose epitaph reads: "I did not think about things which I ought not to: whether I had a previous existence, whether I shall have one in time [to come]."[19] Better to stick to writing praises of the gods and teaching morals.

In the century before Jesus Christ, the Roman Cicero had taught that theology does not speculate on the gap of power between God and man but "on the order, regularity, and beauty that are established and maintained through divine activity."[20] For Cicero this is the key to the difference between *superstitio,* which creates fear, and *religio,* which creates admiration and understanding of order. There is simply no need for a divine will behind or apart from "the entirely rational programming of reality."[21] Why should there be? God cannot improve a perfect design. Consequently, a knowledgeable man prays, not in order to move a god to change things, but in order to align himself with the order in the universe.[22] At least that's how some intellectuals saw it. Most people were happy enough to go along with the popular means of placating and second-guessing the gods.

---

[18]Marcus Aurelius *Meditations* 5.27.
[19]Inscription *IG* XIV [1890] 2068. See Horsley, *New Documents,* 4:32–33.
[20]Dihle, *Theory of Will,* p. 2.
[21]Ibid.
[22]See Seneca *Epistles* 41.1 and Plutarch *Isis and Osiris* 1.

The vast majority of the population had always taken prayer as a means to influence or change a god's mind and will. The desire was also expressed in charms, like this one from Antinoopolis in the third or fourth century:

> I entrust this binding-charm to you gods of the underworld. . . . I conjure all daimones in this place to assist this daimon Antinoos. Rouse yourself for me . . . and bind Ptolemais . . . [to not] provide pleasure to another [read *etero*] man. . . . Drag her by the hair, tear at her guts, until she does not reject me. . . . If you do this, I will release you.[23]

These kinds of mechanisms had great antiquity; they were not a novelty spurred by a new anxiety. It has been commonly assumed that a considerable shift in mood took place in the mid to late empire as it entered, in the words of E. R. Dodds's memorable phrase, "an age of anxiety."[24] More recent studies, while appreciative of Dodds's work, have emphasized the strong continuities across the period. Wherever we can detect changes in the features and prominence of the mystery cults, oracular shrines and dream interpreters, these should be seen as new angles on an old market. As Robin Fox has shown, the "old compound of awe and intimacy" was very old indeed.[25]

Some sought insurance against the gods in oracles, others through dreams:[26]

> Concerning the things about which you asked. You are well. What you desire night and day will be yours. As for what you want the gods will guide you and your livelihood will be for the better and your life will be distinguished.[27]

> Lysanias asks Zeus Naios and Dione whether the child that Annual is carrying is not by him.[28]

> To Ammias, her children and the initiates of the gods set up the altar with the sarcophagus for the priestess of the gods as a memorial. And if anyone wants to learn the truth from me, let him pray at(?) the altar whatever he wants and he will get it, via a vision, during night time and day.[29]

---

[23]Inscription *SEG* 1717. See Horsley, *New Documents*, 1:33–34.

[24]E. R. Dodds, *Pagan and Christian in an Age of Anxiety* (Cambridge: Cambridge University Press, 1965).

[25]Robin Fox, *Pagans and Christians in the Mediterranean World from the Second Century A.D. to the Conversion of Constantine* (London: Penguin, 1988), p. 237.

[26]The shrine likewise held a little insurance against disgruntled clients—a priest could hardly be held accountable for how "the god's natural truthfulness might be interrupted while they come down from heaven" (ibid., p. 215). Having personally grown up under a strong and somewhat ingenious emphasis on finding out the will of God for life choices, I cannot help but notice many strong correlations between the games of Graeco-Roman shrines and oracles and their fundamentalist, evangelical and charismatic counterparts.

[27]Manuscript of unknown provenance, first century A.D.; *P.Vindob. Salomons* I. See Horsley, *New Documents*, 2:37–38.

[28]Inscription from Dodona, second century B.C.; *SIG* 1163. See Horsley, *New Documents*, 4:134–35.

[29]Inscription from Thyatira in Lydia, second or third century A.D.; *EG* IV.119-20, p. 4:136.

A dead priestess was not the only one to offer revelation in a dream. The gods had done so for centuries, and the philosophers had backed them. In a dream, a man's soul was more attuned to the gods and their realm, as even Plato had hinted. A cottage industry developed around the risky art of interpreting these nocturnal visitations—always, of course, in line with a man's rank.[30] Dreams could offer fresh impetus to piety, even conversion:

> It seemed that in his sleep Sarapis was standing beside him and instructing him . . . to give to Eurynomos the letter which was under his pillow. Waking up [Xenainetos] was amazed at his vision and perplexed about what he should do because of the political hostility which he had towards Eurynomos. But falling asleep again, he had the same dream, and when he awoke he discovered the letter under his pillow, just as was indicated to him. When he returned home, he handed the letter to Eurynomos and reported the god's instructions. Eurynomos took the letter and after hearing what Xenainetos said he was perplexed [also]. . . . But when he read the letter and saw its contents were consistent with what had been said beforehand by Xenainetos, he accepted Sarapis and Isis.[31]

Like dreams, mysteries offered the chance of a safe encounter with a god who might control Fate for the one whom he or she favored: "I conquer Fate. It is to me that Fate listens."[32] This sentiment is attested to in inscriptions throughout the empire dating from the second century B.C. to the fourth century A.D. Wherever people sensed a god's presence, there was fear of its potential anger "and a wish to 'placate' it and avert it by correct performance."[33] But the mysteries offered more than safe ritual; they enabled personal faith and encounter.

The appeal of the mystery cults lay in the taste for certainty and dependence via palpable experience. What they offered was a way of detaching the inner life from the normal routine of ceremony and tradition: an immediate enlightenment by revelation leading to union with the god and victory over every evil force. The combination of myth and ritual could create a moment of dramatic experience heightened by the "secrecy" of the ceremony and initiation.

For the most part, however, the mysteries were as public as traditional religions. Thus Lucian complained that his teacher, Demonax, was the only one in Athens *not* initiated into the Eleusinian mysteries. But the image of dark rings of devotees waiting in anticipation and sworn to strictest silence was part of the experience. Some creative special effects could make the encounter even more memorable. For

---

[30]Fox, *Pagans and Christians*, p. 151.
[31]Inscription at Thessalonike in the first century A.D., *IG* x 2255. See Horsley, *New Documents*, 1:29–31.
[32]Inscription *I. Kyme* 41. See Horsley, *New Documents*, 1:18–21.
[33]Fox, *Pagans and Christians*, p. 230.

some, the encounter was nothing less than a rebirth: "It was in her power by divine providence to make them, as it were, new-born. . . . Holy goddess, everlasting savior of mankind, ever generous in your help to mortals, you show a mother's warm love for the misfortunes of those in distress. . . . You can unravel the inextricably tangled web of Fate, you can calm the gales of Fortune."[34]

The terrors and fortunes of the everyday had always weighed on the hearts and minds of the empire. For some this was nowhere stronger than in the face of death. While most educated people saw the other side of the grave much as the philosophers did (as a disembodied soul), there were those who hoped for a pleasurable afterlife. Thus, in the second century there was something of a shift from cremation to inhumation.[35] In the end, immortality might be the only comeback against the fickle fortunes of everyday reality.

Powers and deities could seem too remote to help or too menacingly close. Simple belief was far from simple. With no orthodoxy to restrict one's choices, a man would gather gods as he might friends. The more, the safer. Perhaps he felt particularly close to one. But everyday realities brought a distinctly businesslike mood to the relationship. Regular transactions were needed to balance the accounts between the everyday and that other darker reality.

---

[34]Apuleius *Metamorphoses* 11.21–25.

[35]It should be noted that the evidence is inconclusive. Epitaphs of the period attest both verdicts on the afterlife (see Fox, *Pagans and Christians,* p. 96).

5

RANK, STATUS
& CONVENTION

PHILOSOPHY WAS ALWAYS TIED TO SOCIAL CONVENTION AND POSITION. ALMOST WITHOUT exception philosophers lived among the privileged and generally upheld the social conventions. The sophisticated hierarchies of the philosophers presupposed and reinforced the self-evident rightness of the social pyramid. The power of tradition could absorb and neutralize contradictions and anomalies raised by new ideas. This held true from at least classical times. A quick revisit of the philosophers will show how deeply their ideas were rooted in the conventions and expectations of social rank and status.

Ideals and Social Conformity
Rare was the philosopher who could live where reason led. The atomism of Democritus, a pre-Socratic philosopher, had opened up radical perspectives with the potential to deeply challenge accepted conventions. But the fragments in Stobaeus's *Anthology* suggest that in practice Democritus[1] had remained tied to tradition:

> Men fashioned the image of chance as an excuse for their own thoughtlessness; for chance rarely fights with wisdom, and a man of intelligence will, by foresight, set

---

[1]Some texts attributed to Democritus may be of dubious authenticity. See Jonathon Barnes, *Early Greek Philosophy* (London: Penguin, 1987), pp. 24-35. The following translations from Stobaeus and Clement are by Barnes.

straight most things in his life. (2.8.16)

It is fitting to yield to the law, the rulers, the wiser. (3.1.45)

Chance may be no more than convention and ignorance, but fortune, natural law and civil order remain unshaken. Likewise the ideals of status, balance, temperance, order, discipline and reason:

It is hard to be ruled by an inferior. (4.4.27)

If your character is orderly, your life too will be well-ordered. (3.37.25)

For men gain contentment from moderation and a measured life: deficiencies and excesses tend to change and to produce large movements of the soul, and souls which move across large intervals are neither stable nor content. (3.1.210)

Fortune provides a rich table, temperateness a self-sufficient one. (3.5.26)

The fifth century B.C. had brought new social complexities and laws, changing quickly, without sanction in antiquity and therefore without the traditional hallmark of credibility. Comparative anthropology raised questions about the fixity of law and religious custom. As E. R. Dodds explained, law normally meant "the entire body of traditional usage which governed the whole of [a man's] civic conduct, political, social, and religious."[2] Law was accepted as an unchangeable inheritance. All human laws were sustained by one divine law that stood constant beneath the changes of the everyday. But the debate had begun: Is the social restraint imposed on nature by law good or bad?

For Protagoras, much like Heraclitus, the law may be better or worse from one place to the next, but it stands while the people believe it. The law is king. Yet for Hippias, the law is a tyrant, an artificial bond. So also Euripides' famous line, "There is nothing shocking but thinking makes it so."[3] In this spirit, Antiphon rejected race and class distinctions as arbitrary: "By nature we all stand with a like equipment, whether we are barbarian or Greeks; our natural wants are the same . . . we breathe a common air . . . we feel respect and awe for the nobly born, and for them only: in this matter we behave like barbarians to our own people."[4]

Likewise, Euripides and others were intensely conscious of the rights of individuals against society and felt a concern for the oppressed classes. Alcidamas, Georgias's student, captured the mood: "God has left all men free; Nature has made none a slave."[5] Here were individualists, humanists, secularists and iconoclasts

---

[2] E. R. Dodds, *The Ancient Concept of Progress and Other Essays on Greek Literature and Belief* (Oxford: Oxford University Press, 1973), p. 97.

[3] Fragment 19.

[4] P. Oxy 1364.

[5] Alcidamas in Schol. Aristotle *Rhetoric* 1373b.

with intellectual bonds stronger than arbitrary national customs. Yet confidence in reason did not lead the Sophists to social revolution. Eventually they passed on a thoroughly conventional legacy—"nature is right"—to many conventional sons.

Earlier we noted how Plato's moral teaching and social ideals matched the characteristics of reality and perfection in his cosmology. All moral and social prescription derived from "the Good," the form of absolute beauty and moral perfection:

> We distinguish between the many particular things which we call beautiful or good, and absolute beauty and goodness. Similarly with all other collections of things, we say there is corresponding to each set a single, unique Form which we call an "absolute" reality.[6]

> The Good therefore may be said to be the source not only of the intelligibility of the objects of knowledge, but also of their existence and reality; yet it is not itself identical with reality, but is beyond reality, and superior to it in dignity and power.[7]

Plato's ultimate goal was not a perfect theoretical system but a perfect city-state, ruled by a wise philosopher-king and politically and pedagogically engineered to maintain strict guidelines for social and moral purity. It was a bold vision—a scheme to bring heaven as close to earth as mortals could do.

The decline of the Greek city-states in the fourth century had a huge bearing on the idealism of Plato and Aristotle. In response, they sketched the shape of a society founded on pure rational inquiry, a society structured by the ideals of liberty, autonomy and the rule of law. The noblest citizens of this society, Aristotle argued, will always choose the highest and purest ends: "As an instance of pleasures of the soul, consider the love of distinction in public life or in some branch of learning. The devotee in either case takes pleasure in what he loves without any physical sensations. What he feels is a spiritual or intellectual pleasure, and we do not speak of men who seek that kind of pleasure as 'temperate' or 'intemperate.'"[8]

Speaking in the Lyceum, Aristotle would have been heartily endorsed by the elite for his ideals:

> As for the superior man, since nothing is too good for him, he must be the best of men. For the better a man is, the more he deserves, so that he who deserves most is the best. Therefore, the truly superior man must be a good man. Indeed, greatness in all the virtues is surely what stamps him for what he is. . . . For honor is the guardian of goodness and is awarded to the good. . . . He will rarely undertake anything or, if he does, it will be something great and glorious. . . . He must live his own life uninflu-

---

[6]Plato *Republic* 507B.
[7]Ibid., 509B.
[8]Aristotle *Nicomachean Ethics* 3.10.

enced by anyone, unless perhaps a friend, since to permit such influence would involve some degree of complaisance.[9]

Balanced, temperate, serene, reasonable, superior men; above the irregularities of life and the pettiness of lesser men—such men discern the extremes of the everyday and, guided by reason, choose the middle way:

> Virtue . . . observes the mean relative to us, this being determined by such a rule or principle as would take shape in the mind of a man of sense or practical wisdom. We call it a mean condition as lying between two forms of badness, one being excess and the other deficiency; and also for this reason, that, whereas badness either falls short of or exceeds the right measure in feelings and actions, virtue discovers the mean and deliberately chooses it.[10]

The confidence of materialism reached into every corner of Hellenistic life. In classical times, painting and sculpture had conveyed lofty images of universal ideals. But the emerging individualism of the fourth century made art more realist. Great pressure surfaced at every level to conform to the newly emerging culture. The kings and the rich built vast libraries. New routes and means of trade brought unimagined commodities and treasures. The gap between rich and poor widened dramatically. The old rivalry of cities and aristocratic dynasties extended down the social scale, bringing new players and pressures into the old game of keeping up with the neighbors. Vast expenditure in education and public projects was meant to impress and secure loyalties.

The age brought new access to education, but it was far from egalitarian. Training in rhetoric, the essential preparation for young men entering the burgeoning world of bureaucracy, remained housed in the best gymnasia or with expensive private tutors. The boys of the best families were marked out to "keep up the idealization of the city."[11]

Several Latin writers, notably Cicero, Virgil and Seneca, extolled human cooperation and the brotherhood of man. Posidonius, one of the great intellects of the second and first centuries B.C., combined hopes of a universal commonwealth with the reality of Roman imperial rule. The city of God, the rule of divine providence, had come to earth in the great cosmopolis, the symbol of the unification of human history.

But individualism prevailed. The ideal of the detached, self-sufficient man

---

[9]Ibid., 4.3.

[10]Ibid., 2.6.

[11]Robin Fox, *Pagans and Christians in the Mediterranean World from the Second Century AD to the Conversion of Constantine* (London: Penguin, 1988), p. 343. Note also the *epikrisis* papyri *P.Mich.* XIV 676. For a copy and translation, see Stephen Llewelyn, ed., *New Documents Illustrating Early Christianity* (Sydney: Macquarie University, 1992), 6:132–40.

withdrawn into himself remained. But withdrawal was rarely complete. Philosophers, especially those with Roman connections, usually taught and moved among the ranks of the ambitious. The true test of wisdom was inner and outer serenity. Stoics, Epicureans and Platonists portrayed the sage who stood above the changes of life.[12]

Such was the power of the ideal that Seneca seemed unperturbed about whether such a man had or would ever exist: the ideal sage stood supreme over all other men. He may be defeated in body but never in mind: "Know, therefore, Serenus, that this perfect man, full of virtues human and divine, can lose nothing. . . . The walls which guard the wise man are safe both from flame and assault, they provide no means of entrance—are lofty, impregnable, godlike.[13]

Epictetus also harmonized inner freedom with social conformity.[14] All philosophers agreed that the primary task was to shape the self.[15] The process began with self-knowledge ("know yourself"), proceeded through education in the cardinal virtues (courage, wisdom, justice, self-control), cultivated reason, and pruned back the emotions until *apatheia*, or impassivity, brought its serene rule. To quote Seneca again:

> Do you ask me what you should regard as especially to be avoided? I say, crowds; for as yet you cannot trust yourself to them with safety. I shall admit my own weakness, at any rate; for character that I took abroad with me, something of that which I have forced to be calm within me is disturbed; some of the foes that I have routed return again. But both courses are to be avoided . . . withdraw into yourself as far as you can. Associate with those who will make a better man of you. Welcome those whom you yourself can improve.[16]

The same ideals held for Stoics, Epicureans, Peripatetics and Cynics, irrespective of how they disputed about the value of emotions or of teaching the masses.[17] The *ideal* was all-important, not the particulars of any given situation. A socially well-placed Stoic could point to a fiercely individualist Cynic as the embodiment of the Stoic quest for autonomy, even while he derided the Cynic's antisocial behavior. Self-praise could at the same time be both odious and an accepted tool and right of the philosopher.[18]

---

[12]See J. T. Fitzgerald, *Cracks in an Earthen Vessel: An Examination of the Catalogues of Hardships in the Corinthian Correspondence,* Society of Biblical Literature Dissertation Series 99 (Atlanta: Scholars Press, 1988), pp. 59–65, and the texts cited there.
[13]Seneca *On the Firmness of the Wise Man* 6.3-8.
[14]Epictetus *Discourse* 3.22.38-49, cf. 1.1.22-24.
[15]Ibid., 1.4.18-21; see also Musonius Rufus *What Is the Best Provision for Old Age,* frag. 16.
[16]Seneca *Moral Epistles* 7.1, 8.
[17]E.g., Dio Chrysostom *Oration* 13.13; Seneca *Moral Epistles* 75; Pseudo-Diogenes *Epistle* 29:4-5.
[18]Plutarch *Moralia* 539A-547F.

So much for philosophy. Most people found their direction in folksy maxims and in religion. Religion could be a powerful vehicle for patriotic emotion.[19] Isocrates interpreted the religious agendas of the Egyptian legislator Busiris this way: "He thought that the crowd ought to be habituated to obedience to all the commands of those in authority."[20] Lucretius protested, but the first century scarcely heard such protests. Livy and Virgil glorified Rome and Italy, employing religious myth and themes liberally to do so. No one made more political use of religion than the emperor Augustus. MacMullen notes that, while somewhat sensitive to hypocrisy, the priest-philosopher Plutarch nonetheless concurred "that the masses' faith should be stimulated so as to direct their thoughts upward in reverence for nobility: to be found among the gods, found likewise among the local—nobility."[21]

Whatever private release individuals enjoyed through the cultic mysteries, the cults were carefully monitored and patronized to maintain social order. Individual, aristocratic and civic pride found expression in piety, priesthoods and benefactions. A late-first-century A.D. inscription from Ephesus conventionally links the imperial cult to the celebration of the mysteries of Demeter:

> To Lucius Mestrius Florus, proconsul, from Lucius Pompeius Apollonius of Ephesos. Mysteries and sacrifices are performed every year at Ephesos, sir, to Demeter Karpophoros and Thesmophoros and to the divine Augusti by initiates with much propriety and lawful customs, together with the priestesses; [the mysteries] have been watched over for many years by kings and emperors and the annual proconsul. . . . Accordingly, since the mysteries are soon upon us during your term of office, sir, those who ought to perform the mysteries necessarily petition you through my agency in order that you, recognising their rights.[22]

We leave the religious reinforcement of social convention with another inscription, this time from the mid-second century. Once again, the Ephesian worshipers of Artemis both need and expect Roman imprimatur. The author leaves us in doubt as to the social function of his role, and of his inscription:

> The proconsul Gaius Popillius Carus Pedo states: "I learned from the decree which was sent to me by the most illustrious council of the Ephesians that the honorable proconsuls before me regarded the days of the festival of the Artemisia as holy and have made this clear by edict. This is why I considered it necessary, since I also have regard for the reverence of the goddess and for the honor of the most illustrious city of the Ephesians, to make it known by decree that these days shall be holy and the festal holidays

---

[19]Polybius *Histories* 6.56.

[20]Isocrates *Busiris* 26.

[21]R. MacMullen, *Paganism in the Roman Empire* (New Haven, Conn.: Yale University Press, 1981), p. 59.

[22]Inscription *I.Eph.* II.213. See Greg Horsley, ed., *New Documents Illustrating Early Christianity* (Sydney: Macquarie University Press, 1983), 3:94–95.

will be observed on these days." [This edict was promulgated] while *Titus Aelius Marcianus Priscus*, son of Aelius Priscus, *a man very well thought of and worthy of all honour and acceptance*, was leader of the festival and president of the athletic games.[23]

The sense of primary reality was carried by the conventions of social experience. Intellectualism preferred the abstractions of form and logos, mind and being, Demiurge and the One. Religious sensibility located the "other reality" in dramatic ritual and initiation, and in oracular and miraculous visits from the gods. Popular superstition explained catastrophic, bizarre and everyday occurrences through Fate, Fortune, magic, omens and charms. Social relationships remained fixed in the impenetrable and unquestionable logic of the love of honor *(philotimia)*, the common source of competition and concord.

Social Order and Convention

A great gulf separated local aristocracies from their dependents. The senators and knights of Rome might as well have been the Olympian circle of the gods, so far were they removed from most people's experience, even from the local elites. The presence of the Roman elite, like that of the gods, was felt everywhere, but with little if any familiarity. In an age when realism vied with idealism in art, the grandeur of earlier ages was pressed into imperial coins and statues to present rulers godlike before their far-flung subjects. Even local aristocrats who aped Rome's manners were likely to know this fraction of a percent of the empire more through the erosion of their own rights to govern than through any personal familiarity.

Elitism was not confined to the top. Conventions of distinction and patronage operated across the social pyramid. "Free," "freed" or "slave" stamped a person for life. With little prospect of ever changing rank, the numerous strata of free and freed jealously guarded their pecking orders. On a papyrus from Oxyrhynchos, an application for admitting a son to membership of the gymnasium stretches back six generations on his father's side and eight on his mother's to prove his good stock.[24] Household slaves gave themselves ranks with special prominence for the literate. We find them in the occupational references on their tombstones and in the wills of their masters.[25] A freedman might rise to great prominence, yet never throw off his stigma among the old wealthy and the satirists.

Whatever "inner" meaning a person might find in the Delphic maxims, they spoke to him first of all of his social place:

---

[23]Inscription *I.Eph.* Ia.24. See Ray Oster, "Holy Days in Honour of Artemis," in Horsley, *New Documents,* 4:74–82.

[24]*P.Mich.* XIV 676. See Llewelyn, *New Documents,* 6:132–40.

[25]See *P. Oxy.* 3197, dated 20.10.111. See Horsley, *New Documents,* 1:69–70.

"Know yourself" = know your rank and its obligations

"Nothing to excess" = regulate behavior to what is expected

"Pick your time" = pick the opportune moment to improve status

"A cost to every commitment" = weigh the risk to honor in each relationship

The philosophers did not create the values enshrined in the maxims or cardinal virtues. Nor did they create the ideals of self-sufficiency and impassivity. These were written into the cultural mindset from the earliest expressions of caste. Intellectuals only projected what everybody knew: one must maintain one's rank.[26] The proximity of urban living made everyone's status conspicuous: every day in many subtle and overt ways, every man, woman or child was reminded of his or her rank. Even in death it was important to set the record straight: "Here lies Valeria, daughter of Marcus, *of free-born status* from Caesarea in Mauritania. She was kind, affectionate, dignified, blameless."[27]

Every system creates those who manipulate it. The fixed hierarchy was not always so fixed. New blood entered the knights and senators of Rome as well as the lesser local aristocracies. Roman army veterans could rise to a modest local prominence. A slave in Caesar's household had prospects far superior to that of other slaves, even to many respectable free-born citizens. Occasionally someone might even move down in order to move up: "Gaia greets you as do her children and her husband. Know, then, that Herminos went off to Rome and became a freedman of Caesar in order to take appointments."[28]

Honor could be gained without any change in legal position. Wealth, education, marriage, adoption, administrative or rhetorical talent, piety, virtue and citizenship could each offer a platform for status. The costly business of benefactions brought status to those of means, as Plutarch observed: "Most people think that to be deprived of the chance to display their wealth is to be deprived of wealth itself."[29] The quest for status was upheld as a noble goal even by the exploited. As Edwin Judge noted, those lucky enough to make the climb made sure that others knew about it at the end: "The system of public eulogies is the principle ideological regulator in Greek society under the Empire. It interprets and applies the social position which the notable citizens established through benefactions."[30]

---

[26]Libanius *Orations* 48.31; Cicero *Pro Cnaeo Plancio* 15.

[27]Side 1, inscription at Cairo, late first or early second century A.D., SEG 1536. See Horsley, *New Documents,* 3:40–43, emphasis mine.

[28]*P.Oxy.* 3312. See Horsley, *New Documents,* 3:7–9.

[29]Plutarch *Cato maior* 18.4.

[30]Edwin Judge, *Rank and Status in the World of the Caesars and St. Paul: The Broadhead Memorial Lecture 1981* (Christchurch: University of Canterbury Press, 1982), p. 106.

Note the indicators of prominence in this Roman epitaph: "This is the tomb of Rufinus, whom they used to call Asterios. He left the land of Rome and went to the city of the Nile; and shining out in the progress he made, he provided many things for many people, causing distress to no one, but considered what was just."[31]

No convention surpassed friendship as a means of personal ambition and maintaining a balanced system. Contracts of cooperation *(amicitia)* among aristocrats and others of high office maintained political affiliations and secured election to important posts. These contracts could be reinforced through marriage, divorce and adoption. The patron-client relationship *(clientela)* cemented the bonds between the powerful and the less so. This was an arrangement of mutual self-interest. Money passed downward; political and other support passed up; honor moved both ways. Once entered, the *clientela* bond was for life, even passing through the generations, like the ties of a freedman's family to his previous master. An entire society maintained its ideals and elitism through vast, sometimes complicated quasi-legal networks of obligation.[32] As a specific instance of *clientela,* note the deference of this client to his patron:

> Herm . . . [to Sarapion] . . . greetings, and that you may always remain in good health in your whole person for long years to come, since your good genius allowed us to greet you with respect and salute you. For as you also make mention of us on each occasion by letter, so I here make an act of worship for you in the presence of the lords Dioskouroi and in the presence of the lord Sarapis, and I pray for your safe-keeping during your entire life and for the health of your children and of all your household. Farewell in everything, I beg, my patron and fosterer.[33]

Throughout classical times the honor of a city was a function, not of its size, but of its institutions: the quality of its citizenry, the magnanimity of their benefactions, the antiquity of its law, the prestige of its council, the orderliness of its lawful assemblies, and the impressiveness of its architecture and civic projects.[34] The

---

[31]Inscription at Rome from the third or fourth century A.D., *IG* XIV 1976. See also *CIL* 8.11824 for a record of rural rags-to-riches. See Horsley, *New Documents,* 4:35–38.

[32]Responding to the criticism that Roman systems of *amicitia* and *clientela* did not operate in Greek states, Edwin Judge surveyed the Egyptian papyri for uses of the normal Greek term for a protective guardianship *(prostatēs)* and the technical loan word *(patrōn)* for the Roman arrangement. He concluded, "We can assume a prevailing familiarity with Roman patronal practice and ideals, which were transposed also to international relations, so that it may be taken as a realistic guide to the ethical character of such other conventions of personal dependency as will have existed in the various Greek states" ("Cultural Conformity and Innovation in Paul: Some Clues from Contemporary Documents," *Tyndale Bulletin* 35 [1984]: 20).

[33]Papyri letter of unknown origin in first or second century A.D., CPR 19. See Horsley, *New Documents,* 1:56–57.

[34]The next few paragraphs roughly follow the survey in Wayne Meeks, *The Moral World of the First Christians,* Library of Early Christianity 6 (Philadelphia: Westminster Press, 1986), pp. 19–64.

pride of a city was its autonomy and self-sufficiency. These were the ideals of Plato's Athens. But a bigger political infrastructure had pruned the autonomy of the local elites. Local decisions were increasingly centralized. Dio of Prusa warned the wealthy of Tarsus to make up with the poor linen weavers, else "you may lose the right of free speech altogether."[35] Yet pride in being a local citizen remained. Philosophers still declaimed on political models and ideals no matter how hollow they might sound. Philo followed others in psychologizing the utopian state, not least because of his personal experience of the fickleness of emperors' whims regarding the Jews. Few people entertained agendas for revolution or social transformation, and no institutions existed for such change.

Intellectuals preached on the justice and injustice of contemporary arrangements and their ambiguities. Their ideals of orderliness, perfection and the divinity of nature were used to uphold the rightness of Roman rule. Some professed to be citizens of the universal cosmopolis. Stoics articulated a universal republic, a commonwealth of mankind whose king was nature, whose law was the rational structure of reality and whose citizens were the fortunate few Stoics able to live in harmony with this reason. The mystique of empire and city held as long as no one looked closely at the poor quality of life endured by most inhabitants.

In Hellenistic and imperial times, social exclusion prompted the formation of small associations. These spontaneous associations often formed around people of common trades, creating social bonds otherwise unavailable through households or republic. Like the family and the republic, worship of a patron god gave expression to the unity of the associations, though some were entirely secular. Particularly common in the larger trade centers and in the cities of Asia Minor, these clubs increasingly served an economic function, providing support in hardships and a funeral fund for members, though their activities remained focused in the fellowship of a shared meal. For those with few hopes of public honors, the club's wealthy patron and its elaborate set of titles and regulations mirrored the structures of civic life and offered an outlet for pride, loyalty and ambition.

Each institution—family, republic, club—upheld and reinforced the ideals of order, balance, harmony and self-sufficiency. The conventions of honor and shame created checks and balances to keep people fixed firmly in their places. In the popular intellectualism of Paul's day, the gulf between primary and everyday reality was the everyday experience of living in a social pyramid.

A Tale of Two Realities

"Primary reality" and "everyday reality" are clumsy labels, but the picture is

---

[35]Dio of Prusa *Orations* 34.39.

clear enough. A marked presumption of and deference to a reality beyond the stuff of everyday life colored popular intellectualism from classical times to Paul's day and beyond. At the same time, idealism and abstraction did not erase the priority of everyday living. Intellectuals sought meaning for history, relationships and the everyday. But their methods presupposed and gave priority to the other reality.

Call it what we will, the sense of primary reality persisted in many different, even contradictory senses: that the invisible, unchanging forms are more real than the everyday world of the senses; that there is an inner "core" or "essence" or "first principle" to things; that this essence is somehow more real than the outer trappings; that what never changes is better than what does; that the general is more important than the particular; that the greatest truths are timeless and universal; that a certain aloofness marked heroes and sages of past times, legends and philosophers' ideals; that nature has endowed some men superior to others; that the highest god is unfeeling, unchanging, unmoving, unknowable; that one should know one's place in the world and live up to its expectations; that reason and piety are the paths to immortality; that the highest good is to be found in the speculative, philosophical activity of the mind, the most honorable part of man; that the greatest truths of the gods are to be kept in mysteries; that god is known only where words and logic have ceased. This sense of primary reality lived in art and ritual and architecture, in social rank and civic duty and funeral oratory.

Something within, without, above, below, beyond. Something other than here-and-now, you-and-me. This is the sense of primary reality, of the essence, of the ideal, of the perfect. It is equally the parent of rationalism and irrationalism. Hard-headed logician and contemplative mystic made their home on this foundation. Sophists debunked it while creating their own version of it. Plato sought to name it. Aristotle was equally indebted to it, even as he went about correcting his master. The Delphic maxims presumed it. Moralists argued with one another, yet never moved from this common ground. Art and architecture celebrated and mimicked it. Letters, epitaphs and graffiti presumed it as they mocked it.

The desires of Graeco-Roman intellectuals and the less-educated were as intensely personal as those we will see in Paul. But the outlook was radically different. Somewhat ironically, ancient intellectuals discarded the ordinary in their search for its value. It is not always so different in our own evangelical conventions.

Before we turn to the ways Paul framed his preoccupation with Jesus Christ, the last word on the power of an ideal belongs to Paul's contemporary Seneca, that prince of Roman perfectionists:

> Among the very persons who are making progress there are also great spaces intervening. They fall into three classes, as certain philosophers believe. First come those who

have not yet attained wisdom but have already gained a place near by. Yet even that which is not far away is still outside. . . . The second class is composed of those who have laid aside both the greatest ills of the mind and its passions, but yet are not in assured possession of immunity. . . . The third class are beyond the reach of many of the vices and particularly the great vices, but not beyond the reach of all. . . . There awaits us, if ever we escape from these low dregs to that sublime and lofty height, peace of mind and, when all error has been driven out, perfect liberty. You ask what this freedom is? It means not fearing either men or gods; it means not craving wickedness or excess; it means possessing supreme power over oneself. And it is a priceless good to be master of oneself. Farewell.[36]

---

[36]Seneca *Moral Epistles* 75.9-18

PART 2

PAUL ON JESUS CHRIST
Frames for Telling the Story

6

SOCIAL FRAMES

ALTHOUGH CERTAIN THEMES AND PHRASES RECUR FREQUENTLY IN HIS LETTERS, PAUL HAS no single central theme—neither justification, redemptive history, apocalyptic, personal encounter nor community. There is no single structure to Paul's thought, no single way that he framed his understanding. Quests by New Testament scholars and others to isolate a central theme are ill-conceived from the start. A similar game has evolved among historians to locate Paul within one or another of the formal schools of his time. Paul's letters do not fit these systems of thought, as we shall see in detail in part three. Unlike the various classical and Graeco-Roman models of primary reality, Paul's thought was anchored in the everyday—in the story of a man.

Framing the Story of Jesus Christ
Paul was first of all preoccupied with a person, Jesus Christ. The story of Jesus formed Paul's message or "gospel" of good news. Paul's preoccupation with Christ and his story gave coherence to all his letters and enabled him to translate his message for each new audience and circumstance. In many ways, as we will explore further in part four, Paul was like a jazz musician improvising on a theme. The theme was Christ and his story; the improvisations were the various ways in which he brought his knowledge of Christ to bear upon the changing circumstances of his own life and the lives of those in the fledgling *ekklēsiai*.

This is a far cry from what we have seen of the classical and Graeco-Roman worlds. Paul's thought does not fit the distinction between *primary reality* and *everyday reality*. We will get further by framing his message in terms of three quite ordinary perspectives: (1) social interactions, (2) history, and (3) personal experience (see figure 6.1). Each frame leads to the others.

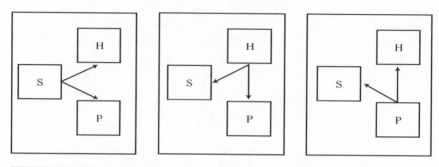

Figure 6.1. The interdependence of the social, the historical and the personal in Paul

We will note this interdependence throughout parts two, three and four. Our aim is not to reduce Paul's life and thought to any system, but to portray the vitality and interdependence of Paul's life and thought as a reference point for new conversations about Paul and evangelicalism.

Respect and Frustration Toward Jerusalem and the Law

Paul appears as a man caught between two worlds. He was the son of a Pharisee. His parents raised him within an orthodox faith and apparently moved to Jerusalem while he was still young. This was perhaps to enable his training at the feet of Gamaliel as a conservative Pharisee. Perhaps also it was the only place where he could receive a thoroughly traditional training in Judaism. His ancestry, heritage, training and progress as a Pharisee were matters of great pride to him for much of his life.[1]

Paul was also a freeborn Roman citizen of Tarsus, a thoroughly Hellenized city, the capital of the Roman province of Cilicia and a significant educational center for studies in philosophy and rhetoric. While some scholars had earlier discounted the possibility of Paul's having received a formal higher education, such an education is the most reasonable and likely explanation for the sophisticated grasp of rhetorical conventions Paul showed in his deeply ironic reply to the Corinthians' accusations.

The contrast seems stark: Paul, the traditional Pharisee and the educated Hellenistic man. But the dichotomy is misleading, for these worlds had long since pene-

---

[1]See Acts 22:3-5; 23:6; 26:4-5; 2 Cor 11:22; Gal 1:13-14; Phil 3:4-7.

trated one another. If Paul had spent any of his childhood education in the synagogue schools of Tarsus, he would have been well trained in Greek and quite familiar with the basic materials of a Greek education. But even if he had received all his education in Jerusalem, the same would apply. The fact is that Jerusalem was in many ways as Hellenistic as any other city of the empire. Martin Hengel's verdict on the relation of "Jewish-Hellenistic" and "genuine Jewish" literature of the centuries immediately before Christ holds also for the two cultural traditions: "There were connections in all directions, and a constant and lively interchange."[2] Just as the older dichotomy of Greek versus Hebrew thought is now seen to rest on false antitheses,[3] much of the effort by New Testament scholars to locate Paul within "Hellenistic Jewish," "Palestinian Jewish" or "purely Hellenistic" cultures is also ill-conceived.

So the gap between these cultural worlds was not always vast. None of this, however, should be seen to minimize the deeply felt convictions of those Jews who labored to educate their countrymen and convert Gentiles to a life shaped by the law and by a high regard for Jerusalem as the city of God.[4]

Paul epitomized this desire. Alongside the status opportunities that the language and education of the Greeks had given him, Saul the Pharisee shared his peers' zeal for their heritage. Although "orthodox" Judaism was reasonably pluralistic, indeed far more than its leaders may have cared to acknowledge, a strident fundamentalism nevertheless came to the fore during times of crisis and threat.[5]

---

[2]Martin Hengel, *The "Hellenization" of Judaea in the First Century After Christ* (London: SCM Press, 1989), p. 26. Hengel's survey of the evidence for educational practices, language, social mobility, architecture and other features of city life highlights the extent to which Jerusalem had absorbed the newer culture. None of this means that the city and its people had lost their linguistic, religious and cultural distinctives. Rather, Hengel's point is that "even where there was opposition and conflict involving vigorous argument with the new pagan civilization . . . people became more strongly 'infected' by it than they realized" (p. 19). An interesting footnote to the extent of this unrealized absorption of culture is the adoption in the Passover meal of the Greek habit of reclining to eat. As Greg Horsley notes, "If the last supper (Jn. 13.22ff) were a Passover meal one might expect that orthodox Jews would not have reclined at least on this occasion, however much they might have done so in other situations . . . [yet this passage may well reveal] how thoroughly normal this Greek fashion was felt to be by pious first-century Jews from rural Galilee" (*New Documents Illustrating Early Christianity* [Sydney: Macquarie University Press, 1981], 1:9; see also 4:233 on Hellenistic customs at Jewish weddings).

[3]See the following surveys on the various false linguistic arguments used to prop up the dichotomy: James Barr, *The Semantics of Biblical Language* (Oxford: Oxford University Press, 1961); Moises Silva, *Biblical Words and Their Meaning: An Introduction to Lexical Semantics* (Grand Rapids, Mich.: Zondervan, 1983); and *God, Language and Scripture: Reading the Bible in the Light of General Linguistics*, Foundations of Contemporary Interpretation 4 (Grand Rapids, Mich.: Zondervan, 1990); Horsley, *New Documents*, vol. 5.

[4]Cf. Philo *On Dreams* 2.245-54.

[5]See Robyn Tracey, "Jewish Renovation of an Amphitheatre," in Horsley, *New Documents*, 4:204.

This nationalistic reaction to crises helps explain several events in the lives of Jesus and Paul: the responses of the Jerusalem leaders to Jesus, Paul's response to the first Christians, and the responses of the Jerusalem leaders and Jewish Christians to Paul's preaching of Messiah Jesus.[6]

We do not need any Hellenistic-Palestinian dichotomy or any stereotype of Judaism as excessively legalistic to understand the tension. Jesus, the first Christians, and the converted Paul each touched a nerve: that deep consciousness of identity and heritage that accompanied the law, the city and the temple. This tension with Jerusalem unavoidably shaped much of Paul's subsequent life and thought.

Paul understood his dramatic conversion as an encounter with the Messiah and as his commission to declare the arrival of his kingdom. The event deeply influenced Paul's thought.[7] It reworked his understanding of his Jewish heritage as well as undermining his confidence in it. He had come from Jerusalem full of zeal and with the blessing of its religious leaders to persecute the followers of Jesus. But now he saw the Christians as the ones who were truly faithful to the God of his fathers. His self-righteousness was shaken, and Jerusalem began to lose its grip on him.

Paul's sense of Jewish heritage did not disappear. He still looked to the Jewish scriptures as his understanding about Christ's fulfillment of Israel's identity and history developed. His teaching consistently respected the divine origin and blessing of Israel's heritage. Although his Hebrew name no longer seemed important to him, he still identified with his countrymen, worked from their synagogues, often conformed to Jewish practice and went to great lengths to support the poor in Jerusalem.[8]

Paul's new message was always likely to antagonize Jerusalem, however. He saw the end of the law in Christ's appearance.[9] His teaching often radically departed from conventional Jewish theology and biblical interpretation.[10] He became exasperated with what he saw as Jewish blindness to prophecy and fulfillment. He was angered by those who placed Jewish constraints on his message and friends. Like Jesus, he knew he did not need approval from the leaders in

---

[6]Luke 13:31—14:14; 19:41—20:39; Acts 22:3–5; Gal 1:13-14; Acts 15:5; 21:20-36.

[7]Acts 9:1-19; cf. 22:3-16; 26:4-18. Seyoon Kim argues that virtually all of Paul's thought flows from his conversion experience (*The Origin of Paul's Gospel* [Grand Rapids, Mich.: Eerdmans, 1981]). While I find his arguments generally persuasive, at times he seems too tied to portraying Paul's thought as a tidy system built on this foundational experience. He helpfully opens up Paul's allusions to the event beyond those passages normally taken to refer to it (viz. 1 Cor 9:1; 15:8-10; Gal 1:13-17; Phil 3:4-11). I will return in part four to the importance of this event for Paul.

[8]Acts 24:10ff; 25:8; 18:6, 23; 16:3; 21:26; 1 Cor 16:1-4; Gal 2:10.

[9]Rom 10:4; Gal 3:25; 6:2; Eph 2:14-15; Col 2:14.

[10]Acts 15:2; 18:2; 21:18, 27-29.

Jerusalem or even from the apostles there.[11]

Paul's refusal to tailor his message to any claimed priority for Jerusalem helps to explain his letter to the Galatians.[12] There is no need to stereotype the Jerusalem group or the Judaizers or Pharisees as having no understanding of grace or mercy. Paul's verdict on their teaching as works flowed from his verdicts on Jerusalem and the law. While he profoundly respected both as the gifts of God, he held that Messiah Jesus had fulfilled them. Paul could live with those who remained attached to Jerusalem so long as they left him and his communities alone.

It was at the point of what he saw as Jewish elitism defrauding his Gentile converts that Paul began his provocative interpretation of the Judaizers' attachment to the city and the law.[13] In his view, the Judaizers did not honor their own commitments.[14] They so badly misunderstood the promises to Abraham and the place of Jerusalem in the biblical story as to prefer "Arabia" and its slavery to the freedom of the new and greater city of their own prophets' hopes.[15] They absurdly promoted Gentiles returning to a law they were never under and promoted slavery in preference to the freedom of the Spirit.[16] The law had reached its end in Christ. When Paul stated that circumcision was now irrelevant, he placed himself socially and intellectually beyond the claims of Jerusalem and the law.

While Christians at Jerusalem hung on to their affiliation with mainstream Judaism, the parting of the ways was clear for Paul.[17] The message of Christ could not be shackled to anachronisms that threatened its freedom of expression. The apostles and brothers at Jerusalem had acknowledged that Gentiles were now included among the people of God, but they did not grasp what Paul knew: that

---

[11]Gal 1:17-24; 2:6-21.

[12]It is also possible that Jewish Christians at Galatia had taken advantage of a likely or actual conflict with the imperial cult to press Gentile converts into seeking refuge under the status of Judaism as a *religio licita*. See Bruce Winter, *Seek the Welfare of the City: Christians as Benefactors and Citizens*, First Century Christians in the Graeco-Roman World 1 (Exeter: Paternoster; and Grand Rapids, Mich.: Eerdmans, 1994), pp. 136–43.

[13]Gal 2:4-13; 4:17-20; 6:12; 2:14-21; 4:21-26.

[14]Gal 2:3, 11-14; 5:2-3, 12; 6:13.

[15]Gal 4:21-31.

[16]Gal 3:1-5; 4:1-11; 5:1-12.

[17]The question of when Christians parted from Judaism ("the parting of the ways") has been traditionally answered in terms of a long history of continued affiliation and confused identity. Edwin Judge argues that the Romans were never confused about the distinctiveness of the Christians ("Judaism and the Rise of Christianity: A Roman Perspective," *Australian Journal of Jewish Studies* 7 [1993]: 82–98). Judge maintains that the confusion seems to have been within the minds of those Jewish Christians who maintained "a vain struggle to contain radical beliefs within the limits of a socially conformist sect devoted in the rabbinical manner to the study of the law" ("The Early Christians as a Scholastic Community," *Journal of Religious History* 1 [1960]: 15). The point may need to be qualified by Gallio's verdict that the Jews' dispute with the Christians was an in-house affair (Acts 18:12-17).

Christ had reconciled Jew and Gentile into one new man.[18]

Reconciliation of Jew and Gentile

The unity of Jew and Gentile was not merely academic for Paul. As we have noted, there was widespread interaction between Jewish culture and the Graeco-Roman world. There were tensions on both sides. Jewish protests in Palestine against Rome were mostly passive. Yet the Romans continued to anticipate trouble and were not above singling out Jews for persecution. There were "continual controversies and periodic violence between gentiles and Jews" in Alexandria in Paul's day.[19] In Palestine considerable loyalty and nationalism attached to the sanctity of Jerusalem, the temple, the law, the Sabbath and the other traditions of the fathers.

Each of these Jewish distinctives could attract curiosity, admiration or derision from Graeco-Romans.[20] There was a long history, especially among prominent women, of Gentiles connecting themselves to Jewish customs and communities.[21] As well as converts, wealthy adherents gave financial and social support to the local synagogues—thus the "God-fearers" of Acts. The Jewish seven-day week held a particularly strong attraction for many as an alternative to the Roman eight-day arrangement. While Jewish scruples curtailed their involvement in some events, inscriptions of the period show them absorbed into normal Graeco-Roman life, including the social conventions of benefaction and honors. There is also considerable evidence that Gentiles incorporated Jewish beliefs into their magical and religious practices and cults.[22]

It is unlikely that Gentiles gave any thought to Paul's Jew-Gentile problem. Eccentric Jewish beliefs and practices and isolated occurrences of extremism did not weigh heavily on Gentile minds. The Graeco-Roman mood preferred intellectual and religious pluralism, though there is also evidence for dogmatism and intolerance (e.g., Acts 19:28). On the Jewish side, even those who had attained prominence in city life might at times feel alienated by their peculiar heritage. A common Jewish response in this environment was to assimilate further into the

---

[18]Acts 15:1-29; cf. 10:9—11:18; Gal 3:28.

[19]Wayne Meeks, *The First Urban Christians: The Social World of the Apostle Paul* (New Haven, Conn.: Yale University Press, 1983), p. 38.

[20]Cf. *Martial* 7.82.

[21]There is some debate as to whether Jews actively proselytized or whether Gentiles were attracted to Judaism without active Jewish effort. For an outline of the issues, see Meeks, *First Urban Christians,* pp. 32–39, 152–53. See also Bradley Blue, "Acts and the House Church," in *The Book of Acts in Its First Century Setting,* vol. 2, *Graeco-Roman Setting,* ed. D. W. J. Gill and C. Gempf (Grand Rapids, Mich.: Eerdmans; and Carlisle: Paternoster, 1994), pp. 178–83.

[22]Rosalind Kearsley, "Angels in Asia Minor," in *New Documents Illustrating Early Christianity,* ed. S. R. Llewelyn (Sydney: Macquarie University Press, 1992), 6:206–9.

patterns of normal city life while still maintaining distinctives within the safe confines of the synagogue community. On the Gentile side we encounter curiosity, indifference and occasional animosity; on the Jewish side, anxiety, opportunism and pride.

Paul's concern and perspectives were innovative within both frames of reference, yet with a distinctively Jewish bent. His message was for the Gentiles, yet it maintained Israel's priority ("to the Jew first"). The Gentiles were incorporated into one new people created around the Jewish Messiah. Paul recalled God's plan to create Israel through the patriarch Abraham and to make this new nation the vehicle of blessing to all nations. Now that the blessing had come, Paul saw that the standing of the Gentiles had to be resolved. His answer was to simultaneously uphold the priority and heritage of Israel *and* to level all racial distinctions under the one common Lord.

Paul's teachings on the reconciliation of Jew and Gentile were highly relevant to those in his *ekklēsiai*. There is evidence that many were affiliated to practices syncretizing Jewish and Gentile beliefs and traditions. This is particularly clear in Paul's response to those Ephesian Christians who feared and were fascinated by angels and powers in the syncretistic cults of Asia Minor. [23]

Life in Ephesus revolved around Artemis and her cult. Tom Moritz has shed useful light on the account in Acts 19 of Paul's confrontation with the followers of Artemis at Ephesus: "On all levels of social existence failure to support the cultic system would entail repression. The basic motivation for compliance with the cult was no doubt the individual's existential fear of the evil powers who needed to be manipulated by the goddess. Compliance with the demands posed by the cult was clearly a matter of social survival and hope for the future."[24]

The mystery rites of Artemis offered protection from the ever-present evil powers and demons.[25] There had been a significant Jewish presence in the city since Hellenistic times, and Jewish magic had become renowned in the first century (cf. Acts 19:17-19). As a result, there were distinctly Jewish elements in the "asceticism, immoral indulgences, esotericism, spiritism, astrology, divination, sacred calendars and magic"[26] that made up the religious and superstitious environment

---

[23]C. E. Arnold, *Ephesians: Power and Magic* (Cambridge: Cambridge University Press, 1989). There is no certainty that Ephesus was the destination of the letter to the Ephesians. Arnold reviews the arguments and helpfully lifts the issue to the larger matter of the place of the city in the life of Asia Minor. See Kearsley, "The Mysteries of Artemis at Ephesus," in Llewelyn, *New Documents*, 6:201–2.

[24]Thomas Moritz, " 'Summing Up All Things': Religious Pluralism and Universalism in Ephesians," in *One God, One Lord in a World of Religious Pluralism* (Cambridge: Tyndale House, 1991), p. 92.

[25]See Arnold, *Ephesians*, pp. 19–40. He has argued that the notion of evil powers and demons was not a second-century development, but is well attested for the first century. He demonstrates the hold these powers had on the mindset of the time.

[26]Moritz, "Summing Up," p. 89.

of Ephesus. There was also a live Jewish-Gentile conflict. Both connections provide important background for Paul's later remarks to the Ephesians on the unity of Jew and Gentile.

At the outset, Paul moved Christ to center stage to preclude syncretism—Christ was head of all things. It did not matter whether one was a Jew or Gentile. What counted was being "found in Christ." The promises of the covenants had been the exclusive privilege of the Jews. However, these privileges alienated Gentiles. But now, in Paul's teaching, the Gentiles too were heirs to the promises, though the law had until now left them drifting in the futility of their darkened minds at the mercy of the powers. Through his death, Christ had torn down the partition, making Gentiles "fellow-citizens with God's people and members of God's household." This inclusion of the Gentiles, Paul believed, was integral to the divine plan.[27] Ethnic distinctions no longer held any privilege since Christ had fulfilled God's intention "to create in himself one new man out of the two."[28] Christ was superior to all the powers.[29] The Ephesian Christians only had to see what they already possessed.[30] There was no need for the visionary-mystical experiences found in Gentile cults or for the Torah observance, asceticism or exorcism of much Jewish mysticism.[31] In Christ, both groups held the same privileges, secure from all powers and beyond the need of cult and magic. Paul's message discredited the walls of social separation and demanded they be torn down within the *ekklēsia*.

Paul was everywhere working to shift his friends' sense of their place in the world. As J. Paul Sampley put it, "Whereas their legitimation formerly came from others and the opinions of others guided their actions, now believers are secure in Christ: they know they are accepted by God and therefore are freed from the world's clutches."[32] Those clutches were not only psychological and intellectual but also social. Paul labored to transform social relationships. No authority attached to Jerusalem or to Jewish (or Gentile) heritage. Ethnicity, sex, culture and social rank no longer defined the person. Social divisions and hostilities were abolished in the one new person.

Radical Social Relationships Within the *ekklēsia*

The Roman historian Suetonius explains that the emperor Claudius had expelled

---

[27]Eph 1:10, 12; 3:1-11; 2:12, 14; 3:6; 2:2-3, 15; 4:17-19; 5:8; 6:12; 2:14-17, 19; 3:1-11.

[28]Eph 2:15; cf. 4:22-24; 1:20-21; cf. 2:4-7; 3:10; 4:8-10; 6:10-11.

[29]Eph 1:20-21; cf. 2:4-7; 3:10; 4:8-10; 6:10-11.

[30]Eph 1:17-23; 3:14-19; 4:14-21.

[31]On the elements of Jewish mysticism that are likely to have been familiar to the Ephesians, see Moritz, "Summing Up"; Arnold, *Ephesians*, pp. 29–34; and Kearsley, *Artemis*, p. 202. See also Kearsley, "Ailments and Remedies" and "Angels," in Llewelyn, *New Documents*, 6:194, 206–9.

[32]J. Paul Sampley, *Walking Between the Times: Paul's Moral Reasoning* (Philadelphia: Fortress, 1991), p. 16.

the Jews from Rome (A.D. 49) "because they were persistently rioting at the instiga-tion of Chrestus."[33] This passage has often been cited as evidence of a substantial, well-organized and independent Christian community at Rome from earliest times, probably planted by Roman converts from the day of Pentecost.[34] Consequently, commentators tend to ignore the possibility of any social context behind Romans and treat the letter as a theological handbook. But a more concrete social picture of life for the Roman Christians is possible.

When Paul wrote from Corinth to Rome, he probably knew of no wider Chris-tian community in the city, only of the household groups associated with his own personal networks (Rom 16). These groups may have been loosely related to one another and still meeting under the auspices of the synagogue. Presumably there had been no prior apostolic ministry at Rome, given Paul's strategy not to build on another's foundation (Rom 15:20). In a sense, this turned back the clock for Paul. Having abandoned his earlier strategy of working from the synagogues to then focus on Gentile audiences, the synagogue might again become his point of entry (Acts 28:15–28). But his experiences in the east would have forewarned him and perhaps hardened his resolve to shape a community independent of the synagogue. He may also have anticipated further factions and elitism like he had encountered at Corinth.[35]

If this reconstruction holds, then the letter may have been a preemptive strike against anticipated social tensions. His experiences elsewhere had taught him to anticipate three such tensions: first, opposition from the Jews; second, Gentile con-fusion about Jewish traditions and the gospel; third, divisions within the *ekklēsia* mirroring the structures and conventions of society.[36] With this in mind, note the relevance of his comments on social structures throughout Romans:[37] his lengthy remarks on Jews and Gentiles, his portrait of a new body unified in Christ, his

---

[33]Claudius *Impulsore Chresto* 25:4, translated in Judge, "Roman Perspective."

[34]*hoi epidemountes Rômaioi* ("visitors from Rome," Acts 2:10 NIV) may be better translated "Roman residents" (i.e., residents of Jerusalem with Roman citizenship-cum-connections) who are "both Jews and proselytes." Also, the reference in Suetonius to "Chrestus" may not be to Jesus Christ but to some passing messianic contender. If these alternate readings hold, then we might reconstruct a very different social setting for Romans. This reconstruction builds on the work of Edwin Judge and G. R. Thomas, "The Origin of the Church at Rome: A New Solution?" *Reformed Theological Review* 25 (1966): 81–94. See also Judge, "Roman Perspective," pp. 87–88. Their hypothesis has met with criticism. See Charles Cranfield, *An Exegetical and Critical Commentary on the Epistle to the Romans*, International Critical Commentary (London: T & T Clark, 1975), 1:16.

[35]Compare 1 Cor 8:1—11:1 and Rom 14:1—15:13; cf. 1 Cor 12—14 and Rom 12:1-21.

[36]Rom 16:17-20. If Paul wrote Philippians from Rome, then his fears eventually materialized in the capital (Phil 1:12-18, 27-30; 3:2-6, 19).

[37]Rom 1—4, 9—11, 15; 12:1-21; 13:1-7; 14:1—15:13.

advice to respect authorities and maintain benefactions for the welfare of the city,[38] and his plea for respect and understanding between social factions.[39]

Romans does not offer a theological, religious or moral system. Neither was it an agenda for revolution or anarchy—Paul expected his converts to maintain their social station (Rom 13:3-4; cf. 1 Cor 7:17-24). Nevertheless, Paul had not resigned himself to the status quo but drew provocative social conclusions from his message. His treatment of the divine plan for human history led to a radical new mindset that had begun to transform everyday relationships away from the social conventions of rank and status (Rom 9:1—12:21).

This radical mindset began in Paul's sense of the impartiality of God's mercies. Paul aimed his critique at the heart of the ideology that propped up the social system. Edwin Judge states that his appeal in Romans 12:2 to no longer be "conformed to the world" echoed "the term that embodied the ideal of the culturally 'well-informed' person . . . (the *euschēmon*) who is entitled to social respect because of cultivation."[40] Whatever their rank, believers must now see themselves and their social priorities based on the mercies of God. The body no longer existed for the individual. Instead, each member had been gifted for the good of the body. Paul was clearly stepping away from convention.

Faced at Corinth with a community of believers fractured by elitism and dissension, Paul unleashed a devastating attack on those who sought to tame the power of his message. Neither the tertiary scholar nor the nobly born nor the grand orator could discern or reveal the mysteries of God in the gospel (1 Cor 1:19-20, 26; 2:4-5, 7-16). Nor could they convey the power of the gospel. God had exposed the

---

[38]Bruce Winter in *Seek the Welfare of the City* has argued that Romans 13 implies Paul urged wealthy Christian converts to continue their patronage and benefactions to the city. See also his "The Public Honouring of Christian Benefactors: Romans 13:3-4 and 1 Peter 2:14-15," *Journal for the Study of the New Testament* 34 (1988): 87–103, and " 'If any man does not wish to work': A Cultural and Historical Setting for 2 Thessalonians 3:6-16," *Tyndale Bulletin* 40 (1989): 303–15. See also Bruce Harris, "St. Paul and the Public Reputation of the Churches," *Reformed Theological Review* 50 (1991): 50–58.

[39]On "the strong and the weak" in 1 Corinthians as indicators of rival groups based on social position and influence, rather than as purely ideological or psychological indicators, see Marshall, "A Metaphor of Social Shame: ΘPIAMBEYEIN in 2 Cor. 2:14," *Novum Testamentum* 25 (1983): 302–17, and *Enmity in Corinth: Social Conventions in Paul's Relations with the Corinthians* (Tübingen: J. C. B. Mohr, 1987). See also Meeks, *Urban Christians*, and " 'Since then you would need to go out of the world': Group Boundaries in Pauline Christianity," in *Critical History and Biblical Faith: New Testament Perspectives*, ed. T. Ryan (Villanova: College Theology Society, 1979), pp. 4–29, and "Judgment and the Brother: Romans 14:1–15:13," in *Tradition and Interpretation in the New Testament*, ed. G. F. Hawthorne and O. Betz (Grand Rapids, Mich.: Eerdmans, 1987), pp. 290–300. See also Gerhard Theissen, *The Social Setting of Pauline Christianity* (Edinburgh: T & T Clark, 1990).

[40]Edwin Judge, "The Interaction of Biblical and Classical Education," *Journal of Christian Education* 77 (1983): 31.

impotence and frailty of their wisdom, social pretense and eloquence. Only the power of the Spirit could serve as a foundation for faith. Thus Paul taught the scandal of the cross, knowing it would be dismissed as foolish and unimpressive (1 Cor 2:1-5).

Refusing the Corinthians' social expectations and ideals, Paul introduced an innovative image of their new relationships (1 Cor 3:10-15).[41] They were a building of which Christ was the foundation and Paul the architect. The metaphor canceled partiality. The strong must disregard their claims to privilege. They must act with new regard toward those they regarded as the weak as those for whom Christ also died (1 Cor 6:12; 8:9-12; 10:23-24).[42] The new freedom offered in Paul's message was the means for building each other up, not for individual license or prestige.

Recalling the interdependence of our frames for Paul's thought, his social perspectives presumed and led onto his sense of the personal and the historical. The arguments he crafted to prize open the grip of Jerusalem, ethnicity and social status rang with the authenticity and congruency of a man who "counted it all nothing" as he stepped down in the world in imitation of his master. His labors to undo the hold of ethnic, religious and social ideals were energized by a larger vision of history.

---

[41]See Edwin Judge, "Cultural Conformity and Innovation in Paul: Some Clues from Contemporary Documents," *Tyndale Bulletin* 35 (1984): 5.

[42]On the identity of the strong and the weak, Chris Forbes notes that " 'weakness' and 'strength' never indicate simply psychological states. . . . 'Weakness' is the state of those without power or status, and 'strength' is the state of those who do have status. 'Weakness' connotes humiliation in the eyes of others, rather than inadequacy in one's own" (" 'Strength' and 'Weakness' as Terminology of Status in St. Paul: The Historical and Literary Roots of a Metaphor, with Special Reference to 1 and 2 Corinthians" [B.A. honors thesis, Macquarie University, Sydney, 1978], pp. 108–9).

7

HISTORICAL FRAMES

PAUL TOLD AND RETOLD THE SAME STORY WHEREVER HE WENT. THE STORY WAS CHRIST'S story. It focused on him, and Paul claimed to have received it directly from him.[1] But the story was also Paul's in that he identified himself with Christ and with his commission to make him known.[2] He was also deeply aware of how it could become "another gospel" or "no gospel at all" (Gal 1:6-9). He labored to tell the story without deceit, pride or empty eloquence.[3] He suffered for it and believed his trials would advance its cause.[4]

In the Fullness of Time

Paul's use of the term *euangelion*, "good news" or "gospel," fits well with the use of the verb form in the Septuagint.[5] His use also drew from the traditions of Jesus' teaching.[6] At the same time, the word was also intelligible to those without a Jew-

---

[1]Rom 15:19; 1 Cor 15:2-7; Gal 1:11-12.

[2]Rom 2:16; 16:25; 1 Cor 1:17; Gal 1:10-17; Eph 3:7; cf. Eph 6:19.

[3]1 Thess 1:5; 2:1-6; cf. 1 Cor 2:1-5; 2 Cor 2:14—3:3; 4:1-3; Phil 1:15-18, 27; 1 Thess 2:9.

[4]Phil 1:12, 16; Philem 13.

[5]Is 40:9; 52:7; 60:6; 61:1. The Septuagint was a Greek translation of the Jewish Scriptures made some two centuries before Paul as an aid to preserving the faith of Jews living outside Palestine. Paul would have been schooled in the Hebrew texts, not the Septuagint. Yet more of his quotes from the Old Testament follow the Septuagint. This suggests among other things that he had spent considerable time relearning his Scriptures in Greek for the task of going to the Gentiles. The standard abbreviation for references to the Septuagint is LXX. For example, a reference to the Septuagint text of Isaiah 40:9 is written as LXX Is 40:9.

[6]1 Cor 15:1-8; Rom 14:17; 1 Cor 6:9; 15:24; Col 1:13; cf. Acts 20:17; 28:23, 31.

ish heritage. Discussing a second century A.D. letter responding to news of a wedding, Greg Horsley cites a wide range of mostly Hellenistic texts using the same *euangel-* family of words:[7]

> You filled us with joy when you announced the *good news* of most noble Sarapion's marriage.

> a slave coming to bring the *good news* of his victory and success . . .

> since I have become aware of the *good news* about the proclamation as Caesar [as Gaius Julius Verus Maximus Augustus] . . .

> [Honors for an individual] giving [largesse] magnanimously at the festival for *"good news"*

Among the texts Horsley discusses are those for festivals conveying news concerning the imperial family. They include an inscription from Sardis proclaiming that a son of Augustus had taken the *toga virilis*. Horsley particularly notes that the word group was associated with royalty and victories and with the benefactions, festivals and sacrifices offered on such occasions.[8]

This marriage of Old Testament hopes with the known use of the word in imperial contexts suited Paul's purposes. His good news proclaimed the long-awaited coming of the royal son of David, now crowned as the Son of God. This coronation marked the "fullness of time." Indeed, Paul understood that the final event of the story, the return of Christ, carried the hopes of the Jewish prophets' great day when the Lord would triumph and be crowned.[9]

Closely related to Paul's use of *euangelion* was his use of another word, *mystērion*, "mystery,"[10] which enabled Paul to convey the sense of making known something that had been hidden for long ages. This mystery had many sides to it.

---

[7]The texts that follow are *P.Oxy.* 3313, 3-4, *P.Giss.* 27, *SB* 1, 421.2 and *IGRR* 4, 860. See Greg Horsley, ed., *New Documents Illustrating Early Christianity* (Sydney: Macquarie University Press, 1983), 3:10-15.

[8]One technical point gives us insight into an interesting innovation. The Graeco-Roman texts almost always use the plural, *good news*. But the New Testament writers consistently used the neuter singular. Horsley concludes that "this specialised usage was the result of conscious choice. Yet we should not lose sight of the relatively widespread occurrence . . . of the neuter plural . . . with a specialized meaning whereby it related to news frequently connected with royalty. . . . While the New Testament usage is distinctive, therefore, it cannot be divorced from the larger context of the *koinē*, within which one other equally distinctive application was widespread, one which provides the stem from which the New Testament usage took root. Whether or not the theological basis can be traced to the Old Testament, philologically and socially it would have been perfectly comprehensible to those living in Graeco-Roman cities in the Roman period" (Horsley, *New Documents*, 3:14–15).

[9]Rom 1:2-4; Gal 4:4; Phil 1:10; 2:16; 1 Thess 1:10; 4:13—5:11; 2 Thess 1—2.

[10]Rom 16:25-27; 1 Cor 2:7-16; 15:51; Eph 1:9-10; 2:11-12; 3:2-13; 6:19; Col 1:23-27; 2:3-4; 4:3.

Its origins lay before creation. The work of Christ had lifted the veil of mystery from the grave. It had baffled the best minds and thwarted the strongest tyrants of human history and could only be known by the Spirit. It was the revelation of God's scheme for human history. It was the inclusion of the Gentiles within the people of God. The mystery of God was "Christ, in whom are hidden all the treasures of wisdom and knowledge" (Col 2:3).

Like *euangelion*, Paul's use of *mystērion* was similarly suited to both Jewish and Graeco-Roman audiences. In LXX Daniel 2:18-47, Nebuchadnezzar, king of Babylon, dreams of the events that are soon to determine the course of human history and the fortunes of the exiled people of Judea. But the dream remains a mystery to the king and to Daniel until God reveals its meaning to the seer. The connections to Paul's use are clear. A similar use of the term emerged in the Jewish literature of the Hellenistic period and gained some currency beyond Jewish audiences.[11] At the same time, Paul's use of the word may have suggested comparisons to the Graeco-Roman mystery cults.[12] Like his use of *euangelion*, Paul almost invariably used the singular *mystērion*, whereas when referring to the Graeco-Roman cults the word is always plural.[13] This might seem to distance Paul's use from the cults. But it may be that Paul had again innovated slightly in order to turn the word for his own use. Perhaps he used the term to help his audiences to compare his message to that of the cults and so to preempt their claims. Rosalind Kearsley concludes that "the passage in Eph 3:9 where stewardship of the mystery *(hē oikonomia tou mystērion)* is referred to may represent an attempt on the part of the author to draw a deliberate contrast between the "new mystery" (that revealed in the New Testament) with the Lydian-Phrygian mysteries and to counter their influence within the Christian churches of the area."[14]

It seems that Paul deliberately used this "preeminently cultic word" in a noncultic manner. If so, then he implied that the open story of the life, death and resurrection of Jesus Christ had eclipsed the esoteric mysteries of Graeco-Roman religion.

---

[11]E.g., 1 Enoch 16:3; 103:2; 104:10; 106:19.

[12]This is *not* to say that Paul's use of the term was based on the Graeco-Roman mystery cults or that the characteristics of these cults should be read into his use of the term. While this was a fashionable hypothesis at one stage, the idea is now widely discredited. See D. H. Wiens, "Mystery Concepts in Primitive Christianity and in its Environment," *Aufstieg und Niedergang der römischen Welt,* 2.23.2 (1980): 1261-65.

[13]Paul's rarer use of the plural generally departs somewhat from the heavily historical orientation he consistently gave to the singular, though it retained the sense of divine disclosure found in the book of Daniel (1 Cor 13:2; 14:2).

[14]Rosalind Kearsley, "The Mysteries of Artemis at Ephesus," in Llewelyn, *New Documents,* 6:202. Kearsley cites E. Harvey as reading the use of *mystērion* in Ephesians in a similar manner: "It does not follow that the writer did not intend, and the reader did not pick up, some echo of the Greek mystery-metaphor."

Paul placed the identity and events of Jesus Christ at the center of human history; they gave meaning to all that had gone before and shape to all that was to come. Time and time again, he framed his immediate concerns within a vision of history as a whole.[15] On its grandest scale, this vision stretched from creation to new creation, even as it narrowed to two men.

Adam, Christ and the Shape of History

The Jewish prophets consistently expected a decisive event to renew the fortunes of their people. Generally these prophecies interwove themes of judgment and promise. Some had spoken of a great day, the day of the Lord, when he would deliver Israel from its enemies and a new era would dawn. So, for example, Isaiah developed this theme when he drew together under the banner of the day of the Lord the ancient holy war traditions and the theme of the nations' arrogance. This was later extended to cosmic proportions. In "that day" the Lord would come as the ancient warrior to destroy the earth and his enemies and to restore his people.[16] By Paul's time, "the day of the Lord" was a known symbol for that time when God would conquer all his enemies and renew the creation. It would be the end of one era and the beginning of another (see figure 7.1).

The Day
of the Lord

Figure 7.1. The prophetic expectation of a decisive turning point in history

Paul was no stranger to this expectation. His portrait of Christ's victorious ascension in Ephesians 4:7-9 drew on Psalm 68, a hymn of praise to the Lord, the warrior king. There are numerous other echoes in Paul of the themes of divine coronation, holy war and re-creation.[17] Christ's return would be the day of the Lord. All of this enriches what we have noted repeatedly: that Paul placed the story of Christ at the center of God's plan for history. In an important sense, then, the future had begun already. The single decisive day of the prophets had become two

---

[15]E.g., Rom 1—4; 9—11; Gal 3—4; Eph 1—3; cf. Rom 1:2-4; 1 Cor 15:21-28; 2 Cor 3:7—4:6; 3:21-26; Col 1:15-20; 2 Tim 1:9-10; 2:8-13; Tit 3:3-7.

[16]Is 13:1-13; 24—27; cf. Joel 3:9-16; Ezek 30:1-4; Zech 9:14-17.

[17]Phil 1:6, 10; 2:6-11; Col 2:15; 1 Thess 5:2; cf. Acts 2:20. See Tremper Longman, "The Divine Warrior: The New Testament Use of an Old Testament Motif," *Westminster Theological Seminary* 44 (1982): 290–307.

days, creating an overlap in the ages, as pictured in figure 7.2.[18]

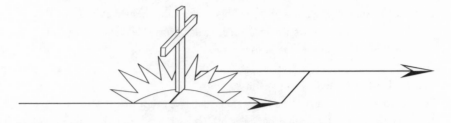

Figure 7.2. The gospel events reworked the prophetic anticipation of the turning point of history

The prophets had anticipated a day of judgment and salvation; Paul believed that both had been revealed in Jesus Christ (Rom 1:17-18; 3:21). In this revelation, Christ had sealed the future of the world and of his people. The future had begun because Christ had entered into the experience of the new creation in his own resurrection—he was the new man (1 Cor 15:45).

This summing up of history within a single person had profound social implications. Christ is "the one new man" in whom Jew and Gentile find a new common identity. Christ draws believers of all sexual, social and cultural distinctions into the one new identity. Through his willing obedience and humiliation, Christ had reversed the arrogance and presumption of the first man and so received the glory and honor due to the image of God (Phil 2:5–11). In so doing, he had become the model for all who would live as the Creator intended.

The same theme occurs on a grander scale in Romans. Anticipating the social tensions likely to exist or develop in and around the believers in Rome, Paul moved quickly in chapter 1 from his summary of Christ's fulfillment of Israel's history to identify Christ as the new and entirely sufficient revelation of God's plans. What follows is a lengthy clarification of the respective lots of Jew and Gentile, beginning and ending with Adam.[19] We must recall here Paul's agenda to preempt the claims of Jerusalem and of social rank and to show how they had been made redundant in the events of his gospel. This clarifies why Paul stresses the common accountability of all people before God at the start of the letter. His portrait of the pitiful state of

---

[18]This reworking is not necessarily Paul's own innovation, given that the model fits the "now-not yet" pattern that shapes Jesus' preaching of the kingdom in the first three Gospels. Figure 7.2 is adapted from Gerhardus Vos, *The Pauline Eschatology* (Grand Rapids, Mich.: Baker, 1930), p. 38. For an elaboration of this model in relation to the possible worldviews of the Ephesian converts, see Clinton E. Arnold, *Ephesians: Power and Magic* (Cambridge: Cambridge University Press, 1989), pp. 145–58.

[19]Rom 1:21-23; 5:12-21. See Morna Hooker, *From Adam to Christ* (Cambridge: Cambridge University Press, 1990), pp. 73–87.

mankind rang true to the social realities of his time and set them in a far larger sweep of history from creation to the final revelation. The first man plunged humanity into its present state; the second man guaranteed the future.

By regarding Adam as the prototype of Christ, Paul characterized the two periods of history by the two men: Adam and Christ.[20] The actions of the two men established the identity and experience of those whom they represented: disobedience, sin, condemnation and death; or obedience, righteousness, justification and life. So the two men characterize two eras of history and two corresponding mindsets and patterns of experience that Paul dubbed "the flesh" and "the spirit" (Rom 6:1–8:17). Those who are in Christ are led by the Spirit and see life from the vantage point of their new identity. They now wait for the final revelation of the new creation where they will regain (surpass?) the original honors of Adam—"the freedom of the glory of the children of God" (Rom 8:18-39).

This same pattern had shaped Paul's earlier portrait of the future of humanity (1 Cor 15:12-57). Jesus was "raised from the dead, the firstfruits of those who have fallen asleep" (v. 20). The metaphor of "firstfruits" belongs to Israel's ancient tradition of presenting the first portions of the harvest to God as a guarantee of the whole.[21] The harvest Paul envisaged was the resurrection of all the people of God at the great day of Christ. Christ himself had been raised as the firstfruits—the guarantee—of all those who would rise from the dead because of him. Jesus was now the second man, the new image of God, characterized by heaven and by the Spirit. There is now a new humanity, patterned after the order of the new man: "And just

---

[20]Rom 5:12-21; cf. 1 Cor 15:20-58. Several scholars have suggested that Paul's treatment of Adam and Christ, especially in 1 Corinthians 15, owes much to Philo's understanding of two Adams in Genesis 1:26-28 and 2:7, though few would argue for any literary dependence. While there are lexical parallels, and while it may well be that Paul knew of this tradition (whether from Philo or another source), Paul's own model differs considerably in places. See also Richard A. Horsley, "'How can some of you say there is no resurrection of the dead?' Spiritual Elitism in Corinth," *Novum Testamentum* 20 (1978): 202–31. Horsley discusses Philo's pattern of two Adams and notes its heavily metaphysical orientation over against Paul's historical perspective. His identification of Philo's pattern, or one like it, as a likely prop to the spiritual elitism of the strong at Corinth resonates with my own comments here and in part three on elitism at Corinth. In terms of Paul's use of the Adam-Christ pattern in both Romans 5 and 1 Corinthians 15, I am more persuaded by the view that Paul has reframed the Old Testament expectations of a decisive historical turning point. For a survey of the issues and bibliography, see Craig A. Evans, *Noncanonical Writings and the New Testament* (Peabody, Mass.: Hendrickson, 1992), pp. 84–86. At the same time, Adam was a favorite subject for Jewish commentators. Paul may reflect this heritage quite independently of Philo. Indeed, there is evidence within the Old Testament itself of an interest in Adam as a symbol of a primal fall and as "the eschatological man" (e.g., Ezek 28:11-19). As a further example of the use of this motif, note the influence of Ezekiel 28 on Luke's portrait of the death of Herod (Acts 12:20-24). See Mark Strom, "An Old Testament Background to Acts 12:20-23," *New Testament Studies* 32 (1985): 289–92.

[21]Lev 23:9-14; 1 Cor 15:20-28.

as we have borne the likeness of the earthly man, so shall we bear the likeness of the man from heaven" (1 Cor 15:49).

Paul was not playing intellectual games with his friends at Corinth or Rome. He used this Adam-Christ pattern to undercut traditional social expectations and conventions. It undermined the logic of comparison, pride and self-sufficiency so critical to the social pyramid. This is clear in the objections that Paul anticipated at Rome: "So, shall we go on sinning that grace may increase? . . . Shall we sin because we are not under law but under grace? . . . Is the law itself sin? . . . Or perhaps that which is good became death for me?" (Rom 6:1, 15; 7:7, 13). The move from one challenge to the next shows Paul trying to cut off every escape route to the law. Paul had put himself out on a limb away from the security of both Jewish and Graeco-Roman conventions and ideals of morality and religious piety. If Christ determined the status of a believer, then what would hold the believer's behavior in check? His detractors argued that he had opened the gate to immorality and impiety.

Traditional moral safeguards centered on nature, law and reason, piety and self-control. Paul's didn't. Instead, he turned his known and would-be slanderers back to the story of Christ. The only strategy congruent with the new relationship was to reaffirm one's new identity, destiny and master. In Paul's terms, believers must continually "reckon" *(logizomai)* themselves as in Christ and live by the promises of God alone.[22] Paul maintained that if a profound regard for Christ's mercies did not bring transformation, neither would anything else. The old maxim was now radically reworked: "Know yourself" (i.e., your place and rank) had become "know yourself in the rank and benefits of Christ."

In Christ

Paul believed that the old era would remain until the triumphant return of the heavenly man and the ensuing judgment. Yet Christ's resurrection had already inaugurated the new order of creation.[23] All of this carried great significance for Paul's understanding of present experience:

> So then we no longer think according to the flesh. Certainly we had regarded Christ according to the flesh, but we no longer know him this way. So then, anyone in Christ is a new creation. The old has gone—the new has come![24]

Central to this affirmation is the phrase "in Christ" (or "with Christ"), which functioned for Paul somewhat like "gospel" and "mystery"—as a shorthand term

---

[22]Rom 4:3-6, 8-11, 22-24; 6:2-14; 12:1-2.
[23]1 Cor 15:23-28; 2 Thess 2:1-8.
[24]2 Cor 5:16-17, my translation.

that could carry one or more of the patterns of Paul's thought. It enabled him to draw into one place Christ's representative role and the contrast of the two ages. It also gave a deeply personal color to these historical pictures. As their representative, Christ had guaranteed the blessings of the new creation for his people even as they lived in a world enslaved to the old order. The tensions between the two ages made every accomplishment of Christ a "now" and "not-yet" experience for Paul. The resolution lay in Christ's own experience—what was "not yet" for Paul was already "now" for Christ.

As the new man, the heavenly man, the man in full possession of the Spirit, Christ fully experiences the arrangements of the new creation. Paul locates all of the benefits of the new order with Christ, whom Paul believes is holding them secure on Paul's behalf until they meet face to face.[25] So the phrase was not about a mystical union, nor about an ideal of a higher spiritual or moral state to attain. There is no shift from history to some more primary reality. It was profoundly personal. As the psalmists saw themselves sheltered from the storms of life by the closeness of the Lord, Paul exulted in Christ as the one who would hold him secure until the final day.[26] This was not a sleight of hand, as though Paul were saying, "I'll act as though you are with me even though I know you are not!" Paul believed that the Spirit interacted with his own spirit to keep his heart and mind in the identity and blessings of the new order even while he lived within a world that was passing away.[27]

Once again, we note how Paul's perspectives meshed together: the historical spills over into the social and the personal. The reshaping of history and humanity in Christ radically reframed Paul's life and thought.

---

[25]Note the benefits associated with the phrase in Eph 1:4-13; 2:4-7; Col 2:9-15.
[26]Col 3:1-4; cf. Ps 16:1.
[27]Rom 8:14-17, 22-27; Gal 4:6; 5:5; 2 Cor 1:22; 3:17-18; 5:1-5; Eph 1:13-14.

8

PERSONAL FRAMES

ADAM AND CHRIST ESTABLISHED THE IDENTITY AND EXPERIENCE OF THOSE WHOM THEY represented (Rom 5:12-21). They characterized two eras and two corresponding mindsets and patterns of experience. Paul dubbed these flesh and spirit (Rom 6:1—8:17). The language sounds dualistic—as though Paul opposed a "spiritual" world to a physical one. We have noted that most of his contemporaries thought in this way. But not Paul. The *language* of Plato or Philo may have come across to Paul, but the *system* did not.[1] Flesh and spirit worked for Paul as metaphors for two eras with opposing ways of living: sin or righteousness; slavery or freedom; foolishness or wisdom; futility or hope; condemnation or justification; death or life.

The Antithesis of Flesh and Spirit
In the last chapter we saw that Paul had built his understanding of the two ages on his awareness of the hopes of Israel's prophets. Something similar may lie behind

---

[1]See Edwin Judge, "St. Paul as a Radical Critic of Society," *Interchange* 16 (1975): 194. I am focusing on the pattern of Paul's thought that he just so happened to articulate in several contexts through the language of *sarx* and *pneuma*. I do not mean to imply that Paul had a developed metaphor in mind whenever he used *sarx* or *pneuma*, such that the terms *meant* the full significance of the metaphor. There were numerous occasions when he used both terms in their everyday senses (e.g., Gal 4:13; 2 Cor 12:7; Col 2:1; 1 Thess 5:23). Moreover, Paul often conveyed the tension without using either of the terms. Neither is there any need to press Paul's terms into any precise anthropological system with sharp differences between flesh *(sarx)* and body *(sōma)*. See Moises Silva, *Biblical Words and Their Meaning: An Introduction to Lexical Semantics* (Grand Rapids, Mich.: Zondervan, 1983) for a critique of these linguistic fallacies.

his characterization of the ages as flesh and spirit. To live in "the fullness of time" is to live in the age when God had poured out his Spirit upon his people.[2] Paul probably saw his own struggles in the prophets' ministries. As men and women of the Spirit thrown into conflict with their hard-hearted contemporaries, they had longed for a day when the Lord would grant his Spirit to all. The Spirit was integral to their wider hopes.[3] So spirit *(pneuma)* would be a natural choice for Paul as a descriptor of the people of the new era. And, perhaps in keeping with contemporary usage, flesh *(sarx)* would serve equally well to capture the life of the old.[4] A further feature of Paul's use makes this background more likely and moves us to a clearer understanding of what he intended by this strong contrast between flesh and spirit.

On several occasions Paul linked the two words to those who still pursued Jerusalem and the law: "Are you so foolish? After beginning with the Spirit, are you now trying to attain your goal by the flesh."[5] We have seen that Paul believed that the story of Christ had made Jerusalem and the law redundant. Any ongoing attachment to them now constituted "works," the antithesis of faith in Christ and the mark of one who still grasped at self-justification. As Albrecht Dihle notes, it was a short step for Paul to combine Jew and Gentile under the common verdict of self-righteousness and to link this to *sarx:*

> *Sarx* (flesh), as opposed to *pneuma* (spirit), denotes rather the empirical condition of man, in which all his activity, including his religious, intellectual, and moral endeavour, finds its ultimate goal in himself. Pride and self-assuredness, for instance, characterize the fleshly existence. The proud man has forgotten that he is a creature of God whose life and salvation depend entirely on the grace of the Creator. . . . The main factor of the life *kata sarka* (according to the flesh) can be seen in man's strong feeling of independence by which he separates himself from his Creator. The most notable result of that separation comes in man's striving for "his own righteousness" or justification.[6]

---

[2]Joel 2:28-32; cf. Acts 2:16-21.

[3]Num 11:26-29; Is 11:1-3; 34:16; 42:1; 44:3; 59:21; Ezek 36:24-27; 37:13-14; 39:29; Joel 2:28-32.

[4]Paul's choice of *sarx* to complete the pair is a little ironic, given its use in the Septuagint version of Ezekiel 36:26: "I will give you a new heart and a new spirit *(pneuma)* I will give you. I will remove the heart of stone from your flesh *(sarkos)* and I will give you a heart of flesh *(sarkinen)*"(my translation). This is why I referred to Paul working backwards from the appropriateness of *pneuma* to characterize the new era. Given the use of *sarx* in LXX Ezekiel 36:26, Paul might have chosen another term to accompany *pneuma*. Most likely his choice of *sarx* simply reflected a common pairing of the terms in his own day.

[5]Gal 3:4 (my translation); see the whole of 3:1—4:7. Note also the proximity of the law to his further remarks on the flesh and spirit in Galatians 5:1-12, 24-26; 6:8.

[6]Albrecht Dihle, *The Theory of Will in Classical Antiquity* (Berkeley: University of California Press, 1982), p. 84.

All sin, Paul believed, is an individual's choice to break faith with God by inverting the Creator-creature relationship (Rom 1:18-32). His Graeco-Roman contemporaries tended to view sin in terms of inadequate reason and the mere fact of
bodily existence (as opposed to the higher forms of intellectual and spiritual life).
Paul uniquely located the problem within a person's pretension to autonomy and
the subsequent rupture in relationship. This same autonomy was at work in the
Jew and the Gentile. Justification before God, however, depended on the sheer
mercy of God. God justifies the sinner and cancels his identity in Adam for a new
identity in Christ. So flesh and spirit do not indicate philosophical or moral categories for Paul, but alternate identities in relationship. According to Paul one who is
in Christ is correspondingly in the Spirit and a slave of righteousness. This is a
given. He or she is *not* in the flesh (Rom 8:9).[7] The reverse holds for those in
Adam—they are in the flesh and slaves to sin and death.

Those who are in Christ may foolishly choose to live and think as if they were in
Adam. Paul's response for them was to reaffirm the character of the relationship
(Rom 6:2-10). The law could not effect transformation (Rom 7:4-6; 8:10-17). Thus
Paul placed an ongoing choice before his converts: to believe the truth about their
new identity or to believe the lie of their old identity (Rom 6:11-14). If they believed
the truth, they would know life and freedom; if the lie, then death and slavery. Or
more correctly, either slavery to Christ, which is true freedom, or slavery to sin and
death, which is bondage indeed (Rom 6:15-18). Paul had moved to a decisive turn
in the argument of Romans.

Believers were previously "free from righteousness"; that is, they had no share
in the righteousness of God.[8] But now they are "slaves of righteousness"; that is,
bound in relationship to Christ (Rom 6:18). They are not under law, and therefore
sin will not be their master; their identity will remain in Christ (Rom 6:14; 7:1-6).
Thus the law itself was never the problem; it only fueled an individual's own inclination to rebellion (Rom 7:7-13). Paul believed this was still a real possibility.
"Whenever I focus on the law," Paul in effect says, "I experience again the curse of
self-justification." This is the crucial and bitter irony of the law: *open rebellion and
exacting obedience both lead to an imprisoned and tormented conscience* (Rom

---

[7]Throughout Romans 6—8, the NIV persistently renders *sarx* as "sinful nature" and frequently supplies the phrase "controlled by" for *en* and *kata*. It thus gives the impression that Paul says believers have two natures: a fleshly nature and a spiritual nature. This is particularly irritating and
misleading in 8:9, where Paul simply says, "However, you are not in the flesh but in the spirit, if
the Spirit of God lives with you" (my translation). The NIV has "You, however, are controlled not by
the sinful nature but by the Spirit, if the Spirit of God lives in you."

[8]Once again, in Romans 6:20, the NIV unhelpfully supplies "the control of," thus tilting the meaning toward cohabiting moral natures and away from the contrast Paul is making between identities based on Adam or Christ.

7:14-25).[9] Paul did not say this from the safety of theory. This had been and at times probably still was his own experience. As Edwin Judge notes, "There is in my view no writer of antiquity who exposes himself so ruthlessly to direct human contact and reveals himself to others with such candour and directness as does St. Paul."[10]

Paul's clarity about how law fed the self-destructiveness of the conscience tightened his insistence on the end of the law in Christ. Again Paul did not criticize the law; he simply stated the futility of trying to live by it. Note how the argument unfolds in Romans 8. The mind set on the flesh negates the law's good intention. God, however, achieved through Christ what could not be done through the law. His sacrifice condemned all attempts at self-rescue once and for all. Ironically, Christ's sacrifice gave believers the very status—that of law-keepers—that they could never attain through the law. The law could not create purity of walk and conscience, but the Spirit does. Thus all attempts to please God through a mind fixed on his law were now doomed. It is the Spirit, then, who brings the power of the sacrifice of Christ to life in the believer's experience. Where the law could only reinforce the futile cycle of self-justification and self-condemnation, the Spirit brings his witness of legitimacy and inheritance, enabling personal intimacy with the Father and providing hope in suffering, and meaning and strength in weakness.

The Spirit, then, enables believers to see and consider themselves as in Christ. He works to embed the understanding and experience of their changed identity. So personal transformation always works from "the mercies of God" (Rom 12:1). The exposure of the old mindset not only brings immorality to light but also exposes the futility of those religious and moral patterns used to maintain one's status in the eyes of the world. Nothing provoked Paul at this point like the image of the dying and rising Christ.

Dying and Rising with Christ

Paul's understanding of the dying and rising of Christ developed in several directions. It was

☐ the most critical moment in human history

☐ the moment of Paul's union with Christ

---

[9] I take Romans 7:25a ("Thanks be to God—through Jesus Christ our Lord") to be like a statement in parentheses. So I see the parallel phrases of v. 25b ("in my mind a slave to God's law . . . in my flesh a slave to sin and death") as roughly synonymous and as continuing the line of v. 24a ("What a wretched man am I!"). Verse 24b ("Who will rescue me from this body of death?") is then a cry of despair, not a glimmer of hope. In other words, Paul maintains his tormented portrait until the very end of v. 25. The real change of tone occurs in 8:1. This way of reading the text removes any need to determine the precise identity of the "I" in 7:14-25. It is the tormented experience of *anyone* who seeks to live by the law or any moral code. On the broader questions of will and conscience in Paul and Graeco-Roman thought, see Dihle, *Theory of Will.*

[10] Judge, "St. Paul as a Radical Critic of Society," p. 193.

☐ the explanation of his life since his encounter with Christ on the Damascus road
☐ the preeminent pattern and motivation for his ongoing life
☐ the guarantee of his own future bodily resurrection

Each of these points warrants some clarification. First, Paul was convinced that Jesus had risen from the dead in recent history. Faith is a sham without the resurrection. Paul consistently anchored his proclamation of Christ on this event, even in the face of disbelief and ridicule.[11]

Second, Paul believed he had been crucified, raised and ascended *with Christ*.[12] This is the crux of much of Paul's subsequent thought about the dying and rising of Christ. The death and resurrection of Christ had transferred Paul from belonging to Adam, to belonging to Christ. As difficult as the idea may seem, Paul believed he had died and risen with Christ not only at the moment of his own dramatic conversion but at the historical moment of Christ's experience. This is critical to Paul's understanding of the security of his relationship with God in Christ.

Third, Paul subsequently saw that the dying and rising of Christ explained his own experiences since the encounter on the way to Damascus. The dying and rising of Christ made sense of what he saw happening to himself as he traveled the eastern Mediterranean on behalf of others: "We always carry around in our body the death of Jesus, so that the life of Jesus may also be revealed in our body" (2 Cor 4:10). His sufferings, persecutions and hardships had been a constant dying. His ministry had been a public spectacle of one being led to death in the arena by Christ.[13]

Fourth, the dying and rising of Christ had become the pattern and the motivation for Paul's continuing life. Imitating Christ meant deliberately conforming to his humiliation and exaltation. Paul extended the theme beyond himself to the new community and their mutual sharing in the sufferings and comfort of Christ.[14]

Finally, Paul expected in time to rise from his own death because Christ had gone before him to secure his resurrection.[15]

The dying and rising of Christ exerted a profound influence over Paul's personal life and over his experience of social conventions and commitments in relationships. We will return to these themes repeatedly in part three. Innovative and often startling formulations appear in his ideas:

---

[11]1 Cor 15:1-20; Acts 13:30-37; 17:3, 31; 22:6-8; 23:6; 26:12-15, 23; Rom 1:4.

[12]Rom 6:4-11; Gal 2:19-20; Eph 2:5-6; Col 2:12-13; 3:1.

[13]2 Cor 11:23-33; 1 Cor 4:9; 2 Cor 2:14; Col 2:15. See Scott Hafemann, *Suffering and Ministry in the Spirit: Paul's Defense of His Ministry in 2 Corinthians 2:14—3:3* (Grand Rapids, Mich.: Eerdmans, 1990), pp. 12–34.

[14]1 Cor 11:1; Gal 6:1-5; 2:1-11; Eph 5:1; 4:20—5:21; Phil 1:3—2:18; 3:10-11; Col 3:12-17.

[15]1 Cor 15:20-23, 51-54; Phil 1:21-23.

☐ The future has broken into the past.

☐ Life is a constant dying.

☐ Dying brings a previously inaccessible life.

☐ Weakness is the vehicle of strength.

☐ Joy expresses meaning in suffering.

Peter Marshall succinctly captures the spirit of these remarkable expectations:

> Death has a positive power. God uses death for good, i.e., uses it transformatively. God has commandeered the power of the old age for his own use and death acts upon the apostle with the contradictory effect of giving and promoting life. Dying as suffering is purposefully related to participation in life for oneself and for life in others. It retains this positive sense through the apostle's continuous participation in dying and rising with Christ as suffering as a power which keeps him from returning to his former trust in himself. Weakness as dying with Christ is the necessary means by which power is brought to perfection. Power and weakness or suffering are no longer polar antitheses but are now brought together in a new relationship as a means by which Paul understands the experiences in his own life and his relationship with others and his world.[16]

The dying and rising of Christ led Paul to step down in the world in terms of personal and social prestige (Phil 3:1-11). It led him to be ridiculed, opposed and rejected. His own converts were embarrassed and scandalized by his choices. His deliberate rejection of the indicators of status and prominence—such as rhetorical flair and impressive leadership—flew in the face of what was entirely normal.[17] Paul sought to adapt himself in each new context. This often included withholding his personal rights.[18] These actions brought a charge of inconstancy and fickleness from certain powerful men at Corinth who then brought to bear the conventions of enmity against him.[19] His letters show that this social demise stung him and that he was not accustomed to such mistreatment.[20] Yet he refused to meet their expectations, for that would be to boast—*the* symbol of the life from which Christ had rescued him.[21]

Even the enmity of relatively powerful men at Corinth provided Paul with new means of modeling and urging conformity to the dying and rising of Christ.[22] By the time Paul wrote 2 Corinthians, this enmity had grown to include a group of pseudo-apostles who happily paraded the marks of their prestige. Paul worked from a radically different set of criteria. His weakness and suffering proved his posses-

---

[16]Peter Marshall, *The Enigmatic Apostle—Paul and Social Change: Did Paul Seek to Change Graeco-Roman Society?* (Melbourne: ITIM, 1993), pp. 22–23.

[17]1 Cor 2:1-5; 2 Cor 10:1, 10.

[18]1 Cor 9:1-23; cf. 2 Cor 11:7-12.

[19]2 Cor 1:12-22; 10:1, 10; 11:7-12; 12:13-18.

[20]2 Cor 6:4-12; 11:1-33.

[21]Rom 3:27; 1 Cor 1:29-31; cf. 2 Cor 10—12.

[22]1 Cor 4:18-21; 10:1—11:15; 12:11-18.

sion of the Spirit and his legitimacy as an apostle.[23] He had suffered numerous brutalities. His close associates had deserted him. He had forsaken his rights to financial support so that he could ply his trade in the sweatshop and offer his message free of charge. The Judaizers pursued him. Through it all, he knew the grace that transforms: "That is why, for Christ's sake, I delight in weaknesses, in insults, in hardships, in persecutions, in difficulties. For when I am weak, then I am strong" (2 Cor 12:10). This was Paul's experience of the dying and rising of Christ.

Perspectives on Paul

We have continually encountered Paul's thought structures as embedded within his own personal experiences. Yet historical and social perspectives were always at hand. Adam and Christ headed up two orders of humanity. The mindsets of the two ages, the flesh and the Spirit, manifested themselves respectively in the perversion and renewal of relationships. Paul's life and thought oscillated between a profound grasp of the historical significance of the dying and rising of Christ, and those personal and social experiences of humiliation that brought new meaning to the story.

Like Polybius and other ancient writers, Paul offered a schema for human history. But Paul was not interested in history as such. He was absorbed with a person and with the implications of the identity and story of this person for others. Even where Paul generalized about humanity as a whole, he did so to illuminate the present circumstances of particular people. It is *our* perspectives that make Paul an historiographer or apocalyptic seer. The idea of history may serve us as a way for peering into Paul's genius, but it remains *our* perspective, not his.[24]

---

[23]2 Cor 2:14—3:6; 4:7-12, 16-18; 6:3-10; 7:5; 11:1—12:10.

[24]I appreciate those who speak in terms of Paul's eschatological or apocalyptic orientation. See for example Gerhardus Vos, *The Pauline Eschatology* (Grand Rapids, Mich.: Baker, 1930), and J. Christian Beker, *Paul the Apostle: The Triumph of God in Life and Thought* (Philadelphia: Fortress, 1980). But this approach has too often, I believe, lifted Paul out of his social orientation in the Graeco-Roman world. This happens principally in two ways. First, Paul's terms of reference are located almost exclusively within Jewish prophetic and visionary writings. Second, these patterns of thought—eschatology and apocalyptic—are virtually made into another order of history lifted above the mundane and social. The effect of this is to create a polarization between so-called social history and redemptive history. Among evangelicals this can become a version of the split between everyday reality and primary reality. The categories of "redemptive history" are allowed to swallow up the details of "social reality." A case in point is the evident reticence of some evangelical scholars to allow that Paul's use of vocabulary such as *euangelion* and *mysterion* may have connected with Graeco-Roman realities as much or more than with the Old Testament. At another extreme, evangelicals have attached ideological significance to the language of the New Testament as a special case. See again the refutations of this in James Barr, *The Semantics of Biblical Language* (Oxford: Oxford University Press, 1961); Silva, *Biblical Words* and *God, Language and Scripture: Reading the Bible in the Light of General Linguistics*. Foundations of Contemporary Interpretation 4 (Grand Rapids, Mich.: Zondervan, 1990); and Greg Horsley, ed., *New Documents Illustrating Early Christianity*, vol. 5 (Sydney: Macquarie University Press, 1989).

The interdependence of these three sets of frames—the social, the historical and the personal—centered in Paul's preoccupation with Jesus Christ. He claimed to *know* Christ, not simply to know *about* him. He claimed a new identity for himself in Christ's personal representation of him. He staked his present and future experience on Christ's historical fulfillment of the hopes of Israel. For Paul, Christ was neither an ideal nor the highest principle of an intellectual system.

The various patterns of Paul's thought that we have surveyed—Jew-Gentile, Adam-Christ, in Christ, flesh and spirit, dying and rising—did *not* function as hierarchies of concepts within an ordered theological system. Each was a perspective, a way of seeing, a means of framing a particular concern around Christ. These perspectives were largely interchangeable. Each could be reworked into the others. Paul did not employ them according to a preset formula or as components of a system of theology. He provoked a knowledge of Christ and a response to him that simultaneously upheld a long tradition and turned traditional expectations and ideals inside out.

Evangelical conversations may be as hindered as they are helped by so-called theologies of Paul. Our conversations around Paul do not need more "objective" scholarly abstractions of his life and thought. We need portraits of a flesh-and-blood Paul, engaged with his Christ and with the cut and thrust of his social milieu. We need portraits of Paul that invite engagement, not armchair reflection. This is the continuing challenge before us in parts three and four.

PART 3

MEETING OF
TWO WORLDS

9

PAUL & PHILOSOPHY

PAUL DID NOT LIVE OR THINK IN A VACUUM. THE BOOK OF ACTS AND HIS LETTERS SHOW him in touch with the ideas and conventions of city and rural life. This is clear from even a brief overview of his encounters.

Luke reports that when the rustic Lycaonians encountered Paul and Barnabas, they mistook the apostles for Hermes and Zeus. A little later, in the Roman colony of Philippi, Paul, Silas and Luke encountered local superstition through a fortune-telling slave girl. Her owners convinced the authorities that Paul and Silas were creating strife and advocating customs unlawful for Romans, and they were beaten and imprisoned. The illegality of their treatment was not lost on Paul, nor on his captors. Traveling on to Athens, Paul's "babbling" attracted an invitation from certain Stoics and Epicureans to address the Areopagus, where he quoted sources familiar to them and alluded to their own theology. No doubt those philosophers converted on this occasion brought new intellectual dimensions into the fledgling *ekklēsia*. Much later, at Ephesus, Paul came into contact with magic, sorcery, a trade association, the cult of Artemis, civic pride and piety, the imperial cult, and Roman social policy. The impression grows of a man familiar with Graeco-Roman thought, custom and lore.[1]

Paul's letters presume that his readers are familiar with customary religious

---

[1]For the events summarized in this paragraph, see Acts 14:8-18; 16:19-21, 37-39; 17:18-34; 19:13-41.

piety, moral precept, rhetorical display and the customs of the Sophists. They had access to education, temples, courts and cults. His associates included prominent men and women, some of whom were members of the local elites and civic leadership. As such they made benefactions and received the due honors. Others received the dole from their patrons and engaged in political intrigues on their behalf. Paul knew the conventions of patronage and friendship only too well: his self-humiliation elicited embarrassment, contempt and enmity from those who took offense at his employment, his refusal of patronage, his disavowal of eloquence and his unseemly changeableness. He showed a good grasp of the legal and social requirements for widows, marriage, divorce, litigation, slavery and manumission, and the privileges and obligations of citizenship.

Paul was conversant with social expectations and the popular intellectual climate. He experienced the common presumptions of the primacy of reason and nature, abstractions about the gods, the expectations and claims for religious ritual and experience, and the idealism of moral preachers. In other words, he understood conventional social practices and the populist patterns of philosophy, theology, religion and morality.

Paul had formed his own opinions of both the social and intellectual patterns of his day. On some occasions he conformed. At other times his perspectives were provocative and critical. On yet further occasions he seems to have charted his own direction. Figure 9.1 models his responses.

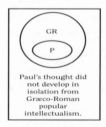   

Figure 9.1. The dynamics of Paul's thought in relation to Graeco-Roman popular intellectualism

The diversity of Paul's interactions with Graeco-Roman society and intellectualism argues against any single picture of his distinctiveness. He was neither wholly absorbed nor thoroughly original. Again we return to Edwin Judge's verdict that Paul may be best understood as an independent thinker, yet located in his surrounding world.[2]

---

[2]Edwin Judge, "St. Paul and Socrates," *Interchange* 14 (1973): 110. While the topics of philosophy, theology, religion and morality were intelligible to Paul and his contemporaries, the boundaries I have imposed between them are artificial. Eventually one has to come down somewhere on

The Rationalist-Irrationalist Tension Within Greek Philosophy

Aspects of our earlier discussions of Graeco-Roman popular intellectualism come into play again here: the location of reason in the soul, the role of reason in comprehending nature and the higher orders of reality, and the corresponding tendency toward abstraction. We have noted how the harsh realities of everyday life could undermine the high claims of abstract theories of reality. Yet in the hands of a skilled orator, those same abstractions could make experience seem like illusion. Reason alone could not deal with the vicissitudes of life, especially moral failure and personal insecurity. This everyday awareness of the value and limits of reason had its intellectual counterpart in the inherent tension within Greek philosophy of what we may loosely call rationalism and irrationalism.

Confidence in reason was both the genius and the Achilles heel of Greek philosophy. The same preoccupation with classification produced both the beauty and precision of Greek geometry and the misguided physiology of Greek medicine. Since reason made nature transparent, medicine already knew in advance what must be true of the body. The intellectual system of the four humors of the body required no autopsy for verification. As Edwin Judge has noted, the tendency of philosophy and science to become detached from people "often locked [them] into an abstract cycle of debate in general terms, driven more by the sheer rationality of the tradition than by reference to any actual social situation."[3]

The sophistication of the Greeks committed them to stepping away from particulars to universal principles. In this sense the principle was reality in Graeco-Roman thought. But for all its self-professed rationalism, philosophy could only proceed by what Judge has called a "leap in the dark":

> [The philosopher depended upon] the mere assumption . . . ungrounded either in experience or in the *elenchus*, that the good exists because he has the call divinely to seek it. So indeed many of the other basic positions of the philosophical schools are necessarily of this kind; for example, the cosmological theories of the Stoics or the physical hypotheses of the Epicureans, to which their ethical systems are necessarily related, are methodologically a leap in the dark. The intellectual enterprise as set up by Socrates and the philosophers is always dependent upon this creative imagination to provide the framework and the goals which direct thought and criticism.[4]

This leap betrayed a lurking irrationalism, the "other side" of Greek philosophy

---

whether, for example, to treat reason under philosophy or morality, or to deal with theology as a separate topic or as a subsection of religion or philosophy. Objectivity or precision is not the point. What matters is whether readers can join the conversation and whether I stay true to the intent of the sources.

[3]Edwin Judge, "St. Paul as a Radical Critic of Society," *Interchange* 16 (1975): 191.
[4]Judge, "St. Paul and Socrates," p. 115.

that eventually became so prominent. A profound shift slowly took place on the character and power of *logos* and on how easily reality yields its secrets to reason. Silence began to replace discourse as the pathway to the deepest levels of reality. Raoul Mortley concludes:

> The disease of which Greek culture eventually died is known by many names . . . scepticism . . . mysticism . . . the Failure of Nerve. My own name for it is systematic irrationalism. . . . For the time being the attack was averted—in part by the development of the Socratic-Platonic philosophy; in part, no doubt, by other agencies which escape us, since they did not express themselves in a literary form. But the germ survived, became endemic, and spread over the whole Greco-Roman world as soon as social conditions were favourable to its development.[5]

In chapter two, we noted how the pre-Socratics viewed *logos* as the rational account that enabled enquirers to validate sense data and ideas. While this brought new awareness of the process of rationality, the pre-Socratics were mostly concerned with the nature and order of reality and with the essential stuffs that made each thing what it was. The Sophists, however, critiqued all presuppositions of a reality underlying appearances. Despite what reason suggested, nonmanifest reality simply did not exist or was unknowable. Thus they stripped reason of its objectivity and foundation. In response, Plato reasserted the older position that there *is* a greater reality and that the function of reason is to bring it to light: "The real lover of knowledge will strive for true being; he will not devote his attention to particular instances, but will pursue things until he comes into contact with this essence. Through 'mingling with genius reality, he would beget intelligence and truth.'"[6]

Plato proceeded by abstraction and negation—the "onion" method: reason strips away mere appearances as it moves toward the essence of things. But while abstraction and negation prepared the way to the summit of reality, something more immediate, something independent of reason and speech was needed to finish the quest. Socrates spoke of a knowledge "born suddenly in the soul, 'like a light . . . fired by a leaping spark' . . . [resulting] not from intense verbal activity, but from continued application and communion with the subject itself."[7] Plato's "Good" made being and knowledge possible but was beyond them both. For his part, Aristotle asserted his confidence in the reality of the objective physical world and in the power of reason to explain it.

The Hellenistic age deeply questioned this classical rationalism, even though the materialism of the Stoics and Epicureans upheld the transparency of nature to

---

[5]Raoul Mortley, *From Word to Silence*, vol. 1, *The Rise and Fall of Logos*, Beitrage zur Religions und Kirchengeschichte des Altertums 30 (Bonn: Hanstein, 1986), p. 90. The following line of argument and several sources borrow from Mortley.

[6]Plato *Republic* 490B.

[7]Mortley, *From Word to Silence*, p. 95, quoting Plato *Phaedrus* 341CD.

reason. Alongside this reality existed another—those "seminal principles" responsible for the generation of the material universe. Thus the Hellenistic materialists maintained that sense of a split reality so characteristic of Greek philosophy, no matter how embarrassing this dualism was to their system.

The shadowy sense of an "Other" lurked in the various Platonic revivals. Driven by the old master's intuition that reason would fail somewhere short of the final goal, they developed options for this last step. Both sides of the tension appeared in the Jewish philosopher Philo. As a traditional Jew, Philo's God was clearly personal and knowable as the Lord of Israel's history and covenants. But as a Platonist, he believed that language could not convey the divine essence. Ultimately, only silence could enable union with the One.

Turning to Paul, we will not find any *explicit* discussion of reason or of the tensions between rationalism and irrationalism or of the drift from word to silence. Yet Paul was aware of the social impacts of the high place given to reason.

In our own day, we can see both sides at work in evangelical life and thought. At the broadest level, there are those more disposed to rigorous exegesis and theology, and those who emphasize matters of the heart. Strident forms of Reformed evangelicalism tend to be rationalist. Like the systems of the pre-Socratics and Plato, evangelical theology in this tradition values and promotes universal ideas and ideals, couched in the form of exegesis and theology, over everyday experience. Experience is swept aside in the name of objective, timeless truths. Theological formulations hedge church systems from sustained incredulity despite their almost palpable irrelevance. On the other side, piety and faith substitute for thoughtful, rigorous reading of the Bible. In some quarters a spiritual pride feeds an anti-intellectual fuzziness. Theology removed from life experience—or theology detached from scrutiny? Our polarization precludes the conversations we most desire.

Paul and the Renewal of the Mind in Christ
Paul's hearers were likely to regard him as a sophist or philosopher though he never described himself in either way. His message and itinerant lifestyle led audiences to link him in some way to rhetoric. At Corinth, a city Dio noted for its oversupply of aggressive sophists,[8] Paul had alienated certain parties by his refusal to play the part of a professional orator operating under their patronage. He had neither arrived, preached, profited or assumed airs like a Sophist, yet he had fallen under the close scrutiny, comparison and rejection of other Sophists.[9]

From the outset, Paul deliberately distanced himself from the Corinthian

---

[8]Dio Chrysostom *Oration* 8.9-12.
[9]1 Cor 2:1-5; 2 Cor 10:10; cf. 1 Thess 2:1-12.

sophistic tradition.[10] Where oratory was central to success, rhetorical skill was *"power,* whether for good or for ill."[11] Paul knew this and also knew that his refusal to use oratory went against the normal codes of sophistic ambition and excellence.[12] His choice to labor with his hands was an affront, earning him the formal enmity of the aggrieved powerbrokers.[13] Their offer—patronage with the usual expectation of honor returned—had been entirely unexceptional. They would have provided Paul with a platform for his Corinthian career in exchange for his professional services and his support of their privileged position. But to Paul, conformity with these expectations meant refusing to identify with the crucified Christ. Oratory would compromise the message of the cross and empty it of its true power.

Paul was deeply aware of how reason and oratory aided the status of the educated. It is against this background that we should note the intellectual dimension of his calls to obedience and conformity to Christ, particularly where his readers had contact with local philosophy and wisdom traditions.[14] He sharply criticized the arrogance and deceit that lurked in the claims and counterclaims of philosophers. He dismissed philosophy as having failed to deliver the certainty and right behavior it promised (Eph 4:17-19). The best of human intellectual endeavor inverted the roles of Creator and creature (Rom 1:18-32). The mind must serve the

---

[10]For an extensive discussion of the Corinthian sophistic tradition and the implications of Paul's refusal to comply, see Bruce Winter, "Philo and Paul Among the Sophists: Hellenistic Jewish and Christian Responses" (Ph.D. diss., Macquarie University, 1988). Winter has also brought the same perspectives to bear on the Thessalonian correspondence; see "The Entries and Ethics of Orators and Paul (1 Thessalonians 2:1-12)," *Tyndale Bulletin* 44 (1993): 55–74, and "Is Paul Among the Sophists?" *Reformed Theological Review* 53 (1994): 28-38. These articles, together with his wider studies of benefactors, suggest a portrait of Paul's struggles to convey his message in the context of higher education, wealth and influence. See also Winter's *Seek the Welfare of the City: Christians as Benefactors and Citizens*, First Century Christians in the Graeco-Roman World 1 (Exeter: Paternoster; and Grand Rapids, Mich.: Eerdmans, 1994).

[11]Conrad Gempf, "Public Speaking and Published Accounts," in *The Book of Acts in Its First Century Setting*, vol. 1, *Ancient Literary Setting*, ed. B. W. Winter and A. D. Clarke (Grand Rapids, Mich.: Eerdmans; and Carlisle: Paternoster, 1993), p. 260; emphasis his.

[12]In addition to Paul's failure as a sophist, Peter Marshall notes how the image of the triumph served as a metaphor of shame and social disadvantage in Paul's account of the enmity between himself and the Corinthian elite (2 Cor 2:14-16; 1 Cor 4:9-13). See Marshall, "A Metaphor of Social Shame: ΘΡΙΑΜΒΕΥΕΙΝ in 2 Cor. 2:14," *Novum Testamentum* 25 (1983): 302–17. His suffering and humiliation authenticated him as apostle and bearer of the Spirit. See Scott Hafemann, *Suffering and Ministry in the Spirit: Paul's Defense of His Ministry in 2 Corinthians 2:14—3:3* (Grand Rapids, Mich.: Eerdmans, 1990).

[13]On the conventions of friendship (patronage) and enmity and Paul's struggles at Corinth, see Peter Marshall, *Enmity in Corinth: Social Conventions in Paul's Relations with the Corinthians* (Tübingen: J. C. B. Mohr, 1987). His suggestion that the Corinthian elite have charged him with inconstancy is particularly relevant given the ideals of conformity and stability in Graeco-Roman morality (pp. 281–339).

[14]Eph 4:17-24; Col 2:2-8.

life of love lived before God and one's neighbor. Nowhere was this clearer than in his struggle with the intellectual and social conceit of influential members of the Corinthian *ekklēsia*.[15]

The factionalism[16] at Corinth betrayed an intellectual and social arrogance: "The Corinthians have treated their teachers as if each represented yet another philosophical school competing to outdo all the others."[17] Paul's censure of their arrogance aggravated the already delicate situation created by his refusal to accept their patronage. They had taken his refusal as a snub. The relationship reached its low point in the alliance between those he had snubbed and certain Judaizing "super-apostles"[18] who had recently arrived in Corinth. In his study of boasting in Paul and Graeco-Roman sources, Chris Forbes notes that his opponents had likely vilified Paul as "inconsistent, and hence as a flatterer (*kolax*), and possibly also as insincere, and hence as an *eirōn* (self-deprecator) as well. It also took the form of studied mutual comparisons among the leaders of the alliance, most probably in terms of friendly rivalry and mutual esteem, while the real cutting edge of the comparisons was directed at Paul."[19]

Paul's social standing at Corinth had, in fact, never been ideal, given the weakness of his plying a trade. Moreover, his remarks in his first letter to the effect that philosophy, rhetoric and education were weakness and folly had been a slap in the face to men of means. These eminent Corinthians now related to Paul in the conventions of enmity. His social disgrace was now made worse by his ironic reply. He countered by attempting to reframe his relationships through the images of a parent and ambassador.[20] At the same time, he attacked the conceit of those who had dismissed him.

---

[15] 1 Cor 1:26-31; 4:10-13; 2 Cor 10:1-6.

[16] Chris Forbes suggests it is better to understand the "strong" as "an ad-hoc alliance, for diverse social and theological purposes" ("Comparison, Self-Praise and Irony: Paul's Boasting and Conventions in Hellenistic Rhetoric," *New Testament Studies* 32 [1986]: 15).

[17] Stanley Stowers, "Paul on the Use and Abuse of Reason," in *Greeks, Romans, and Christians: Essays in Honor of Abraham J. Malherbe*, ed. D. L. Balch, E. Ferguson and W. A. Meeks (Minneapolis: Fortress, 1990), p. 258. My discussion of Paul and the Corinthians in relation to intellectual elitism in part follows Stowers's study on Paul and reason. At times his reconstructions depend on tight parallels to philosophical schools. Like Chris Forbes ("Comparison"), I regard the Corinthian elite as much more eclectic in their intellectualism and often unaware of the origins of "their" ideas. The rivalry between philosophers and rhetors may have been of little account to their audiences, who were likely to synthesize ideas without the agenda of any one school. On the social position of the Corinthian elites, see Winter, *Seek the Welfare*, pp. 179–97, and David Gill, "In Search of the Social Elite in the Corinthian Church," *Tyndale Bulletin* 44 (1993): 323–37, and "Acts and the Urban Elites," in *The Book of Acts in Its First Century Setting*, vol. 2, *Graeco-Roman Setting*, ed. D. W. J. Gill and C. Gempf (Grand Rapids, Mich.: Eerdmans; and Carlisle: Paternoster, 1994), pp. 105–18.

[18] *tōn hyperlian apostōn*, 2 Cor 11:5.

[19] Forbes, "Comparison," p. 15.

[20] 1 Cor 4:14-16; 2 Cor 6:11-13; 11:2; 12:14-15.

The images of weapons and a fortress in 2 Corinthians 10:3-6 may reflect Cynic and Stoic self-understanding. Yet they were also widely used in Paul's time without any necessary links to the philosophical schools. Stoics and others treated emotions as diseases to be overcome by reason, which guards a man like a fortress: "Know, therefore, Serenus, that this perfect man, full of virtues human and divine, can lose nothing. . . . The walls which guard the wise man are safe both from flame and assault, they provide no means of entrance—are lofty, impregnable, godlike."[21]

Whatever the origin of his images, Paul was convinced that though he lived in the (age of the) flesh he was nevertheless *not* using its weapons (2 Cor 10:3). Rather, he used the power of God to take captive all arguments (*logismoi*) and to demolish the Corinthians' stronghold of reason. Paul had turned the image inside out. Instead of viewing reason (*logos*) as a fortress repelling the onslaughts of emotion and passion, the knowledge of God would demolish every stronghold of argument (*logismous*) opposed to Christ. It was precisely this point, Paul implied, that his opponents did not understand—they had not grasped how the dying and rising of Christ had discredited intellectual and social elitism.[22] How did Paul overcome these strongholds? Paul alluded to a demonstration of power (perhaps) beyond words.[23] The tone is deeply ironic: the impressive power of Christ and the Spirit would be manifested in the weak words and wonders of the unimpressive apostle.

We must not miss Paul's innovation in basing thought on the revelation of God in Christ and the Spirit. He was not pitting faith against reason. Rather, he was confronting the arrogant *disposition* that accompanied the intellectualism of the strong (1 Cor 4:18-21). In other words, his remarks on reason had a primarily social orientation. This is important for understanding 1 Corinthians 1—2. Paul was not presenting a quasi-philosophical theory about revelation and reason. Stanley Stowers recognizes this but loses too much when he claims that Paul did not sharply contrast the Spirit with reason as the means of coming to faith.[24] Likewise, he suggests that the mysteries imparted by the Spirit to which Paul refers (1 Cor 2:6—3:4) were not "the basic beliefs about God and the narrative of Jesus' life, death, and resurrection," but "something entirely different . . . [and] apparently unessential to their Christian life."[25] This seems to lose Paul's point, his intent to undermine intellectual arrogance.

The transition from 1 Corinthians 2:5 to 2:6 is not from the gospel to a *new*

---

[21]Seneca *On the Firmness of the Wise Man* 6.3-8. This view had also found a home in Judaism (cf. 4 Macc 7:4-5, 20; 14:11—16:12).

[22]2 Cor 1:9-10; 2:14-16; 4:7-18; 6:3-10; 12:7-10.

[23]2 Cor 10:6, 11; 12:12—13:10; cf. 1 Cor 2:4; 5:3-5.

[24]Stowers, "Paul on the Use and Abuse of Reason," pp. 255–56.

[25]Ibid., pp. 262, 261.

message for the Corinthians—not a shift from central to peripheral matters—but a development of his remark that faith must rest on the Spirit and not on human wisdom. There is no reason-revelation dichotomy here in the sense that many theologians have subsequently presumed. Yet Paul did present an antithesis: human (intellectual) autonomy could not attain what only the Spirit could reveal (1 Cor 2:14-16). In this sense, Paul did have a distinct perspective on rationality. The gospel had created an entirely different framework for the exercise of the mind. In place of arrogance, the Spirit created the new norms of faithfulness, cooperation and edification (1 Cor 3:5-15). By placing the mind in service of others, Paul had no choice but to spell out the social and personal implications of this reframing to the Corinthian elitists, even challenging the behavior of those with whom he otherwise agreed.

Stowers suggests that 1 Corinthians 6:12-20 is "a dialogue between Paul and an imaginary debater who represents the 'libertine position.' "[26] "All things are permitted" may thus be akin to the Stoic slogan "Only the wise man is truly free." Other Corinthian slogans may have included "It is good for a man not to touch a woman" (1 Cor 7:1). According to Stowers, the strong had adopted "a therapeutic model . . . part of the philosophical *koinē* known to cultured and educated people in the empire."[27] This amounted to the use of reason to improve the weak by correcting each faulty belief. The cure came in the form of philosophical and moral arguments and sayings to drive out false beliefs. Stowers hears echoes of these in the "we know" slogans and confession (1 Cor 8:1-6).[28] As a further example, the strong may have championed the knowledge that an idol is "nothing" in order to heal the weak of their religious scruples.[29]

Paul sought to demolish the elitism of those who presumed to know best. At the same time, he seemed to play into the hands of the pretentious Corinthians by emphasizing his own weakness (1 Cor 4:11-13). Whether or not Paul was consciously inverting the philosophers' use of hardship catalogues remains a somewhat open question. What *is* clear is that Paul understood the success of his ministry not to have come *in spite of* his hardships and vulnerability, but precisely *because of* and *through* these. His suffering had opened the way for the power of his message and the Spirit.[30] Thus Paul and those who called themselves the strong held vastly different criteria for apostolic authority and authenticity.[31]

---

[26]Ibid., p. 263.
[27]Ibid., pp. 274–75.
[28]Ibid., p. 275.
[29]1 Cor 8:5-6; cf. Gal 4:8-10, 1 Thess 1:9.
[30]1 Cor 2:1-16; 2 Cor 4:7-18.
[31]2 Cor 1:12-14; 10:10; 11:6.

The fundamental disagreement between them reached its climax in 2 Corinthians 10:1—12:10, one of the most perplexing passages in either of the letters, a startling self-disclosure that drew heavily on the conventions of irony, boasting, self-praise and encomium. The traditional conventions of rhetoric were widespread and well understood in Paul's day. There were clear "rules" about comparison, self-praise and boasting, and equally clear criteria for judging when and how an exception could be made. Chris Forbes clarifies the relevance of the conventions of self-praise: "It is fair to say that the educated Hellenistic world in which Paul moved knew of conventions of self-praise, but believed that they required great delicacy if they were not to be misused, as they led all too easily to *alazōneia* and *hyperopsia*, which were closely related to *hybris*."[32]

In regard to irony, there is no way to know if the "rules" were widely known in Paul's day, but it was a topic "of considerable interest for rhetorical writers, and hence, most probably, for students and practitioners of rhetoric."[33] The pretentious or boastful man *(alazōn)* was the opposite of the ironic man. Paul's argument turned on an ironic parody of the self-praise, boasting and comparisons of his opponents and their "super-apostles": "[It was] a ruthless parody of the pretensions of his opponents . . . [but] while holding to the traditional forms of encomium, and following common topics, he radically inverts the content . . . he amplifies what he should minimize, and minimizes what he should amplify."[34]

Having spoken of his relation to Christ, instead of proceeding to the customary delineation of personal honors, Paul speaks of his humiliations, disgrace and hardship, culminating in his confession of personal weakness (2 Cor 11:29). This weakness was primarily social, not psychological—the helplessness of one who had chosen little power or status, and his humiliation in the eyes of those who were honored. These trials were the test of his work: "Paul is presenting a case for a radically different conception of apostolic authority through his irony . . . [he] has taken several steps beyond the Hellenistic tradition in his attitude to self-praise. [Unlike Plutarch,] for Paul *self*-praise is never legitimate: boasting that is not 'in the Lord' is 'beyond measure' and 'senseless.' "[35]

The place Paul gave to the intellect was thus radically different from the prevailing norms. He subverted the claims of the strong to be demonstrably superior. He

---

[32]Forbes, "Comparison," p. 10.

[33]Ibid., p. 11. "Without following the entire trail, it is possible to show that the definitions of *alazoneia* persisted down to Paul's time and well beyond" (p. 13).

[34]Ibid., pp. 18-19. Paul must have seemed frustratingly enigmatic and fickle to some Corinthians. As Winter points out, "He refused to use rhetorical devices to persuade in his preaching . . . yet he could make use of rhetorical forms in his letters when it suited his purposes" ("Philo and Paul," p. 251).

[35]Forbes, "Comparison," p. 20.

did not challenge their perceptions of idols per se. Neither did he ask them to comply with the false beliefs of the weak, nor did he gag dialogue. Rather, he urged the strong to be sensitive to the pain of the weak. Love, not ideological precision, must color all.[36] Stowers captures the spirit of this subversion:

> Those who want a more rational view of religion are not to act as if the goal of life in Christ is to relieve the weak of every irrational belief by means of arguments over arguments. Paul again identifies himself with the more rational. They are right, but he wants to make it clear that the goal of the kind of community that he advocates is not minds purged of all irrational belief. In fact, the point of the section as a whole is that such a narrow view is counterproductive in achieving an inclusive and mutually enhancing community.[37]

For Paul, the problem with reason was not intellectual but relational. The mind cannot be partitioned from sin as the soul is from the body in so many of the philosophers' accounts. Paul never explained sin in dualistic terms: sin is not an inherent source of vice in a creation fashioned out of the tension of reason and matter. Sin entered the *kosmos* through the history of a man—a patent absurdity to Greeks, for whom the *kosmos* was the perfect, ordered totality. The dying and rising of Christ located the problem of humanity within the person but put the solution in the hands of the one to whom he was accountable. Being in Christ transformed the mind as an aspect of relationship.[38] The power of Paul's explanation lay in his ability to quarry his own inner man, correctly observing his own self-contradiction and frustration. For Paul, the common struggle of mankind was intensely personal and relational, not philosophical.

There are uncomfortable links between the Corinthians and much that passes as sound theology and ministry in evangelical circles. Paul confronted the arrogant disposition that accompanied the intellectualism of the strong. They had adopted a common therapeutic model of reason to improve the weak by correcting each faulty belief. The cure came through sermons to drive out false beliefs. Paul had no such agenda. He promoted love rather than precision and conformity. He urged the strong to be sensitive to the pain of the weak rather than to correct every inadequate belief.

Much evangelical theology and preaching sides with the Corinthians over against Paul. In some circles a simplistic logic links preaching with objectivity and with the authority of the Bible, portraying the preacher as the last line of defense against the evils of relativism. The outcome is an obsession among some clergy and

---

[36]1 Cor 8:10-11; 13:2, 8-13; 2 Cor 13:11; cf. Rom 14:1.

[37]Stowers, "Paul on the Use and Abuse of Reason," pp. 283–84.

[38]Rom 12:1-2; Eph 4:17-24; Col 2:2-6.

congregations with driving out every vestige of thought deemed less than truly evangelical. This mindset has spawned generations of zealous preachers who have harassed their captive audiences into needless guilt and dubious "work for the Lord." Unable or unwilling to step down from their own presumptions of theological and ministerial superiority, they preach to cast out error, while never facing the pain of those who hear.

10

PAUL & THEOLOGY

IN THE MID TO LATE THIRD CENTURY B.C., OENOANDA IN LYCIA BOASTED MOST OF THE
refinements of a small town eager to show its Hellenized civility. Earlier that century one Diogenes had bequeathed the city a sermon of Epicurean wisdom on the
gods—a forty-meter-long "vast wayside pulpit of stone."[1] It seems, however, that
the citizens of Oenoanda valued the sermon's "atheism" far less than its architec-
tural potential. Piece by piece they had dismantled it over the centuries for repairs
to buildings and walls. A new inscription, high over the outer eastern gate of the
town and positioned to catch the first rays of daylight, bore witness to a more popular theology:

> Self-existent, untaught, without a mother, undisturbed, of many names although not
> spreading abroad his name, dwelling in fire: this is God, and we messengers are a small
> portion of God. To those enquiring about God, who he is, this is what it (i.e., the ora-
> cle) said: that Aither is the all-seeing God, looking to whom pray at dawn as you look
> towards the east.[2]

The connection to local oracles and the ritual suggested by the final line bear
out the general testimony that theology was never divorced from popular religious
understanding and practice. *Theologoi* were frequently located at oracular shrines,

---

[1]Greg Horsley, ed., *New Documents Illustrating Early Christianity* (Sydney: Macquarie University
Press, 1987), 4:73.
[2]Inscription *SEG* 27 (1977) 933, in Horsley, *New Documents*, 2:39.

where they "wrote hymns to the gods" and "made this language the language of the gods" about whom worshipers had come to inquire.[3] An epitaph at Rome to an "expounder of the numinous to others," himself from a town not so far from Oenoanda, reveals the potpourri of philosophy that these men attached to the oracles:

> To the underworld gods. I was like I was in my speech, spirit, and form, possessing the implanted soul of a person just born, happy in friendship and fortunate in my mind, holding the view "nothing in excess," and viewing everything as mortal. I came (i.e., into the world), I departed blameless, I did not think about things which I ought not to: whether I had a previous existence, whether I shall have one in time [to come]. I was educated, I educated [others], I shackled the vault of the universe, declaring to men the divine virtues which proceed from the gods. The dear earth conceals me; yet what was my pure name? I was Philetos, a man beloved by all, from Limyra in Lykia.[4]

The inscription from Oenoanda was at least partly an answer from an oracle. Great confidence was placed in oracles to reveal the mind and character of a god. Such confidence had torn up Diogenes' sermon at Oenoanda. His Epicurean "atheism" was no match for a dawn ritual with a sprinkling of theology. While the philosophical schools preferred to keep theology at a safe distance from popular religion, communities generally had no scruples about blending the two.

Theology and the Constraint of God

The Oenoanda text quoted above named God as much by the absence of his name as by his assorted titles and characteristics: "of many names although not spreading abroad his name." The paradox was as old as Heraclitus and "well attested in pagan hymns and theology by the first century A.D."[5] Less frequently attested was the "motherless" origin of God.[6] "We messengers" *(angeloi)* is not likely to refer to Oenoanda's leading citizens, but to the intermediary gods who each form a portion of the one God. Greg Horsley notes that the way the inscription absorbs the lesser gods *(angeloi)* into one God is "a remarkable indicator of the trend towards monotheism" in the second and third centuries A.D.[7] But the language may simply reflect the influence of Jewish angel mysticism in western Asia Minor. The inscription may not point to faith in one God as much as to "an hierarchical

---

[3]Robin Fox, *Pagans and Christians in the Mediterranean World from the Second Century AD to the Conversion of Constantine* (London: Penguin, 1988), pp. 152, 260.
[4]Inscription *IG* XIV (1890) 2068 in Horsley, *New Documents*, 4:32–33. Horsley considers that Philetos's self-description fits that of a *theologos*.
[5]Fox, *Pagans and Christians*, p. 170.
[6]Cf. Philo *On the Universe*, p. 100.
[7]Horsley, *New Documents*, 2:39. See also 3:48.

arrangement where one god is proclaimed supreme over others."[8]

If the inscription was monotheistic, the mention of Aither, the One "dwelling in fire," nonetheless moves toward the murkier waters of a primary element in the cosmos shaping reality through intelligence and power. Plato had linked the Demiurge to his fourth element, fire. Aristotle then added Aither to Plato's fire, and in time the two became the one principle.[9] As the worshipers of Oenoanda prayed at dawn looking toward the east, their thoughts may well have swung between God as self-existent One and God as (a principle of) Nature. Both lines of thought were old and well-made.

We have noted on several occasions how Greek philosophy worked by the "onion principle" of abstraction. Theology shared the same tool and its presuppositions: (1) reality is layered; (2) understanding proceeds by mentally peeling back these layers toward (3) the goal of uncovering the essence of reality. This is reflected in the Oenoanda inscription: we know God by what he is *not*—"self-existent, untaught, without a mother, undisturbed."[10] This kind of negative theology was standard fare, especially for those with Platonic leanings: "[God is] incorporeal, one, immeasurable, begetter of everything . . . blessed and beneficent, the best, in lack of nothing, himself bearing all things, celestial, ineffable, unnamable, and as [Plato] himself says, 'invisible, unconquerable—whose nature is difficult to find and if found cannot be expressed among the many.'"[11]

Time and again we have noted the primacy of reason and nature within philosophical thought, including the common subjection of men and gods to the rules of reason.[12] This confidence in reason created a split attitude toward describing God in human terms (anthropomorphism). On the one hand, anthropomorphism could be dismissed as mere superstition.[13] On the other hand, if reason is the basis of our knowledge of God, then theology must be natural theology—we infer what God is like from understanding nature. This meant arguing in a circle: first, from man to God (if man is xyz then so is God, only "bigger"); second, from God back to man (if God is xyz then so is man, only "smaller"). Cicero sensed the circularity: "It follows that they possess the same faculty of reason as the human race, and that both have the same apprehension of truth and the same law enjoining what is right and what is wrong. Hence we see that wisdom and intelli-

---

[8]Rosalind Kearsley, "Angels in Asia Minor," in *New Documents Illustrating Early Christianity*, ed. S. R. Llewelyn (Sydney: Macquarie University Press, 1992), 6:208.

[9]Cf. Cicero *On the Nature of the Gods* 1.39.

[10]Cf. Plotinus 6.5.1.

[11]Apuleius *On the Teaching of Plato* 1.5; the quote is from Plato *Timaeus* 28E.

[12]E.g., Pliny the Elder *Natural History* 2.27; Seneca *Epistles* 95.49.

[13]Lucretius *On the Rule of Nature* 1.62-72.

gence also have been derived by men from the gods."[14]

Rationalism, abstraction and anthropomorphism found a home in negative theology. First, only reason could reveal God (to whatever degree). Second, only reason could remove those layers of matter and faulty reasoning that darkened our comprehension of God. Third, if reason is the highest faculty of the noblest part of the most divine creature, then theology must begin with man in order to go beyond him. God thus lies beyond the limitations of our best and worst qualities.[15]

Philosophical perspectives on the gods and the cosmos emphasized that gods and men must both conform to the order of nature and to reason as the key to understanding that order.[16] Nature determines the character of God and man. It was only a short step from here to the divine providence of Graeco-Roman theology and religion.[17] At times the divinity of providence seems to have allowed it to trade by many names, including the largely interchangeable terms "providence," "acts of God" and "Zeus." To Stoics, providence was the most plausible and important basis for meditation, personal piety and worship, and it was a model for correcting ignorant superstitions: "From everything that happens in the universe it is easy for a man to find occasion to praise providence, if he has within himself these two qualities: the faculty of taking a comprehensive view of what has happened in each individual instance, and the sense of gratitude."[18]

Although providence suggested divine favor and care, there was little if any room for mercy in the god of the Stoics. Despite the many lengthy praises of the gods that survive, few note mercy as a divine quality. Yet as classicist Bruce Harris notes, the tale of Apuleius's *Metamorphoses* turned on Lucius's experience of the tenderness of the goddess Isis: "Holy goddess, everlasting saviour of mankind, ever generous in your help to mortals you show a mother's warm love for the misfortunes of those in distress. . . . You can unravel the inextricably tangled web of Fate, you can calm the gales of Fortune."[19]

The same tone appeared in aretalogies to Isis, such as the following inscription

---

[14]Cicero *On the Nature of the Gods* 2.31.78-79.

[15]Raoul Mortley has shown that certain philosophers of late antiquity regarded negative theology as still too "positive" and limiting of the One. They sought to go beyond negation to silence. See Mortley, *From Word to Silence*, vol. 2, *The Way of Negation, Christian and Greek*, Beitrage zur Religions und Kirchengeschichte des Altertums 31 (Bonn: Hanstein, 1986), p. 90.

[16]Pseudo-Aristotle *On the Universe* 401AB; Hierocles *On Duties* 1.3.53-54.

[17]It also featured in some Jewish thought. Horsley notes that "its occurrence in Philo suggests . . . it had currency in educated Jewish circles" by the first century (Horsley, *New Documents*, 3:143; cf. Philo, in *Flacc* 125).

[18]Epictetus *Discourses* 1.6.1-2; cf. 3.22.50-51. Also Cicero *On Nature* 1.3-4, 117, 2.72.

[19]Apuleius *Metamorphoses* 11.22, 25. I am indebted to Bruce Harris for many of the texts and, in places, the line of argument that follows. See his "St. Paul and the Public Reputation of the Churches," *Reformed Theological Review* 50 (1991): 50–58.

at Maroneia from the second or first century B.C., in which she is praised as the benefactor and savior of her followers: "I am completely confident that you will come [to my aid] again. For since you came when called for my salvation, how would you not come for your own honor?"[20]

Isis's mercy, however, was not quite what it seemed: "I inflict vengeance on those who do unjust things. I legislated for mercy *(elean)* to be shown to suppliants. I have regard for those who defend themselves with justification *(dikaiōs)*."[21] Isis ordained mercy for those who could defend themselves according to justice. In other words, she defended the defensible—mercy was held within the constraints of justice.

The fact that God did not immediately exact punishment on all evildoers appears as a theme in religious and philosophical literature since at least the sixth century B.C. In *On God's Slowness to Punish*, Plutarch, a contemporary of Paul, advances several reasons for the divine delay. First, the more obvious reasons: to provide an example or pattern for curbing passion, to allow time for improvement, to bring good out of evil and to ensure the most fitting moment of punishment. Second, the more philosophical reason: that God actually *is* punishing evildoers, the problem being our inability to perceive this.[22] Somewhat like the sentiment that Isis will defend the defensible, Plutarch pictures God delaying judgment on those whose "innate nobility" may yet be enough to produce repentance and change:

> It is reasonable to assume, however, that God takes a careful look at the emotions of the sick minds to which he is dispensing punishment, to see if they have the slightest possible tendency and inclination towards remorse, and that he determines how much time should elapse for those people whose nature is not absolutely and incorrigibly evil. You see, God knows the amount of goodness which the minds bore when they left him and proceeded to birth, and he knows how solid and substantial their innate nobility is. . . . So, because he knows all this, he doesn't hastily impose the same punishment on everyone: he wastes no time in mowing down and removing from life anything which is irredeemable . . . but he gives time, the chance to change, to people whose sinfulness has probably taken root because they didn't know what was right.[23]

People were more likely to encounter mercy in the political arena—not in any personal experience, but on the imperial propaganda of coins ("Clementia Caesaris") and marketplace inscriptions. Gods and great men alike represented the same principle: "If the gods, merciful and just, do not immediately pursue with the thun-

---

[20]Inscription *SEG* 821, in Horsley, *New Documents*, 1:11–12.
[21]Inscription *I. Kyme* 41, in Horsley, *New Documents*, 1:18–20. See also inscription *SEG* 821 on pp. 10–12.
[22]Plutarch *Moralia* 550C-557E.
[23]Ibid., 551D.

derbolt the sins of the mighty, how much more just is it for a man set over his fellows to exert his authority with a mild spirit."[24] At least that was the *ideal*. The reality was far tougher both on earth and in the heavens. As Bruce Harris notes, "We may conclude that in the mind of ordinary Greeks and Romans of the first century 'clemency' was a quality which by and large men of power had arrogated to themselves and their own use. There was a hardness and political realism which left little room for the more humane feelings of pity and tenderness associated with it."[25]

All of this recalls what we noted in chapter five of the links between the social experience of rank and the various theories of multiple levels of reality. Mercy must conform to the age-old patterns of self-sufficiency and personal honor: "Self-interest and the perpetuation of power are the obvious motives for [a display of mercy], beyond any possible reflection of divine beneficence."[26] The gods, like the wise man, were bound to Nature and Fate and to the ideals of an undisturbed inner peace. They were also equally preoccupied with their own ambitions. Pity, a "sadness at misfortunes which one believes are happening to the undeserving," must be shunned as far as possible in the interests of self-sufficiency.[27] "Remember," intoned the sage, "let nothing be to excess."

There was an exception to prove this rule. In the center of Statius's Athens, without image or ritual, stood the Altar of Mercy. It was a place of refuge for the wretched. It was not for the noble, whose lives were shielded from Fate and Fortune and the whims of rulers.[28] The noble prided themselves on having no need of mercy, divine or human, other than that which befitted their piety and civic virtue. The less fortunate dared to hope for mercy at the altar—perhaps from an Unknown God. As Paul stood to speak before the council at the Areopagus, writes Harris, "the idea of divine mercy was not far away . . . and we may guess that Paul himself knew of the Altar of Mercy in the city, and was aware that the supreme mercy was among the attributes of the 'unknown god' he was now expounding to the Athenians."[29]

Paul on the Areopagus at Athens
Paul was invited to present his credentials before the Areopagus, the body responsible for "surveillance over the introduction of foreign divinities" to Athens.[30] The

---

[24]Seneca *Epistles* 1.7.2.
[25]Harris, "St. Paul and the Public Reputation," p. 78.
[26]Ibid., pp. 98–99.
[27]Seneca *Epistles* 2.5.4; cf. Epictetus *Manual* 16.
[28]*Thebaid* 12.503-5.
[29]Harris, "St. Paul and the Public Reputation," p. 103.
[30]Horsley, *New Documents*, 1:31.

Stoics and Epicureans present in the marketplace seemed to have understood him as introducing two new deities, Jesus and Anastasis (Acts 17:18).[31]

Certain aspects of Paul's speech seem close to Stoic philosophy and theology. David Balch emphasizes that after Posidonius, Stoic philosophy had reached a rapprochement with popular religion such that Stoics had openly defended the place of temples (Acts 17:23-24, 29).[32] In Luke's account, Paul's disavowal of temples and idols would cast him as the "true" Stoic returning to the original doctrine of Posidonius. Paul's treatment of providence in nature and history, and even of judgment, is also said to be compatible with Stoic teaching (Acts 17:23, 25-28, 30-31).[33] Jerome Neyrey emphasizes those aspects of Paul's message likely to be out of step with Epicurean teaching, such as his supposed theodicy and his appeal to providence.[34] In this case, Paul is seen to be siding with the Stoics and forcing a split between the two groups, just as he did later between the Pharisees and Sadducees (Acts 23:6-7).

But there are problems with these theses. On the one hand, Paul's "conformity" to the Stoics seems particularly overstated. On the other hand, Bruce Winter has shown that Paul may have been closer to Epicurean interests than Neyrey considers.[35] Their suggestions also do not account for the split verdict of the council— some sneered, while others believed—neither response indicating that Paul has conformed to "orthodox" Stoicism.

Colin Hemer's conclusions seem more judicious.[36] To a large degree, Paul structured his address around his audience's perspectives,[37] even including their own sources.[38] Nevertheless, his message was confronting. The whole address was deeply ironic as Paul pitted the Stoics and Epicureans against each other. The Epicurean God needed nothing; the Stoic divinity was the source of life. Paul's God was personal, not the alternatively transcendent and pantheistic force of Sto-

---

[31]Paul's audience must have mistaken his mention of Jesus' resurrection *(anastasis)* as reference to a second deity.

[32]See David Balch, "The Areopagus Speech: An Appeal to the Stoic Historian Poidonius against Later Stoics and the Epicureans," in *Greeks, Romans, and Christians: Essays in Honor of Abraham J. Malherbe*, ed. D. L. Balch, E. Ferguson and W. A. Meeks (Minneapolis: Fortress, 1990), pp. 67–72.

[33]Ibid., pp. 58–67.

[34]Jerome Neyrey, "Acts 17, Epicureans, and Theodicy: A Study in Stereotypes," in *Greeks, Romans, and Christians*, pp. 124–33.

[35]Bruce Winter, "In Public and in Private: Early Christians and Religious Pluralism," in *One God, One Lord in a World of Religious Pluralism* (Cambridge: Tyndale House, 1991), pp. 123–24.

[36]See Colin Hemer, *The Book of Acts in the Setting of Hellenistic History*, Wissenschaftliche Untersuchungen zum Neuen Testament 49 (Tübingen: Mohr, 1989); and "The Speeches of Acts: II— The Areopagus Address," *Tyndale Bulletin* 40 (1989): 239–59.

[37]Paul may even have used a set pattern for theological debate like Cicero's *On the Nature of the Gods*. See Winter, "In Public and in Private," pp. 118, 122.

[38]Aratus *Phenomena* 7; Cleanthes *Aristobulus*, fragment 4.6.

icism.[39] The Stoics' God is not like men, yet they uphold man-made images. The philosophers pride themselves on their superior wisdom, yet they worship an "unknown" God. The "babbler" Paul must enlighten them.[40] The Epicureans, whose God is supremely disinterested, are lumped with those who are wary of the anger of a neglected deity. In the heart of Athenian racial supremacy and religious renown, Paul declares that all men are from the one stock and that God needs no temple.

Paul's allusion to Epimenides—"in him we live and move and have our being" (Acts 17:28)—linked his message to Athenian tradition. Epimenides was a significant figure in Athenian religion. More specifically, he figures in the explanation for the altars to the unknown god(s) as told in the story by Diogenes Laertius.[41] Paul's closing remark also called to mind another Athenian treasure. Legend told that when the Areopagus was founded it was dedicated with the words, "When a man dies the earth drinks up his blood, there is no resurrection."[42] Hemer notes that this declaration "must have been familiar to every cultivated Athenian in that audience and the crucial point of Paul's encounter with the beliefs of his hearers."[43] Beginning with their own poets, Paul steered his message to the central place of Christ in human history, and Christ as the revelation of the character and purposes of God. Having begun with theology, he ended by disallowing it.[44]

Paul and the Free Mercy of God in Christ
The themes Paul stressed in the ancient capital of philosophy were also relevant for

---

[39]Paul always spoke of God as the Creator and Redeemer whom he knew in close personal relationship. According to A. A. Long, this contrasted sharply with Greek theologies: "Their conception of the divine, even when expressed in highly personal language, never suggests that the supreme being is an individual to whom someone might be related in the manner of an Abraham or a Job" ("Epicureans and Stoics," in *Classical Mediterranean Spirituality: Egyptian, Greek, Roman*, ed. A. H. Armstrong [London: Routledge and Kegan Paul, 1986], p. 136).

[40]Hemer cites the sources that imply that *spermologos* (babbler) was a piece of Athenian slang (*Book of Acts*, p. 117).

[41]Diogenes Laertius *Lives of the Philosophers* 1.110-12. Colin Hemer notes that "we cannot now specify how far Paul's knowledge of the intricacies of Athenian tradition extended, but it suffices to show that he had struck some significant vein of the richer hidden complexity" ("Speeches of Acts," p. 246). He also notes in another place that the apparent discrepancy between the plural *gods* and Paul's singular *God* is not the difficulty it seems (*Book of Acts*, p. 117).

[42]Aeschylus *Eumenides* 647.

[43]Hemer, "Speeches of Acts," p. 2.

[44]Paul's portrait of God's involvement in human affairs (Acts 17:24-28) bears only a superficial resemblance to providence as the philosophers understood it. Paul never used the common phrase *theia pronoia* (Horsley, *New Documents*, 3:143 and 5:145). His only use of *pronoia* (Rom 13:14) does not carry the sense of providence. Paul is more likely to have based his understanding on Old Testament sources such as Psalm 19. I suggest that providence is not an apt term for Paul's thought. See my remarks on Romans below.

his readers in the imperial capital, Rome. Paul's understanding of the character and purposes of God would have been immediately intelligible to Jewish readers but highly irregular to many others. Perhaps mindful of how both Jewish and Graeco-Roman interests might distort his message, Paul began Romans with themes implying the eclipse of both Graeco-Roman natural theology and Jewish nationalistic theology (Rom 1:16—3:20).

As in his speech to the Areopagus, the letter to Rome worked around the themes of judgment, religious practice, God's provision of the necessities of life, his forbearance with human ignorance and his relation to all peoples (Rom 1:18—2:16). At first the language seems close to Plato's *Timaeus* and even to the inscription at Oenoanda. The creation shows God's invisible qualities *(ta aorata)*, his eternal power *(aidios autou dynamis)* and his divine nature *(theiotēs)*.[45] Paul's themes have the appearance of theology, but the resemblance is superficial. As in the Areopagus speech, Paul's subsequent handling of his topic and his wider vision caution against any simple identification of his message with theology. Just as Paul had concluded his speech at Athens with Christ, the divinely appointed judge of all people, so in Romans he pictured both the former and present eras of human history as a divine stay of execution before the day "when God will judge men's secrets through Jesus Christ."[46] Also like his Athens speech, Paul located the character of God in the person and story of Christ. While nature reveals God to some degree, it is inadequate. It is through Christ that believers know God.

Paul bypassed both Jewish law and the Graeco-Roman understanding of nature by locating the revelation of the justice of God *(dikaiosynē theou)* in Christ.[47] In so doing, he harmonized what Graeco-Romans regarded as mutually exclusive—the justice and unmerited mercy of God. Having dismissed pity *(misericordia)* as a mental fault, Seneca sought to preserve a place for mercy *(clementia)*.[48] But just as the wise man or ruler ought not to allow pity to ruin his inner serenity, neither should he show mercy except where it is in the best interests of the subject. Such discernment clearly lay with the superior man—mercy belonged only to those who deserved it. The congruence we have seen between Stoic moral ideals and theology held here too: God must not compromise his own perfection by pardoning the undeserving.

---

[45]Rom 1:20; cf. 1 Tim 1:17. An even closer parallel of expression occurs between 1 Cor 8:6 and Marcus Aurelius, who praises Nature with the appellations "All things are from you . . . in you . . . [and] for you" (*Meditations* 4.23).

[46]Rom 2:16; cf. 1:18; 2:4; 3:19-20, 25.

[47]Rom 1:17; 3:21; cf. 1:18.

[48]Seneca *Epistles* 2.7.3; cf. Cicero *Tusculan Disputations* 3.20.

Paul put the matter on an entirely different footing: "God shows no favoritism" (Rom 2:11). God in his mercy had justified the ungodly. Where a man might dare to pay the ultimate cost for a patron of great significance, the Son of God sacrificed himself for the powerless, the impious and the guilty.[49] God had *not* set aside his justice in order to grant mercy but had revealed his justice in the judgment of his Son on behalf of those who would believe in him (Rom 1:17; 3:21-22, 25-26). The sacrifice of Christ only deepened the sense of anomaly for Gentile readers. As Martin Hengel has shown, the idea of atonement by human self-sacrifice may well have been comprehensible, but it nevertheless "must have seemed aesthetically and ethically repulsive to them and to be in conflict with the philosophically purified nature of the gods."[50]

The same scandal would follow Paul's conclusion that believers in Christ had lost all ground for boasting (Rom 3:27-31). This loss was complete: personally, they must depend on the mercy of God as Abraham had done (Rom 4:1-25); historically, they had been grafted onto God's Jewish vine (Rom 11:11-32); socially, the loss of grounds for boasting was only the first of the changes implicit in Paul's message. Paul recorded two responses to this message. First, he praised God, not for the amorphous qualities of an abstract deity, but for his mercies revealed in the stories of Israel and Christ. Second, he called for a personal transformation displacing social convention and status (Rom 11:33—12:4).

Our previous discussion of mercy, justice and social ideals looms large here. In effect, in Romans 12—13 Paul urged the Christians to base their lives on a God whom the best of theology would discredit. They should resist the unquestionable ideals of personal self-sufficiency and serenity. Putting their normal means of recourse to justice to one side, they were to show mercy in their leadership and benefactions to the less fortunate. Moreover, they were not to act from the normal presumption of superiority. They were to start from the radical self-awareness that, though undeserving, they had received their place in the new social structure of the body of Christ by the mercies of God.

Paul's portraits of God stood in stark relief to Graeco-Roman theology. Nevertheless, it is remarkable how quickly subsequent generations conformed his message to the theological patterns of the philosophers.[51] While Justin Martyr and

---

[49]Dio Chrysostom *Orations* 32.50; Rom 5:6-8.

[50]Martin Hengel, *The Atonement: The Origins of the Doctrine in the New Testament* (Philadelphia: Fortress, 1981), p. 31.

[51]The subject of the early apologists' and fathers' realignment of Paul's message with theology is vast. For the basic themes, see Robert Grant, *Gods and the One God,* Library of Early Christianity 1 (Philadelphia: Westminster Press, 1986), pp. 84–175. For the Roman perspective, see Robert Wilken, *The Christians as the Romans Saw Them* (New Haven, Conn.: Yale University Press, 1984). Particularly out-

others for the most part presented Christ in a manner congruent with Paul's message, the abstraction inherent in Greek theology drove upon them a pressing new need to uncover the essence of Christ that lay behind the story. Little more than a hundred years after Paul, the God of Christian *apologia* resembled Plato's Demiurge more than the one "who is rich in mercy": "We have brought before you a God who is uncreated, eternal, invisible, impassible, incomprehensible, and infinite, who can be apprehended by mind alone, who is encompassed by light, beauty, spirit, and indescribable power, and who created and now rules the world through the Logos who issues from him."[52]

Evangelicals have benefited enormously from the faithful and creative labors of many theologians. I certainly acknowledge that for myself. But there are other less acknowledged sides to the story of theology: its inability to connect with everyday concerns; its use to patronize and disdain others; its role in propping up an elitist system of leadership; its deadening effects on young theological students; its promotion of pedantry and destructive debate; its second-hand character that minimizes genuine creativity and new perspective; the ways it imposes law in the name of protecting grace; the ways it preempts and gags conversations that might otherwise break new ground in integrating faith and life. There is great value in laying a foundation of beliefs. But the methods and disposition of theology have failed to deliver its promise of a richer personal knowledge of God. Theology and church have by and large abducted the conversations that rightfully stand at the heart of the gathering.

---

standing are the sections on "Biblical and Related Citations" and "Ecclesiastica" in most volumes of the series *New Documents Illustrating Early Christianity*, ed. Greg Horsley (1981–1989) and Stephen Llewelyn (1992, 1995, 1998) and ongoing (Sydney: Macquarie University Press). The value of the series in this regard lies in the degree to which we can juxtapose the development of popular intellectualism and piety among the early Christians with those of their pagan neighbors.
[52]Athenagoras *Embassy for the Christians* 8-9.

11

PAUL & RELIGION

EPICUREANS AND SKEPTICS ATTACKED WHAT THEY SAW AS THE CRUDEST RELIGIOUS MYTHS and practices. What particularly mattered to many philosophers was not so much cultic observance as a piety that reinforced the life of reason:

> Now the best and also the purest and holiest worship of the gods, and that which is the most pious, is that we should ever venerate them with an undefiled, undivided and untainted mind and voice.[1]

Such piety neither scorned the cult nor needed it. Speaking of late Platonists and the Hermetist groups, Robin Fox notes that they "dwelt on the various paths by which people could come to God. They could turn inwards and contemplate their soul, learning to approach God by the old Apolline principle of knowing themselves. Alternatively, they could turn outwards and marvel at the beauty of the world. . . . These two fine paths became the neutral property of educated men."[2]

We should not conclude that Graeco-Roman religion was fundamentally intellectual and meditative, however. Both the humble and the elite preferred to be over-insured with religion rather than to be caught unprotected and unaided in their struggle against forces larger than themselves. The ever-present statues in

---

[1]Cicero *On the Nature of the Gods* 228.71; cf. Philo *Principles of Allegory* 3.27; Marcus Aurelius *Meditations* 5.27.
[2]Robin Fox, *Pagans and Christians in the Mediterranean World from the Second Century AD to the Conversion of Constantine* (London: Penguin, 1988), p. 94.

homes, civic places and shrines continued to shape popular understanding of the gods and to maintain the sense of their presence.

Awe and Intimacy

The gods provoked not only contemplation but also awe and fear. Epiphany, oracle and cult shared common ground: the pervasive presence of the gods, the acute awareness of their potential anger, and the constant need to placate them. In this sense, religious experience turned on the tensions of awe and intimacy. Fear and the need for propitiation sponsored various techniques for drawing closer to the gods. When the gods did draw near, they could be relied on to be swift to help—or to punish. When they seemed far away, they elicited deep admiration and awe—and the cold dread of their unpredictability and indifference.

The gods inhabited every corner of life. Clients had plenty of incentive to petition the gods on their patrons' behalf. A letter of greeting from the first or second century is typical:

> Herm . . . [to Sarapion] . . . greetings, and that you may always remain in good health in your whole person for long years to come, since your good genius allowed us to greet you with respect and salute you. For as you also make mention of us on each occasion by letter so I here make an act of worship for you in the presence of the lords Dioskouroi and in the presence of the lord Sarapis, and I pray for your safe-keeping during your entire life and for the health of your children and of all your household. Farewell in everything, I beg, my patron and fosterer. . . . All the gods here, male and female, greet you.[3]

A client's opportunities for fraternity, security and ambition largely rested on his inclusion in his patron's household. This is partly the background to the *klinē*, those small private dinners hosted by a patron devotee over which Sarapis presided:

> Nikephoros asks you to dine at a banquet of the lord Sarapis in the Birth-House on the 23rd, from the 9th hour.[4]

> The god calls you to a banquet being held in the Thoerion tomorrow from the 9th hour.[5]

Clubs played an increasingly important role in Graeco-Roman cities. They could extend the patron-client relationship or provide some of the same benefits for those without such an arrangement. Religious observance marked the group's activities just as they did for family, civic life and the state:

---

[3]Inscription *CPR* 19, in Greg Horsley, ed., *New Documents Illustrating Early Christianity* (Sydney: Macquarie University Press, 1981), 1:56–57.
[4]Inscription *P Coll. Youtie* 51, in Horsley, *New Documents,* 1:5–9.
[5]Inscription *ZPE* 1 [1967] 121-26, in Horsley, *New Documents*.

It is decreed that no associations and clubs be tolerated . . . [however] to hold meetings for religious purposes is not restricted so long as the Senate resolution forbidding unpermitted clubs is not thereby contravened.[6]

Those at the bottom of society might hope for a master's religious goodwill at the end:

In this place Chrestos buried aged Italos; he wept for his faithful slave when he died. In return for [Italos's] good life and industrious servitude [Chrestos] fulfilled these sacred rites for him as a favour.[7]

For those devoid of legal protection, Pythian Apollo might offer hope of being freed:

[When N. N. was archon in the month of] [. . . N. N. gave up to Pythian Apollo] [a male slave by the name of Theophanes, by race . . .] [for the price of X silver minae and] [he has the entire price, just as Theophan]es entrusted the sale to the god [on condition that he be free and not be seized as a slave by] anyone for the duration of his life. . . . Witnesses are the priests] of Apollo.[8]

The gods were present at dinners, clubs, funerals and manumissions and at every other family, fraternal and civic occasion. We should not be misled by the blandness with which the documents record the divine presence. A late Hellenistic inscription at Arsada left testimony "for the sake of heartfelt love to the gods."[9] Love, however, was not the only emotion on hand. When mortals prayed, fear was close by; even thanksgivings were "interwoven with ideas of propitiation."[10] Intellectuals inferred that prayer was a matter of aligning oneself with the *logos* embedded in the universe, not with moving the gods to change things.[11] But popular religion never accepted this abstraction. High and low alike prayed to bargain with the gods.

Intrinsic to these bargains was the need to ensure the due honor of the gods. While they might be moved to benevolence, their anger could flare, wreaking havoc and misfortune. The most tangible safeguard was to take absolute care in ritual. In the case of the cult of Men Tyrannos, purity depended on a careful execution of the prescribed bathings and sacrifices. Failure could incur a sin beyond expiation, such as in the following inscription at Sounion (Attika) from the second or third century:

Xanthos the Lykian, slave (/) of Gaius Orbius, set up the temple of Men Tyrannos—the god having chosen him—for good fortune. And no-one impure is to draw near; but let

---

[6]Marcian *Digest* 4722.1.

[7]Inscription *I. Bithynia* III.12, first century, in Horsley, *New Documents,* 3:39.

[8]Inscription *BCH* 105 [1981] 461–63 at Delphi from first century B.C., in Stephen Llewelyn, ed., *New Documents Illustrating Early Christianity* (Sydney: Macquarie University Press, 1992), 6:72–73.

[9]Inscription *ZPE* 24 (1977) 276, in Horsley, *New Documents,* 4:80.

[10]Fox, *Pagans and Christians,* p. 38.

[11]Seneca *Epistles* 411; Plutarch *Isis and Osiris* 1.

him be purified from garlic and swine and woman. When members have bathed from
head to foot, on the same day they are to enter. And a woman, having washed from
head to foot seven days after menstruation, is to enter on the same day. . . . If anyone
violates [these provisions] his sacrifice will be unacceptable to the god. He is to provide what is appropriate for the god . . . and may the god be very merciful to those who
serve in simpleness of soul. . . . Anyone who interferes with the god's possessions or is
meddlesome, let him incur sin against Men Tyrannos which he certainly cannot expi-
ate.[12]

Cultic failure carried dire threats:

Do not harm the sacred fish, nor damage any of the goddess' utensils, nor carry anything out of the sanctuary to steal it. May the one who does any of these things be
destroyed wretchedly by a terrible destruction, being eaten by fish.[13]

If anyone urinates here, Hekate is filled with wrath against him.[14]

The need for ritual precision is further underscored in inscriptions of ransoms
for personal sins. Pointing out that the *symbolaphoroi* appear to have had the task
of carrying certain sacred objects in religious processions, Greg Horsley records
the possibility "that a mishap during one such occasion involving these carriers
and the three brothers offended the god, and caused them to seek release from
some punishment by public confession of their fault":[15]

To Artemis Anaeitis and Men of Tiamos, Alexander, Timothy (and) Glykon, sons of Bol-
las, and the *symbolaphoroi*, having ransomed themselves, set up [this stele].[16]

To Men the ancestral god they all set up this altar, equally and all of them after ade-
quate prayers. [For . . .] from the friendly home of our kind rearer we all made a vow
and gave our hair [. . .] as is the custom and holy ransom. Markos, Hilaros, Epityncha-
nos, Peitheros, Loukilios.[17]

Oracles and divinations frequently attributed sickness to ritual defilement, even if
the worshiper was unaware of any defilement:

I have been punished by the god—enos; however because I was willing [to ask the God

---

[12]*IG* II.1366, in Horsley, *New Documents,* 3:31.

[13]Inscription *SIG* 997 at Smyrna from first century B.C., in R. A. Connolly, "Standing on Sacred
Ground," in Horsley, *New Documents,* 4:105–12.

[14]Inscription *I Eph.* II.567, in Horsley, *New Documents,* 4:175–76; also *I. Eph.* II.569. David Gill
notes that Hekate was a particular colleague of Pan, often linking up to "instill irrational fear (lit-
erally 'Pan-ic') in travellers." See his "Behind the Classical Facade: Local Religions of the Roman
Empire," in *One God, One Lord in a World of Religious Pluralism* (Cambridge: Tyndale House,
1991), pp. 72–87.

[15]Horsley, *New Documents,* 3:73.

[16]Inscription *CMRDM* 157, in ibid., 3:72–75.

[17]Inscription *CMRDM* 4, in Horsley, *New Documents.*

which sin I committed] and having received an omen telling me: "You are defiled," after having made a vow I have dedicated this stone.[18]

The personal devotion of worshipers to their gods was objectified in the sacred places, utensils, rites and days that demarcated ritual purity. The devout worshiper must approach at the right time, in the right place and in the manner authorized by the bearers of the tradition:

> For good fortune. Summary of an ancestral law: The *prytanis* is to light the fire . . . [lengthy cultic legislation follows] . . . according to the ancestral practices and at which it is necessary to pray on behalf of the sacred senate and the people of Rome and the people of Ephesos . . . [more cultic legislation]. . . . If any single point of the afore-said matters is left out by the person serving as *prytanis* . . . [penalties follow] . . . and the *kouretes* and the hierophant are to make exaction for the failure to mind each single point as has been written above.[19]

> [I]t is decreed that the entire month Artemision be sacred for all its days, and that . . . throughout the year, feasts and the festival and the sacrifices of the Artemisia are to be conducted.[20]

When it came to a god's honor, there were clear limits to religious pluralism. An inscription at Sardis from the first or second century A.D. employed a text from the fourth century B.C. to warn worshipers against polluting their devotion to Zeus through fraternizing with another cult:

> [Droaphernes] instructs [Zeus's] temple-warden devotees who enter the innermost sanctum and who serve and crown the god, not to participate in the mysteries of Saba-zios with those who bring the burnt offerings and [the mysteries] of Agdistis and Ma. They instruct Dorates the temple-warden to keep away from these mysteries.[21]

Purity was not the only motive for upholding the honor of the gods. A city's honor rested in part on its cults.[22] Likewise, the link between religious benefaction and personal honors was well understood. Equally clear was the sale and use of priesthoods to consolidate social and political control.[23] Note the conclusion to this inscription from the mid-second century at Ephesus:

> The proconsul Gaius Popillius Carus Pedo states: "I learned from the decree which was sent to me by the most illustrious council of the Ephesians. . . . This is why I consid-

---

[18]*Pleket* 14, in Rosalind Kearsley, "Ailments and Remedies," in Llewelyn, *New Documents*, 6:192.

[19]Inscription *I. Eph.* Ia.10, in Connolly, "Standing on Sacred Ground," pp. 106–7.

[20]Inscription *I. Eph.* Ia.24, in Ray Oster, "Holy Days in Honour of Artemis," in Horsley, *New Documents*, 4:75–76.

[21]Inscription *CRAI* 1975, 306-30, in Horsley, *New Documents*, 1:21–23.

[22]Fox, *Pagans and Christians*, pp. 27–63; cf. Horsley, *New Documents*, 4:81.

[23]Fox, *Pagans and Christians*, pp. 52–63, 76–82, 223–29.

ered it necessary, since I also have regard for the reverence of the goddess and for the honour of the most illustrious city of the Ephesians, to make it known by decree that these days shall be holy and the festal holidays will be observed on these days." [This edict was promulgated] while Titus Aelius Marcianus Priscus, son of Aelius Priscus, a man very well thought of and worthy of all honour and acceptance, was leader of the festival and president of the athletic games.[24]

Ancient civic and religious ideals lived on partly through wealthy families who ensured the city's renown and custom. Grave markers resounded these honors and traditions. Some recalled the dead as "manifest heroes" or "manifest gods." In these epithets, "manifest" implied far more than "distinguished": "it meant that these people had appeared in dreams and visions and, in one or two cases, worked wonders to help the living."[25] The gods could also be manifest in art and procession and festival or through a departed loved one. In a second or third century memorial to a woman that was set up by her family and the members of her cult at Thyatira, the former priestess extended an open invitation:

> To Ammias, her children and the initiates of the gods set up the altar with the sarcophagus for the priestess of the gods as a memorial. And if anyone wants to learn the truth from me, let him pray at(?) the altar whatever he wants and he will get it, via a vision, during nighttime and day.[26]

Ammias's invitation may well have been "addressed to seekers after truth on a metaphysical level."[27] Indeed, our inscription high on the wall at Oenoanda offers a glimpse of an intellectual inquiry that may have prompted the god's reply. But for the most part, oracles answered those everyday questions which articulated a brooding opportunity and dread:[28]

> Am I to remain where I am going? Am I to be sold? Am I to obtain profit from my friend? Is it permitted me to make a contract with another? Am I to be restored to my position? . . . Am I to profit from the affair? . . . Am I to become successful? . . . Am I to become a senator? . . . Am I to be separated from my wife? Have I been poisoned? Am I to get a legacy?[29]

> Your first wife is not to remain with you. You are to become a dekaprotos. . . . You are

---

[24]Inscription *I. Eph.* Ia.24, in Oster, "Holy Days," p. 75.

[25]Fox, *Pagans and Christians*, p. 132.

[26]Inscription *EG* IV.119-20, in Horsley, *New Documents,* 4:134–36.

[27]Ibid.

[28]For an extensive discussion of the nature and function of oracles in Graeco-Roman religion, see Fox, *Pagans and Christians*, pp. 168–261. It has been somewhat commonplace among scholars to presume that oracles had declined in frequency and importance during this period. Fox demonstrates that this was not the case. Some shrines had even boomed in this time.

[29]*P Oxy.* 2833, in Horsley, *New Documents,* 2:43–44.

to finish what you undertake. You are not to get a legacy. You have not been poisoned. . . . You will see a death which you did not wish. You are not to win. Persevere. You are not to inherit. . . . She is to miscarry and she is to be in danger. Lend with a mortgage. . . . You are not to get the woman you want.[30]

The questions seem pedestrian and mask their intensity. The religious life of Graeco-Roman people was not simply routine or mechanical. Personal devotion could be vibrant, fueled by palpable experiences of the divine in cult and oracle and dream. Fox writes, "As night fell, they recaptured the lost ideal of Phaeacia and the pre-Homeric past. . . . [I]f we miss this nightly screening of the gods, we reduce pagan religiousness to a 'paganism' of cult acts, brightened only by personal cults which appealed to the emotions and made their worshipers 'new.' "[31]

Cultic acts and dreams could powerfully rekindle piety.[32] An inscription from North Africa in the third century conveys a similar warmth in a dedication to mark the fulfillment of a vow:

I Manius discharged my vow and dedicated a sacrifice for the proving of my faith and the preservation of my health. He discharged his vow with a willing spirit.[33]

Dreams, sacrifices and vows found poignant meaning in the face of Fate, Fortune and the stars. Few epithets to the gods held such strength of desire as "[my god] controls Fate." Alongside reassurances that the god stood ready to help, various techniques flourished to make the divine presence even more secure in the struggle against oppressive powers.[34] It seems there was no shortage of work for those who practiced the arts of divination during the imperial period (Acts 19:13-19). None of this was new. People were no more anxious, oppressed or uncertain in imperial times than in any other age in which they had anticipated the nearness and danger of the gods.

The "rise" of the mystery cults signaled neither the decline of the old gods and rituals nor that paganism was pressing on to its doom. Rather, the religious "innovations" of the Graeco-Roman period were a final breaking through of elements built up over centuries. What we see as the rise of the mystery cults was perhaps a greater public prominence of cults long active among the lower ranks. There was

---

[30]*P Oxy.* 1477, in ibid.

[31]Fox, *Pagans and Christians*, p. 164.

[32]See the inscription *IG* x 2255, in Horsley, *New Documents,* 1:29–31. See also *I. Nikaia* II, 1.1071, in Horsley, *New Documents,* 4:176.

[33]Inscription *CRAI* [1975] 111-18, in Horsley, *New Documents,* 1:23–25.

[34]Not every charm was prompted by fear: "Bring Termoutis whom Sophia bore, to Zoel whom Droser bore, with crazed and unceasing, everlasting love, now quickly!" (unknown origin and date; *SEG* 1243, in Horsley, *New Documents,* 2:45–46).

little sense of competition between the older and newer cults, and concurrent priesthoods were common enough. Although pluralism held sway, worshipers did not simply swallow any bizarre claim. Admittedly the tendency to laud an unusual event had not died out.[35] But it was never a case of anything goes; certain cults and orgiastic rites, for example, were expressly forbidden. Nor was religion simply mechanical—the marked devotion of some worshipers clearly dispels such a caricature. Nor were the cults, even the imperial cult, merely vehicles of state or elite propaganda and control, though they could be exactly that. Despite the authorized special effects of some shrines, worshipers of this period were no more gullible than those of any other time.[36] They did not believe that statues were gods, though in certain contexts the link was very close. Nor were the mystery cults normally sinister or on the social fringe.

Over against all such stereotypes of Graeco-Roman religion, we have seen the awe and intimacy of devotion to the gods. We have also seen the ever-present fear and uncertainty of people about powers larger and darker than themselves.

Paul, Local Religion and the Imperial Cult

It is difficult to align Paul with Graeco-Roman religion. It was common for someone to begin a cult in commemoration of a hero or god. But Paul's adoration and understanding of Christ moved in a very different direction. His speech before the council at Athens offered no common ground with their religious orientation (Acts 17:16-31). This was neither Paul's first nor his last confrontation with Graeco-Roman religion.

Acts 14 records that after fleeing a combined Jewish-Gentile plot against them in Iconium, Paul and Barnabas moved to Lystra, where they performed a healing miracle for a man crippled from birth. To the rustic Lycaonians, the apostles' miracle was taken as an epiphany of Zeus (Barnabas) and Hermes (Paul).[37] Their ensuing reception—enthusiastic, misinformed and short-lived— matches what we have seen of Graeco-Roman religious awe and the need to

---

[35]One particularly celebrated case was the cult that flourished from the death of Antinous, the favorite boy of Hadrian, at the Nile in the second century A.D. See Robert Grant, *Gods and the One God,* Library of Early Christianity 1 (Philadelphia: Westminster Press, 1986), pp. 255–56.

[36]Robin Fox gives a lively account of how the ingenious plumbing of some statues and shrines could add dramatic effect during rituals. He also demonstrates that for the most part this "deceit" was well understood and expected (*Pagans and Christians,* pp. 135–36). Note also Lucian's account of the charlatan Alexander (pp. 241–50).

[37]On the possibility of a local legend as the background to the Lycaonians' enthusiasm to make proper propitiation to Zeus and Hermes, see Bruce Winter, "In Public and in Private: Early Christians and Religious Pluralism," in *One God, One Lord in a World of Religious Pluralism* (Cambridge: Tyndale House, 1991), pp. 116–17. Note also Horsley, *New Documents,* 4:241, on shouted acclamations.

appease the gods.[38] Paul's plea that they turn to the living God from "these worthless things" reveals his opinion of their entire religious orientation.

Later, at Corinth, certain Jewish leaders tried to have Paul indicted for breaching his obligations to the imperial cult (Acts 18:12-16). The Jews were exempt from these obligations under the status of Judaism as a legal cult *(religio licita)*. Paul could lay claim to this exemption. It seems that both Paul and the Jewish leaders understood his message as falling outside the limits of Judaism (itself a diverse and complex religion). Much to the Jews' dismay, Gallio ruled that the dispute only involved matters related to the Jews' own law. Thus he effectively affirmed the protection of Paul (and the local Christians?) under the legal exemption granted to Jews.

We do not know whether this ruling was mirrored or applied in other places where Paul traveled. Yet the alliance between Jewish leaders and prominent Gentiles to hound Paul shows how far the Jews wanted to dissociate themselves from Paul and his new groups. It also suggests that certain Graeco-Roman civic leaders did not want the status of *religio licita* to be extended to the Christians (Acts 13:50–14:19). Bruce Winter suggests that this may shed new light on the ways in which *both Jews and Gentiles* could use the obligations of the imperial cult as a means of harassing the Christians:

> Given the exclusion from the Jewish synagogues, how would rank and file Christians cope with the [imperial] cult? It is being suggested that, from within the ranks of the Christian communities in Galatia, there were Jewish Christians who counseled evasive action. They sought to place all Christians, whether Jew or Gentile, under a Jewish, as distinct from a synagogue, umbrella. Some may even have been tempted to portray the house church in which they met as a Christian "place of prayer" (προσευχή). There was, in the end, a clear way for the Christian community to escape the obligation of the imperial cult *viz.* by appearing to be wholly Jewish.[39]

Those from Jerusalem may have used the pressure of obligation to the imperial cult to press their own agendas, particularly circumcision and the Sabbath, onto Gentile converts. At the same time, those who had taken the drastic step of circumcision (an outrage and crime to most Graeco-Romans) would have welcomed an ideological foundation for their new religious adherence. Given the pervasiveness

---

[38]David Gill and Bruce Winter note that the episode "raises the question of how far Paul was encountering people in the Roman eastern provinces whose worship of natural features, such as rocks and plants, derived from a much earlier period." See their "Acts and Roman Religion," in *The Book of Acts in Its First Century Setting*, vol. 2, *Graeco-Roman Setting*, ed. D. W. J. Gill and C. Gempf, p. 79, in which they survey the evidence for local cults and superstitions at the places visited by Paul.

[39]Bruce Winter, *Seek the Welfare of the City: Christians as Benefactors and Citizens*, First Century Christians in the Graeco-Roman World 1 (Exeter: Paternoster; and Grand Rapids, Mich.: Eerdmans, 1994), p. 136.

of the imperial cult, Paul must have known a confrontation was likely. His episodes at Athens, and particularly Ephesus, show how real this was.

Paul's remarks at Athens touched political sensitivities since the Areopagus was part of the "effective government of Roman Athens and its chief court."[40] The agora was the site for numerous dedications to the imperial family. As Paul entered the agora and later looked down from the hill as he spoke, he could have seen several prominent shrines and statues to the emperors. David Gill notes a strong link between Paul's vocabulary *(sebasmata)* and "the worship of the imperial family, usually in a Sebasteion" (Acts 17:23).[41]

The close links between the imperial cult and those of other deities at Ephesus clarifies the risks Paul faced because of his "irreligious" stance (Acts 19:11-23). He found himself thrust into controversy with a highly esteemed symbol of Graeco-Roman religious life: the temple and cult of Artemis. He was also embroiled in the powerful networks of political and economic life that were inextricable from the glories of the goddess and the city (Acts 19:24-41).[42]

Paul's initial exploits at Ephesus, though dramatic enough, did not specifically touch on Artemis. Against a background of widespread beliefs in divine healing, sorcery and demonic powers, the apostle's miracles elicited awe and fear (Acts 19:17).[43] Some who believed were sorcerers who now willingly and publicly burnt the parchments of their trade.[44] The value of the books indicates reasonable wealth

---

[40]David Gill, "Achaia," in Gill and Gempf, *Graeco-Roman Setting*, p. 447.

[41]Ibid.

[42]Several discussions in *New Documents* vol. 4 help to clarify the connections between the issues. First, Rosalind Kearsley's discussion, "Some *asiarchs* at Ephesos" (pp. 46–55), clarifies that this role should not be confused with that of the *archiereus* who presided over the imperial cult. But there is clear documentation in at least one case, the career of Aristio, that the two roles were held by the same person, though not concurrently. Given the designation of Paul's friends as *asiarchs*, we can only wonder at the potential for complications in his relationship to these leaders and to other leading members of Ephesian society. Second, Ray Oster's discussion of the inscription *I. Eph.* Ia.24 (pp. 74–82), which I reproduced in part earlier, notes that there was often "joint veneration of the Emperor and the Ephesian goddess" (p. 76). Third, Greg Horsley notes the same kind of link in relation to the mystery cult of Demeter (pp. 94–95). Finally, the inscription *I. Eph.* II.251 on the base of a statue from the first century B.C. underscores the connections between the veneration of emperors and local deities: Julius Caesar is "the god manifest from Ares and Aphrodite, and the general saviour of human life" (p. 148).

[43]Rosalind Kearsley notes that while "at several points in both the gospels and Acts, magical belief impinges on the miraculous nature of healing by both Jesus and the apostles . . . none of the characteristic features of magic is found in the actions of the apostles themselves or the beliefs expressed in the NT documents, and it is through the reactions of others to the miracles of healing performed by Jesus and the apostles that the element of magic enters the NT world." See her "Ailments and Remedies," in *New Documents*, 6:195–96.

[44]Trebilco notes other instances of public book burnings, often involving perceived threats to political and religious stability. See his "Asia," in Gill and Gempf, *Graeco-Roman Setting*, p. 315. Normally this was involuntary.

on the part of their owners and thus some prominence of social position. Whatever impact Paul had on local religion, his message now touched the nerve of the "strong and expansionist cult" of Artemis, and the pride and wealth of Ephesus, the guardian of the goddess.[45] Earlier, we noted an inscription showing the importance to the Ephesian city officials of setting aside an entire month of holy days in honor of Artemis. Of particular significance in this context are the strong links between religious and civic pride and success: "With the improvement of the honoring of the goddess, our city will remain more illustrious and more blessed for all time."[46]

Three further features of Luke's account in Acts 19 stand out. First, Demetrius claimed that Paul had denigrated the idols as man-made and therefore as no divinities at all. The pattern of Paul's speeches at Lystra and Athens makes it possible that he had again dismissed local idols and their associated religious paraphernalia as empty and futile. Second, the clerk refuted Demetrius's serious charges: Paul was guilty neither of sacrilege *(hierosylous)* nor blasphemy *(blasphēmountas)*. Third, the town clerk appealed to the divine origin of the image of Artemis. In itself, this was a standard enough claim for any cult. The town clerk's "defense" of Paul *and* Artemis suggests that while Demetrius had probably exaggerated Paul's "crimes," the clerk could not simply afford to ignore the suspicions attaching to Paul. What mattered to the clerk was civic order, the good will of the Romans, and the reputation of the city and goddess. What mattered to Paul was the proclamation of his message and the well-being of the *ekklēsia*. In Paul's eyes, the nexus of religion and social prestige unleashed havoc on himself and threatened the cohesion of the *ekklēsia*.

Paul and the Presence of God in the *ekklēsia*

Certain brothers from Jerusalem had pressured Gentile Christians in the Galatian *ekklēsiai* to conform to Judaism. Their agendas may have been indirectly aided by elements of religious syncretism. Leisured festival days were a feature of Graeco-Roman religious and civic life, and some now had links to Jewish practice. For example, the Jewish Sabbath was well known, even admired, and both Philo and Josephus had used the Graeco-Roman terminology of cultic festival days to characterize their own Jewish Sabbath. But this preference for sacred days found no equivalent in Paul's gospel: "Since nascent Pauline Christianity regarded holy days at best as *adiaphora* (Rom 14:5-12) and at worst as antithetical to the Gospel (Gal 4:8-10; Col 2:16), a Christian living in the shadow of Paul's Gospel would have little

---

[45]Ibid., p. 336.
[46]Inscription *I. Eph.* Ia.24, in Oster, "Holy Days," pp. 74–82. Oster surveys the inscriptional evidence for Artemis and Ephesus. For a discussion in relation to Acts 19, see Trebilco, "Asia," pp. 312–57.

hope of finding an equivalent to this regulated component of his previous piety."[47]

The ease with which Paul shifted his indictment of religion from a Jewish frame of reference to a Graeco-Roman one underscores his common verdict: both were slavery; both were incompatible with his message.[48] The presence of God was no longer available to the Galatians through ritual observance, either Jewish or Graeco-Roman. God was present with his people as the Spirit made himself known in their conversation and prayer together and in their acts of compassion.

This displacement of the cult by the conversation of believers also appears in Ephesians. Graeco-Roman religion employed cult, oracle, epiphany, dream and magical technique to access the presence and will of God; Paul located these in the person of Christ.[49] There was no deeper divine presence or will to attain or discern, only a deepening awe and intimacy grounded in the story of Christ. The believers' new security from the darker forces freed them from having to honor or manipulate these powers through ritual or magical technique.[50] Without shrine or image, the gathering retained none of the standard religious features of an association. The emphasis fell instead on the people and their common relationship to Christ, and on using Christ's gifts in conversation and acts of compassion to promote understanding and love among themselves. In place of priesthood and ritual, they are to "speak the truth to one another in love." The contrast to Graeco-Roman belief and practice was stark.[51]

Similar themes were at work at Colossae. The syncretism of Colossians 2:11-23 provides a portrait of the struggles of an *ekklēsia* and of Paul's repudiation of religion. Once again his indictment covered both Jewish and Graeco-Roman themes and the links between them. Referring briefly to Colossians 2:18, Kearsley notes that the Hellenistic synthesis of the Jewish theme of angels into their own worship, typified in the cult of Hosios and Dikaios, may help explain the fascination of some

---

[47]Oster, "Holy Days," p. 78.

[48]Gal 3:1—4:9, 12-20; 5:1-12.

[49]Eph 1:3-14; 2:21-22; 3:2-11. I do not mean to gloss over those places where Paul's language sounded similar to conventional deference to the will of the gods (e.g., Rom 1:10; 15:32; 1 Cor 4:9). See Horsley, *New Documents*, 1:51–54, for the Graeco-Roman side. Even in these contexts, Paul's use seems tied to his more frequent images of the will of God as the plan of salvation and re-creation revealed in Christ. In this sense, *will of God* and *gospel* were virtual synonyms for Paul.

[50]Eph 2:1-10; 3:10; 6:10-18. See C. E. Arnold, *Ephesians: Power and Magic* (Cambridge: Cambridge University Press, 1989), pp. 51–59, for a succinct summary of the supremacy of Christ over the powers in Ephesians. It should be noted that no consensus exists about the identity of these powers. Over against the interpretation of them as social and political forces, which is the plainest sense of the vocabulary *(archai, dynameis, exousiai)*, I find myself drawn to reconsider them in terms of both Jewish and Graeco-Roman beliefs about demonic powers.

[51]Eph 4:1-16 versus 17-19.

Colossians for angels. This fascination was part of a potpourri of religious legisla-
tion, asceticism and philosophy.[52] Paul's verdict was sharp: these traditions appear
wise and valuable, but are actually useless. There was no place for religious practice
and elitism: every legitimate goal—wisdom, freedom, security, intimacy with God,
certainty, fullness, hope beyond the grave—was already guaranteed by the death
and resurrection of Christ. Their access to these gifts lay through the Spirit manifested in conversation and love to one another.

The link between religious practice and elitism draws us back once more to
Corinth. There was a religious dimension to the elitism of "the strong" within the
Corinthian *ekklēsia*. But unlike the *ekklēsiai* at Galatia, Ephesus and Colossae, the
Corinthian elite had (partly) inverted Graeco-Roman religiosity as well as accom-
modating it. Their slogan, "We know that an idol is nothing" seized on Paul's radically irreligious message. They had also seen through the false claims to divinity of
those so-called gods on earth, the past and current emperors (1 Cor 8:4-6). But
they were still not attuned to the dying and rising of Christ. Nor did they recognize
that the religious pluralism of Corinth threatened their allegiance to Christ, even
as idolatry had brought Israel down in the desert (1 Cor 10:1-22). No doubt Paul
agreed with their slogan. But the conclusions they drew had lost sight of Christ's
lordship and the equality of the believers (1 Cor 9:1-27; 10:23—11:1). To excuse
one's elitist behavior on the grounds of the radicalness of the gospel was more than
a fallacy—it could destroy the one for whom Christ had died.

The background to all this largely concerned invitations to a *klinē*, a meal
between friends or associates held by invitation of some deity.[53] The meals were
commonly held in homes or within the side rooms of a temple. In either case, the
hosts performed the customary libations. Apparently Paul did not object to attendance on the basis of the obvious religious connotations, and he appeared to have
no scruples about accepting these invitations to join pagan hosts and guests.[54]
What did concern him, however, was the possible loss of reputation for his message
in the eyes of unbelievers who could not fathom the Christians' freedom from religious convention. He was also concerned that "weak" believers might sear their
own ill-informed consciences (1 Cor 10:28—11:1).

---

[52]Kearsley, "Angels in Asia Minor," in *New Documents,* 6:209.

[53]1 Cor 10:22; see Horsley, *New Documents,* 1:5-9.

[54]However, Ben Witherington ("Not So Idle Thoughts About *EIDOLOTHUTON*," *Tyndale Bulletin*
44 [1993]: 237–54) argues that *eidōlothyton* in both Acts 15:29 and 1 Cor 10:19 refers to meat
sacrificed and eaten in the temple precincts. He deduces from this that both passages were
intended to prohibit attendance at pagan festivals and banquets. Witherington may well be right
about the matter of attendance at the temples, but 1 Cor 10:27-30 still left the way open for
Corinthian Christians to be guests at private meals (often held in temple dining rooms) where
their hosts would observe customary religious practice.

The "irreligion" of the strong did not stop them from mimicking the prestige attached to cultic piety and leadership. David Gill notes that Paul's argument against men covering their heads during the gatherings (1 Cor 11:4-10) may reflect their imitation of an officiating priest in the local cult.[55] Once again, social rank was the issue, since priesthoods were "frequently named alongside other civic positions of authority in public inscriptions."[56] The elite may well have maintained the conventional marks of religious leadership in order to parade their status over the have-nots.

Chris Forbes argues that the divisions and disorder evident in the Corinthian assemblies were likewise about social elitism and exclusivism.[57] Contrary to the consensus opinion, he demonstrates that there is no evidence that Christian *glossalalia* had parallels in the prophetic or ecstatic practices of Graeco-Roman cultic and oracular shrines. Paul's concern was not about Christian versus Hellenistic models of prophecy or ecstatic speech, but about elitism. Although the Corinthian *ekklēsia* did not observe the standard religious conventions, certain socially prominent members were nonetheless willing to turn prophecy and the other gifts of the Spirit meant for the well-being of the body into marks of their own religious and civic status.

The End of Religion in the *ekklēsiai*

To what extent is it accurate to view Paul's message and *ekklēsiai* as religious? Edwin Judge has argued that to do so is to mislocate them under an "unhistorical rubric."[58] By this he drew attention to the ways religion was redefined in the later merger of Christian tradition and the classical heritage. The Christian emphasis on a body of belief became absorbed into religious experience. Consequently, the West inherited a conflated definition: religion equals ritual (classical tradition) plus belief (Christian tradition). Instead of examining religion as it was in Paul's day, scholars read the *later* definition back into Paul's letters. Since it is easy to find the *beliefs* in Paul, these scholars only have to find evidence of a *ritual*.[59] Baptism and the meal in 1 Corinthians 11 are traditionally the prime candidates. It is in this

---

[55] See David Gill, "The Importance of Roman Portraiture for Head Coverings in 1 Corinthians 11:2-16," *Tyndale Bulletin* 41 (1990): 247–48.

[56] Ibid., p. 248.

[57] See 1 Cor 11—12; 14. Chris Forbes, "Prophecy and Inspired Speech in Early Christianity and Its Hellenistic Environment" (Ph.D. thesis, Macquarie University, Sydney, 1987).

[58] Edwin Judge, "The Social Identity of the First Christians," *Journal of Religious History* 11 (1980): 212.

[59] It is interesting that many scholars who are aware of the Graeco-Roman intellectual and social milieu still read into Paul the conventions of later traditions like liturgy, sacraments and ordination.

sense that Wayne Meeks insists, contra Judge, that Paul was religious: "Christianity did not yet have a *cultus* of the sort that most established cultic associations practised . . . [and] differed in significant ways from the initiatory mysteries . . . [but] it did have an initiatory ritual . . . a ritual meal central to its common life, and rapidly growing traditions of other sorts of ritualized behaviour."[60]

Certainly Paul's *ekklēsiai* had ritual practices in the sense of routine events of deep significance. So did other Graeco-Roman *non*-cultic groups and civic occasions. But to argue from the presence of a repeated significant event to the conclusion that Paul's *ekklēsiai* were religious begs too many questions about both Graeco-Roman religion and Paul's *ekklēsiai*. On the Graeco-Roman side, even the more contemplative and moralistic expressions of piety did not exist in isolation from cult. On Paul's side, the communal meal might be seen by analogy as some kind of extended *klinē* held at the standing invitation of Christ. But while the meals certainly took on a religious character in subsequent generations, they would not have seemed so to Paul's contemporaries. As Greg Horsley notes, "Those to whom cult associations . . . were the norm must have found the Christians distinctly peculiar in their religious habits, if not downright irreligious. Where were their specially set-aside cult centres, their statues of the god, their cultic acts (mysteries, sacrifices, etc.), and their official hierarchy?"[61]

Paul's *ekklēsiai* struggled with the lingering impact of the conventions of religion and their social implications. But his message left no room for rapprochement. Religion in any form suppressed the truth. It was a captivity to the elemental spirits. It was the futility of a world passing away.[62] The "worship" that Paul endorsed was a transformation of everyday experience evidenced in part by a refusal to accept the religious mindset (Rom 12:1-2). It did not take long, however, for religion to reassert its hold.[63]

At first glance, the world of Graeco-Roman religion seems far removed from our

---

[60]Wayne Meeks, *The First Urban Christians: The Social World of the Apostle Paul* (New Haven, Conn.: Yale University Press, 1983), p. 84; cf. pp. 140–42.

[61]Horsley, *New Documents*, 1:23.

[62]Rom 1:18-25; Gal 4:9; Col 2:20-23; Eph 4:17-19.

[63]Like the drift into theology in the early church, the subject of the resurgence of religious conventions is vast (Fox, *Pagans and Christians*, pp. 263–681). See the sections on "Biblical and Related Citations" and "Ecclesiastica" in most volumes of the series *New Documents Illustrating Early Christianity* (ed. Horsley, 1981–1989; ed. Llewelyn, 1992, 1995, 1998 and ongoing). Particularly relevant are the numerous examples of the adoption in the first few centuries after Paul of religious language and conventions such as charms, holy places, relics, imprecations on epitaphs, providence, ritual purity, Fate, rites for healing, and so forth. The religious formulae of Christian and pagan papyri are so close as to make difficult their respective classification. Llewelyn provides a succinct summary of the shifts in his comparison of the use of *leitourgia* in Paul and Clement (7:105–11).

own. But there are suggestive links. The devout Graeco-Roman worshiper had to approach his god at the right time, in the right place and in the manner authorized by the bearers of the tradition. This is not so dissimilar to the spirit of traditional evangelical church services and theology.

Evangelicals like to distance themselves from the ritual traditions of Catholicism and Orthodoxy. To be sure, we are a long way from the more overt religiosity of the Graeco-Roman cults and clubs. Yet when we consider the entirely nonreligious character of Paul's *ekklēsiai* and his struggle to keep them free from the religious mindset, we may well ask how much of that same mindset *we* have perpetuated. Church services are religious occasions structured around formal proceedings conducted by authorized leaders—a far cry from the spontaneity of the *ekklēsia* and the central place it gave to conversation between all participants. Even more informal and relaxed modes of meeting, such as seeker services and "sharing times," remain more in the domain of entertainment or of a token nod in the direction of egalitarianism. Rarely do they accord the dignity and freedom that Paul attributed to the conversations within his *ekklēsiai*.

How far have we drifted from the spirit of Paul? We need only consider our loss of the capacity for sustained conversation about Christ and the affairs of our everyday lives. It is no wonder so many struggle to imagine a world of rich conversation integrating faith and everyday life, a world of sustained conversation unfettered by irrelevant sermons and theological disputes, a world of sustained conversation freed from the confining agendas of the professional elites of clergy and theologians.

12

PAUL & MORALITY

IDEALISM PERVADED THE INTELLECTUAL AND SOCIAL PATTERNS OF THE GRAECO-ROMAN WORLD.
Philosophers predominantly came from positions of social privilege in touch with
civic and political affairs.[1] Whether deliberately or otherwise, they articulated "the
good" in line with prevailing social expectations and ideals. Nature and reason
revealed the propriety of rank, vindicating both the lofty stations of superior men
and the vast gulf separating them from their inferiors. In practice, the adornment
of soul so prized by the moral preachers was as close as a eulogy given to a powerful
independent man sanitized of his everyday passions.

The ideal man, the goal of the moral philosophers, was truly free, without fear,
doing nothing to excess, the epitome of self-control, in total mastery of his inner
self, clothed in virtue, and safe from assault.[2] This is the man "who lives as he wills,
who is subject neither to compulsion, nor hindrance, nor force, whose choices are
unhampered, whose desires attain their end, whose aversions do not fall into what
they would avoid."[3] His superiority is assured.[4] Such a man is in full possession of

---

[1]Dio echoes the commonly attested virtue of a long history of family benefaction to a city: "Now
with reference to my father, there is no need for me to tell whether he was a good man, for you are
always singing his praises, both collectively and individually, whenever you refer to him, as being
no ordinary citizen. . . . Again, no one could say of my grandfather either that he disgraced the city
or that he spent nothing on it out of his own means. For he spent on public benefactions all that
he had from his father and his grandfather, so that he had nothing left at all" (*Orations* 46.2-3).
[2]Seneca *On the Firmness of the Wise Man* 6.3-8.
[3]Epictetus *Discourse* 4.1.1-2.
[4]Dio Chrysostom *Oration* 49.11.

the salvation that philosophy alone can offer.

Not all philosophers agreed on the goals, means and success of philosophical enlightenment. Plutarch sought a truer experience of being in conformity to the divine character: "As Plato says, [God] offers himself to all as a pattern of every excellence, thus rendering human virtue, which is in some sort an assimilation to himself, accessible to all who can 'follow God.' "[5] Stoics likewise sought this conformity.

While Plutarch's ideal left a place for the emotions, Musonius's ideal man had eliminated emotion along with all other "externals": "Therefore, as God, through the possession of these virtues, is unconquered by pleasure or greed; is superior to desire, envy and jealousy; is high-minded, beneficent, and kindly (for such is our conception of God), so also man in the image of Him, when living in accord with nature, should be thought of as being like Him."[6]

Few Epicureans, if any, pursued the kind of hedonism for which they have been maligned. Although they preferred their communities to public life, and disdained the philosophic self-image of hardship, the pleasure they sought lay in tranquillity and moderation: "When, therefore, we maintain that pleasure is the end, we do not mean the pleasures of profligates and those that consist in sensuality . . . but sober reasoning, searching out the motives . . . and banishing mere opinions."[7]

Diogenes, the Cynic, would have had nothing of this. Nature has been so obscured by convention that the one who seeks self-sufficiency *(autarkeia)* must steel himself for a rigorous life: "Poor soul, there is no harsher burden for you than the ways of your forefathers and of the tyrants . . . you need a whip and an overlord and not someone who will admire and flatter you."[8]

Moral Philosophy and the Pathway to Progress and Perfection

Though the moralists differed about the ideal life, most agreed on the role of reason and nature, and likewise on their social agendas. Each cultivated a stable and serene inner life in accord with nature. None had any serious agenda to subvert the structures of society—neither the small communities of Epicureans, nor even the shameless idealized Cynics.[9] The common task was to adorn the soul through rea-

---

[5]Plutarch *Moralia* 550D.

[6]Musonius Rufus *Fragment* 17. Cf. Plutarch *Moralia* 440D.

[7]Diogenes Laertius *Lives of Eminent Philosophers* 10.131.

[8]Pseudo-Diogenes *Epistle* 29:4-5.

[9]The image of Cynics as generally vulgar and repulsive is misleading. As Abraham Malherbe notes, it "reflects a view presented in many of Lucian's satires; but that view hardly fits Lucian's view of Demonax, or with the writings of Dio Chrysostom, who, even during his Cynic period, could hardly have been accused of vulgarity." See Malherbe, *Social Aspects of Early Christianity* (Baton Rouge: University of Louisiana Press, 1977), p. 49.

son, lifting it above those internal and external forces that rob it of its power and serenity.[10] Armed by reason and rigorous self-examination against every vice and passion, the philosopher was the model of the ideal and noble character.[11]

It was axiomatic in the philosophers' world that the perfect is unchanging and cannot be improved. The true sage was thus unmoved in his inner man, no matter how he was buffeted from without. Change of character indicated the baser passions. But the sage was an ideal few philosophers claimed to have attained. Instead, they emphasized progress in the virtues of the philosophic life. This progress focused on self-development and usually entailed a strict regime. Indeed, moral progress was the philosopher's righteousness.[12]

Plutarch's essay *On Being Aware of Moral Progress* encapsulates many of the common perceptions of progress held by educated people in the first century. Beneath progress stood the twin pillars of reason and that "exalted, divine state" of absolute detachment:

> People who are progressing, and who have already "fashioned a fine foundation" for their life (as if it were a home for the gods and kings), do not admit things chosen at random, but use reason as a straight-edge by which to apply and fit every single part together.
>
> In the same way, people whose irrational aspect has been tamed and civilised and checked by reason find that it loses its readiness to use its desires to act outrageously and unconventionally. . . . If as a result of training, detachment can gain control over even the body . . . then naturally this increases the plausibility of suggesting that training can take hold of the emotional part of the mind and, so to speak, smooth it and regularise it by suppressing its illusions and impressions at all levels, including dreaming.[13]

When reason and detachment have their way, the arduous journey toward progress becomes easier: "The path ceases being steep or excessively sheer: it becomes easy, level and manageable. It is as if repeated effort levels the path, as though the journey creates a light and a brightness in philosophy, to replace the perplexity, uncertainty and vacillation which students of philosophy come across at first."[14]

The philosopher's success as a guide depended on the state of his students. In the story of the conversion of Polemo, his aptitude for philosophy was taken to

---

[10]Musonius Rufus *Fragment* 16; Dio Chrysostom *Orations* 78.37-45; Epictetus *Discourse* 3.22.38-49.

[11]Dio Chrysostom *Oration* 17.1-11; 32.7-12; Julian *Oration* 6.200-201; Plutarch, *Fragment* 148; Epictetus *Discourse* 1.4.18-21; Seneca *Epistles* 52.1-9; Dio Chrysostom *Oration* 77/78.37-45.

[12]Seneca *On the Firmness of the Wise Man* 6.

[13]In order: Plutarch *Moralia* 83E, 86A, 83BC.

[14]Plutarch *Moralia* 77D.

indicate a natural endowment of wisdom. His progress began the transformation that would return him to his true nature.[15] Yet "not all who listen to philosophers go away enraptured and wounded, but only those who previously had in their nature some secret bond of kinship with philosophy."[16] The more private philosophers were generally optimistic about the human condition, while the experience of the masses made the more public philosophers pessimistic.[17] The Cynic was convinced that only the tough would progress.[18] In an image recalling Plato's famous cave simile, Maximus of Tyre vividly contrasted the slavery of all men and the goal of freedom that led the Cynic to choose a life without commitments.[19] Stoics tended toward the middle ground: a man might move from vice to virtue, but it was unlikely. In this spirit, Seneca offered a typology of the progress men make and of the likelihood of their going further.[20] The upshot of this was that "one must not talk to a man unless he is willing to listen . . . [unlike the Cynics] who employed an undiscriminating freedom of speech and offered advice to any who came in their way."[21] A student must face the challenge and make every effort without being disheartened by his slow progress.[22]

Vice, however, turns progress into a fight. To the Cynic, a man's vices showed the absurdity of his life.[23] The Stoic faced irrational matter armed with reason: "Some things are high above us, as though they had come forth from the purest substance and are moving evenly while all things in them are accomplished according to the principles of nature . . . but others are earthly exactly as if they had sediment and mud as the substance of nature."[24]

Self-control was the key to imitating the order of the gods and nature. Moralists produced lists of vices and virtues to base morality on the order of nature, particularly in the realm of the household relationships.[25] Philosophers focused on the order of nature that holds for social relationships. Nature itself showed the propri-

---

[15]Lucian *The Double Indictment* 17; cf. Musonius Rufus *Fragment* 2.

[16]Lucian *Nigrinus* 37.

[17]Musonius Rufus *Fragment* 2; cf. Dio Chrysostom *Oration* 13.13.

[18]Pseudo-Diogenes *Epistle* 29.4-5.

[19]Maximus of Tyre *Discourse* 36.

[20]Seneca *Epistles* 52.1-9; also Plutarch *On Listening to Lectures* 46D-47D.

[21]Seneca *Epistles* 29.2.

[22]Plutarch *On Listening to Lectures* 46D-47D.

[23]Dio Chrysostom *Oration* 4.83-96.

[24]Hierocles *On Duties* 1.3.53-54; cf. Plato *Timaeus* 42D-43C.

[25]On the household codes, see Abraham Malherbe, *Moral Exhortation: A Greco-Roman Sourcebook*, Library of Early Christianity 4 (Philadelphia: Westminster Press, 1986), pp. 85–104, 124–29. For a discussion of a *koinē* paraphrase (*P. Haun.* II.13) of the *Letter of Melissa*, a well-known exhortation to feminine piety and virtue from the Pythagorean corpus, see Stephen Llewelyn, ed., *New Documents Illustrating Early Christianity* (Sydney: Macquarie University Press, 1992), 6:18–23.

ety of superior-to-inferior in social relationships.[26] Likewise a man's leadership of his household revealed his potential for civic affairs.[27] Most philosophers regarded withdrawal from public life as the way of ignorant men.[28] Once again, the social position of the philosophers was always close at hand. Many moralists favored or even undertook small amounts of personal labor to set an example of industry or simplicity. But for the most part they held labors, trades and merchandizing to be beneath a rational and dignified man.[29]

A philosopher who called men to imitate him had to show the highest integrity.[30] He must speak without affectation.[31] He must discern the timing of a word.[32] His speech and writing should be dignified, measured and capable of bringing about change. He will not work the crowd as the orators do, but will remain wary of public admonition that may only harden the audience.[33] He will genuinely seek to aid his hearers' progress, yet remain wary of adapting himself too far to his audience.[34] Commitment and community must give way to independence and self-development.

Nowhere was the moralist's integrity more critical than in the face of hardships. The wise man does not choose hardships, nor does he flee them; he engages them for his progress and to justify his superiority. Hardships are opponents for the philosopher to conquer as he furthers his quest for happiness and virtue.[35] Adversity tested and revealed the wise man's virtues and glory; it showed "what sort of person a man is who follows the will of nature."[36]

Of such were the moralists' ideals of conformity, progress and perfection.

Honor, Obligation and Virtue

The broad themes of this idealism were well known through the preaching of sophists and other popularizes of philosophy. Yet very few people consciously based their lives on the ideals of the philosophers. For most people, high and low, morality was shaped by their social experiences of obligation and virtue. This was true even for the intellectual elite. What mattered to Pseudo-Isocrates, for example, was

---

[26]Hierocles *On Duties* 4.22.21-24, 4.27.20-23.
[27]Plutarch *Advice to Bride and Groom* 144CD.
[28]Seneca *Moral Epistles* 68.3-6.
[29]Musonius Rufus *Fragment* 11; Philodemus *On Edification* 23; Cicero *On Duties* 1.150-151.
[30]Pseudo-Diogenes *Epistle* 15; Julian *Oration* 7.214; Lucian *Icaromenippus* 29.311.
[31]Seneca *Epistles* 75.
[32]Plutarch *How to Tell a Flatterer from a Friend* 73C-74E.
[33]Seneca *Epistles* 40.1-8, 13-14; Plutarch *How to Tell a Flatterer* 70D-71C.
[34]Dio Chrysostom *Oration* 77/78.37-45.
[35]Ibid., 8.9-16.
[36]Epictetus *Discourse* 3.20.13; cf. 3.10.11.

that one "do honor to the divine power at all times, but especially on occasions of public worship; for thus you will have the reputation both of sacrificing to the gods and of abiding by the laws."[37] The everyday realities of urban behavior clearly show that the moral ideology of Graeco-Roman cities was maintained first and foremost in those traditions that upheld rank and status. The chief means of regulating this ideology were the traditions of benefaction and patronage, the conventions of reciprocity, and the associated inscriptions of honor and virtue.

Benefactions and honors maintained the good order of society. Much of the cost and oversight of major public works was carried by individuals through their public benefactions.[38] Over and above the concerns of economic and physical well-being, a city's social health depended in no small way on its civic pride and spirit. Love of honor marked the man in whom the whole city could find reason for pride and emulation. The public largesse of the elite perpetuated their prestige and power, confirming their place as the carriers of tradition. A benefactor's virtue included his faithfulness to his family's reputation of generosity toward the city.[39] A great man's gifts validated his piety; the gods loved a cheerful giver with an eye to cultic proprieties. Benefactions for sacrifices, banquets, public spectacles and festivals galvanized not only the donor's piety, prestige and power but also the due order of society. Likewise, the honors returned by the city ensured its own pride and reputation. Both the donor and the recipients received what they paid for.

A society needs a means of enshrining its pride and moral code. Graeco-Roman cities did so through public inscriptions to the honor, piety and virtues of their benefactors. These inscriptions portrayed affairs on earth as replicas of the divine order: the honorific inscriptions of notable citizens mirrored the gods' benefactions to mankind. While reason was the mark of godlikeness to the philosopher, public generosity communicated the same ideal to a far wider audience. Few actions so clearly demonstrated the "divinity" of a great man as his gifts, and his beneficiaries were keen to record in stone his magnanimity to

---

[37]Pseudo-Isocrates *To Demonicus* 13. The close connections of philosophers and sophists to civic affairs is underscored in honorific inscriptions that variously praise them as benefactors in the more usual sense, and also for their "gifts" of philosophy to a city. For a discussion of several of these texts, with passing comments on the proximity of the teaching of the more "formal" philosophers to that espoused by the popularizers, see Greg Horsley, ed., *New Documents Illustrating Early Christianity* (Sydney: Macquarie University, 1987), 4:67–73, also pp. 43–46.

[38]A mid-third century inscription from Ephesus honors one M. Aurelius who "oversaw the most important tasks of the state" (*I. Eph* VII 1.3071).

[39]In the Graeco-Roman period, the lauding of ancestry and tradition was widespread: "It is certain that the whole cultural tradition underwent a process of crystallisation during the first century of our era. Classicism now emerged" (Edwin Judge, *Rank and Status in the World of the Caesars and St. Paul: The Broadhead Memorial Lecture 1981* [Christchurch: University of Canterbury Press, 1982], p. 18).

them as the hallmark of piety and virtue.

Benefactions and inscriptions underscored the respective roles of the greater and the lesser, securing the inherent rightness of the social hierarchy. A man only had to pass through the markets and temple precincts to know his place. If the formal inscriptions escaped his attention, he could always read the graffiti:

> Greetings, Eulalios, a revered person desired by the gods. May you live forever, and forever let your life increase. For you provide friendship to everyone, with good foresight, together with the gifts and joyous banquets of the ambrosian [plenty] which you possess.[40]

Graveyards preached the same sermon. Epitaphs on the tombs of both great and small captured the sentiments of popular philosophy, piety and morality:

> As you look at this image reflect upon your end and do not treat life as though you had forever to live.[41]

In death, if not in life, men would note those who had conformed to the order that marked a cultured city:

> Since Theophilos . . . is of very noble ancestral stock, having contributed all good-will towards his country . . . being amicable to the citizens and in concord with his wife Apphia . . . it is resolved that Theophilus be honored with a painted portrait and a gold bust and a marble statue . . . and that this decree be read aloud [published?] so that all may know that such people who exercise their life on behalf of their country meet with such a testimony.[42]

Epitaphs could also ensure that passers-by noted the piety and virtue of the *living*:

> Out of respect and love for what is good her husband, Lucius Dexios from Herculaneum, buried her.[43]

> In this place Chrestos buried aged Italos . . . [and] fulfilled these sacred rites for him as a favour.[44]

Morality was more than the obligations and courtesies of rank. For many it was deeply intertwined with the piety, ritual exactitude and fraternity of small cultic associations. Devotion to the gods and to the fraternity of members bound the initiate to household and civic obligations and scruples exceeding those of outsiders. Yet a person's rank *was* his or her morality in the profoundly important sense that the vast bulk of expectations that shaped public behavior were nested in a

---

[40]Inscription *I. Eph.* II.555, in Horsley, *New Documents*, 4:153.
[41]Inscription *Pfuhl/Möbius* I.847, in Horsley, *New Documents*, 4:43-44.
[42]75/76AD, *AE* 808, in Horsley, *New Documents*, 2:58–60.
[43]Cairo, first or second century, *SEG* 1536, in Horsley, *New Documents*, 3:40–43.
[44]Inscription from first century, *I. Bithynia* III.12, in Horsley, *New Documents*, 3:39.

person's social position. If the cultic fraternities indicate a growing failure of the household and the city to adequately satisfy a man's sense of purpose, it was not because his behavior was less structured by patronage and rank but because these mechanisms continued to define his moral experience, albeit unsatisfactorily.

Everyday realities were never as fixed as theorists' models. This was certainly true of the social hierarchy and its morality. Benefactions and inscriptions not only marked the rigidity of rank in the Graeco-Roman world but also the dynamics of status. Following Edwin Judge,[45] we may define *rank* as a social (and usually legal) position that carried responsibilities and obligations to others, especially to those of other ranks. *Status*, on the other hand, was the prestige of a rank without its obligations. Ambition was generally applauded, and where it flourished, status tended to convert itself into rank. Rank thus tended to be the fossilized status of the past. In this sense, honorific inscriptions and graffiti recorded the evolution of social order. They portrayed both the aspirations and means of ambition and, in due time, the public endorsements that in effect created new rank from status.[46]

Honorific and eulogistic inscriptions portrayed the ideal of the well-rounded man—good family, dignified manner, strong character, just, pious, ambitious for honor, moderate in everything, progressing in stature:

> embellishing by his dignified behaviour the progress towards betterment which Fortune has bestowed.[47]

> good bearing, treating them with respect . . . with understatement and moderation . . . hating the bad and loving the good, in nothing neglectful of what relates to honor and fame for the sake of the memorable and praiseworthy establishment of his existing preference for the best . . . guiding everyone to become emulators of excellent deeds, delegating men to bring forward a proposal for the honors. . . . And the people, being familiar both with the man's love of fame and with his justice.[48]

> (This honours) Heraclides, [priest] of Artemis, and benefactor of the people, for his

---

[45] Judge, *Rank and Status*. The delineation and distinction of rank and status in the Graeco-Roman world has been a hallmark of Judge's perspectives on the social identity of Paul and his associates, *ekklesiai* and opponents.

[46] R. MacMullen notes the profound influence of status and ambition over the society of Paul's day: "Philotimia . . . No word, understood to its depths, goes further to explain the Graeco-Roman achievement" (*Roman Social Relations: 50 B.C. to A.D. 284* [New Haven, Conn.: Yale University Press, 1974], p. 215).

[47] Inscription *I. Eph.* 1a27, in Horsley, *New Documents*, 4:36.

[48] Inscription *I. Eph.* 6. This and the following texts are from the seminar notes by Edwin Judge, "Benefactors at Ephesus" and "Ethical Ideals in St. Paul and the Inscriptions of Ephesus," in *Ephesus and the World of St Paul: The Inscriptions of an Ancient Metropolis and the Social Con-*

own comprehensive virtue and for his piety towards Artemis and for his scholarly power and trustworthiness and for his public goodwill . . . [and honours his wife] for her own moderation.[49]

The sage and the great man were hewn from the same rock. The philosophers' man was not an individualist; he was the city's man, the one motivated by social propriety. The sage took seriously his divine commission to guide; and no one flinched at the benefactor's love of personal honor.

Nothing conveyed this spirit of self-interest within social harmony more simply and clearly than those punchy little imperatives, the maxims cherished by elite and folksy alike:

☐ Know yourself.

☐ Nothing to excess.

☐ Pick your time.

☐ A cost to every commitment.

The maxims echoed the social world of honors and the obligations and opportunities of friendship.[50] One should "obey" and "honor" the "good man" and "yield to the just." A gentleman "loves friendship" and is quick to "grant" and "return a favor." Moderation is paramount to one who pursues "nothing in excess." The tempered man guards his speech; keeps anger, envy and strife in check; and is careful to "speak well of all." He is able to look within himself without accusation or regret; for as much as he must "fear what controls" him, and "think as a mortal," he knows to "grieve not at life," "neither worry about everything." Right knowledge of oneself is to "pursue glory" and to "respect oneself." His life is held in check from the cradle to the grave: "As a child well behaved . . . in youth restrained . . . in middle life just . . . in old age prudent . . . at the end not worrying." Self-interested, self-protecting, moderate, courteous, harmonious: the quintessential family and civic man.

Philosophers' ideals, social conventions of rank and status, and the maxims reinforced one another (see figure 12.1). Each upheld the ideals of *conformity* and *progress*:

---

text of Early Christianity (North Ryde: Ancient History Documentary Research Centre, Macquarie University, 1993), pp. 19–29, 45–49. His translations are deliberately stilted: "A fluent translation only breaks up the pattern of thought, vital to the impact of a eulogistic text" (p. 19).

[49]Inscription *I. Eph.* 683A. Although honorific inscriptions for wealthy women benefactors often used the same vocabulary as those for men, the contrast in this text captures the broader cultural realities well: the husband's *success*; the wife's *moderation*.

[50]The quotations of maxims are from Judge, "Benefactors at Ephesus." The specific texts are Stobaeus, *Eclogae* III 1.173; *I. Kyzikos* II 2, the Aï-*Khanum* stele; and *P. Athen. Univ.* 2782.

	Philosophers' ideals	Social structure	Maxims
Norm for conformity	nature	social ranking	the individual
Goal of conformity	self-development, piety, independence	personal honors, piety, independence	self-knowledge, piety, independence
Means of conformity	reason	obligations of rank	moderation
Focus for progress	reason as therapy, contemplation	ambition for status, promotion in rank	ambition within harmony
Means of progress	enlightenment, hardship, imitation	patronage, friendship, wealth, benefaction, education, eulogy	courtesy, prudence, resourcefulness, apt timing, praise
Indicators of moral progress	serenity, greatness of soul	transparent superiority or acquiescence	self-respect, self-reliance, reputation

Figure 12.1. The ideals of conformity and progress in Graeco-Roman moral traditions

The "good" of ethical theorists translated into the social systems of rank, friendship, benefaction, reciprocity and honor. The philosophers simply presumed the mechanisms of society as the rough shape of their own moral ideals. Maxims distilled these ideals. Or was it the reverse—the ideal giving voice to an even older tradition? Likewise with the maxims and social structure. Maxims provided a ready reckoner for obligation and prestige. At the same time, they expressed that ancient moderation between ambition and courtesy that the great sons of the *polis* had mastered.

Each tradition recalled the hallmarks of primary reality—serenity, order, unchangeableness. They made the social system self-evidently right and proper: a system able to hold the have-nots in their place while trading status as the currency of new rank.

Paul and the Transformation of the Person in Christ
An intelligent, experienced man who spoke and wrote on topics of personal and social behavior would inevitably echo the conventions of Graeco-Roman households and civic life, those "widespread sapiential traditions" of his day.[51] Paul was

---

[51]Malherbe, "Social Aspects," p. 42.

no exception. In fact, he is easier to fit here than to the other three patterns.

Our survey of Graeco-Roman morality cautions us against identifying Paul with any one tradition or philosophical school. Private and public morality was not a matter of theoretical systems but of exhortations and aphorisms broadcast from ornaments, gymnasia, festivals, city walls, statues, graveyards and the sundry paraphernalia of daily life. The philosophy most people encountered was eclectic, blending Epicurean realism, Platonic vision, Stoic austerity and more. The interdependence of the traditions alone makes it both pertinent and potentially misleading to compare Paul at any one point with the philosophical schools.[52]

In Romans, Paul portrayed the believer as one granted righteousness *(dikaiosynē)* in Christ. This had considerable links to Graeco-Roman morality. We have encountered *dikaiosynē* and related terms as part of the vocabulary of virtue and moral behavior in aphorisms and in honorific and eulogistic texts.[53] What images would a Graeco-Roman reader call to mind at the mention that "no one is righteous" or of one whose "faith is reckoned as righteousness," now "declared righteous" and given "honor" (Rom 3:10, 26; 4:5, 24; 8:21)?

Clearly Paul drew on the Old Testament in his use of *dikaiosynē* and related terms and for the shape of his thoughts about justification.[54] Yet his message was still intelligible to a Graeco-Roman audience without the benefit of a Jewish heritage or a Greek translation of the Jewish scriptures. The vocabulary of "righteousness" was not the exclusive property of Jews. No doubt Paul intended to enlighten these Gentiles with his use of the Jewish scriptures. Yet his portrait of justification would have made startling and provocative sense to those familiar with the terms from social and religious contexts of reputation and approval.

Every city boasted those who were publicly and privately lauded for their good will and blamelessness. Rome perhaps most of all. The use of *dikaiosynē* on statues and graffiti would call to mind those who had conspicuously excelled in civic life and piety. Indeed, the critical importance of one's reputation as good or just partly explains the rampant litigation in Graeco-Roman city life. In a legal context a man's *dikaiosynē* was to be unimpeachable before the courts. In a cultic context,

---

[52]See Edwin Judge, "'Antike und Christentum': Some Recent Work from Cologne," *Prudentia* 5 (1973): 110. Notwithstanding Judge's caution, it is important to note something of the vast literature comparing Paul to the moral philosophers. Some of this falls prey to Judge's criticism. Others do not. Although Paul knew the contemporary philosophical traditions "first hand," Malherbe argues, he nevertheless "used these traditions with as much originality as his contemporaries did" (*Paul and the Popular Philosophers* [Minneapolis: Fortress, 1989], p. 8). From this platform Malherbe helpfully discusses Paul in relation to Plutarch, the Epicureans and, particularly, the Cynics. For the broad similarities, see Malherbe, "Social Aspects," p. 20–28.

[53]E.g., Stobaeus, *Eclogae* III 1.173, *l.* 5, 27, 64, 84, 145; *GVI* 1693; *I. Eph.* Ia.6.

[54]E.g., Gen 15:6; Hab 2:4; Rom 1:17; 4:3; cf. Rom 1:2-4; 1:16—5:21; 9:1—11:36.

the *dikaios* was a man conspicuous for his blamelessness in the duty he rendered to the gods.[55] So there was common ground between those who spoke of divine *dikaiosynē* and of that "quality exhibited by a superior to an inferior."[56] These social contexts located *dikaiosynē* as a key term of a man's standing before the gods and men.[57]

Paul's message concerning the righteous man could not avoid this ideology. His proclamation that there were none good, righteous or honorable outside Christ must have been deeply offensive to Graeco-Roman sensibilities. His message confronted the mainstream beliefs and expectations of what made a man socially and religiously acceptable. The message would equally anger intellectuals. Greek thought began with man. Paul's did not. He was convinced that neither intellectual serenity nor social reputation could avert the searching judgment of God's *dikaiosynē*. Likewise, no intellectual, social or religious progress could secure a man's *dikaiosynē*. Only one *dikaios* (righteous man) mattered now. By his death and resurrection, Christ had revealed the *dikaiosynē* of God as the verdict of justification.

Righteousness and honor did not attach to rank or reputation but were granted as unmerited favors to those who welcomed the promise of justification. Whereas Graeco-Roman morality assured a place for boasting, it was entirely excluded in Paul's message. The futility and hypocrisy of religious and moral self-development was unmasked. The Spirit alone revealed the believer's *dikaiosynē* and brought assurance of the adoption and other honors that God had guaranteed in Christ.

Paul was not seeking to marginalize the Roman Christians. On the contrary, he urged them to maintain social good will through benefaction and obedience to the authorities. He did not seek to overthrow rank, yet he was merciless toward status. Paul's innovations were not an agenda to subvert the social order but a radical repudiation of the elitism and self-interest that maintained it. He thus set himself on a collision course with the contemporary culture of personal honor and self-development.

Where virtue was tied to stability of character, personal change was liable to be censured. This is not to say that the moralists and philosophers had no interest in change or progress. We have clearly noted the contrary. For his part, Paul spoke of personal transformation and the renewal of the mind. The models sound similar but were not the same.

---

[55]A. D. Clarke, "The Good and the Just in Romans 5:7," *Tyndale Bulletin* 41 (1990): 134.

[56]Horsley, *New Documents*, 4:145.

[57]In a personal communication, Brian Powell indicated to me that *dikaiosynē* "is prominent in both Plutarch and Philo as a social virtue, especially expected of the powerful. It is only a minor virtue term for Epictetus and seems to denote conformity to principle rather than right social action and relating (he is ambivalent about social obligation)." For a fuller discussion, see his "The Cardinal Virtues in Paul, Philo, Plutarch (*Lives*), and Epictetus" (Ph.D. diss., Macquarie University, Sydney, 1996).

Moralists generally presumed that one who showed promise of progress, particularly the young sons of the nobility, had been born with the seeds of reason and virtue. They only needed to be guided toward self-control and mastery of the virtues. Paul assumed the moral slavery of all.[58] Moreover, he used the common metaphor of the *polis* as a body to invert the conventional priorities of the one and the many. Whereas the moralists regarded the community as the context and means for the *individual's* honor, Paul urged a radical humility from those whose personal identity now rested on the grace of God. The moralists' ideals of supremacy, serenity and self-sufficiency gave way to the radical personal cost of love (Rom 12:1-21).

The revelation of God's *dikaiosynē* in Christ led Paul away from the ideal of personal progress. Graeco-Roman morality was grounded in abstract ideals and focused on the individual's progress toward perfection. History had considerable educational value, but mostly only to illustrate ideals. Paul's moral innovations were tied to his understanding of Christ as the focal point of human history. This perspective enabled him to dispense with progress as such. The ordering of history in Christ made each moment as significant as any other. No time was now more sacred than another. No time was loaded with the urgency of ambition and progress. The dying and rising of Christ shaped every moment in anticipation of the justification and honors of the children of God in a renewed creation. This was neither utopian idealism nor other-worldly abstraction. Idealism gave way to relationship. The proof, as we will see in part four, was in Paul's own experience of self-humiliation.

Meeting of Three Worlds

Paul's perspectives were not always unique. Others had objected to the status quo and had reworked its traditions. Paul was not isolated from these traditions, but he freely adopted and adapted them in line with his own goals. We have seen definite points of contact between Paul and the patterns of philosophy, theology, religion and morality. Moreover, these were the perspectives Paul's hearers were likely to use to understand his message and life. Yet the very familiarity of these patterns to his *ekklēsiai* created confusion for them. Paul's departures from the norm were not easy to understand. Their heritage continued to exert a powerful influence over their thought and behavior. Paul encountered interpretations of his message at Galatia, Colossae, Corinth, Ephesus and Thessalonica that realigned it with the conventions he repudiated. To identify Paul with these patterns is to lose more than we gain.

We are left with two profoundly different worldviews. Graeco-Roman traditions

---

[58]Rom 6:1—7:25; cf. Epictetus *Discourse* 4.1.1-5.

presumed a reality that transcended the personal and the everyday, a reality grasped in theoretical constructs and generalizations, a reality to be imitated in the models and ideals of intellectual and social life. The educated man sought the perfection of his soul through conformity to those conventions of nature and society which best imitated the "other" reality. Notwithstanding the profound differences between philosophers, religious groups and moralists, this perspective pervaded the literary and nonliterary sources for the intellectual and social life of Graeco-Roman society.

Steeped in the Jewish Scriptures and tradition, Paul brought all questions back to the character and purposes of God as revealed in the history and relationships of his covenant people. Where Paul parted from Judaism, it was not to defer to the abstraction of the Graeco-Roman tradition but to ground all of life in the recent historical events of a Jewish Messiah, Jesus of Nazareth. To be sure, Paul's thought presupposed that the God of Israel and Christ was not bound to human history and experience. But Paul showed no interest in taking this further through theological abstraction. He never developed an image of God-in-his-being in the style of the Graeco-Roman philosophers and theologians. His understanding and proclamation of God remained firmly rooted in the past, present and future events of human history, particularly as they now hinged on the personal past, present and future of Jesus Christ. These same perspectives removed Paul's experience and the character of the *ekklēsia* from the paradigms of religion. The gospel discredited all intellectual autonomy and elitism.

There is a third world to consider. We who are evangelicals like to think our beliefs and practice derive from Paul without a trace of the worldviews he rejected. But our heritage is not so clean. We are the children of both parents. We have already traced something of this confused heritage in relation to philosophy, theology and religion. We have noted the broad similarities between the Graeco-Roman patterns and our elitist intellectual games, our own methods of theology and our own religiosity. Our preaching owes more to the oratory of sophists and super-apostles, and to the tradition of reason as therapy for the soul, than to Paul's disavowal of eloquence or to his preference for love over precision.

The same confused heritage lives on in our ideals of supremacy, serenity and self-sufficiency for leaders. Once again, Paul largely lost the battle. In the generations following Paul, his radical teachings were largely neutralized by the prevailing paradigms of Graeco-Roman moral leadership to produce the basic shape of what we know as *clergy*. A millennium and a half later, the Reformers recovered a great deal about grace for the unconverted, but expected them to live by law in the church. We still do.

Like the idealized sage of the moral preachers and the sanitized inscriptions to benefactors, we teach and expect our leaders to hide personal weakness, insecurity or doubt. Many years ago I studied for the professional pastoral ministry. I vividly recall a professor warning me and my peers against drawing close to congregations or allowing them to see our own struggles. Such advice dooms many clergy to loneliness and a nagging sense of inhabiting a world removed from their congregations. Powerful ideals of ministerial success and self-sufficiency lock many leaders into winning approval from mentors and boards. This pretense contributes to the high rate of depression, breakdown and premature resignation among clergy. Relationships become bounded by law even as the rhetoric of grace flows. We preach grace, then subtly demand performance. We preach grace, then purge those deemed to be in error. We preach grace, then too often ignore the cries of the abused, the weak and the hurting. We preach grace, then gag those conversations that we cannot control.

All of this owes too much to Graeco-Roman ideals and conventions, and it is a far cry from Paul's radical framing of grace and conversation in Christ. We turn now to trace the ways that the dying and rising of Christ shaped Paul's own life, the misunderstanding and enmity he endured, and the profound legacy he left for us of grace and freedom, improvisation and conversation.

PART 4

FRAMES FOR GRACE & CONVERSATION

13

DYING TO RISE

PAUL'S LIFE WAS FAR REMOVED FROM THE SERENE INDEPENDENCE THAT MARKED THE Graeco-Roman ideals of the wise man. Identifying with the crucified and risen Christ cost Paul deeply in physical suffering, emotional anguish and social ostracism. The latter was made worse by his ruthless exposure of his own inner man. Unlike those who maintained an appearance of control and success, Paul paraded his weaknesses and vulnerability as the marks that he was an authentic apostle and bearer of the Spirit. There is a strong link here between Paul's longing, his almost reckless candor about himself, and his sense of freedom. He understood himself as having been made a "slave" to Christ and as having been set free from the bondage of sin and death. This was not abstract theologizing.

The Experience of Knowing Christ
Jerusalem and the law no longer held Paul's allegiance. He regarded himself as free of all men, yet he made himself the slave of all in order to establish communities free from the distinctions of race, gender or rank. He tirelessly worked to free his *ekklēsiai* from enslaving social patterns. His identity was not shaped by his social position, piety or moral progress. He strove to know Christ and to make him known, not to enhance his own reputation. His self-understanding and reflection were born and nurtured in the concrete realities of conflict, enmity, labor, partnership and affection. His freedom and desire had sprung to life on the Damascus road and had matured in the sweatshops,

homes, highways, marketplaces and prisons of Asia Minor, Macedonia and Achaia. Rather than withdraw from the world, he had engaged with others in synagogues, marketplaces, public halls, private residences and the places of his occupation. Imprisonments, court appearances, harassment by crowds—each became opportunities to proclaim the message.[1] As he engaged with people, he saw himself anew. As he grappled with his own humiliations, he recreated the meaning of the dying and rising of Christ.

We distort Paul's message if we dissociate it from his experience. The unmistakably autobiographical tone of his letters show how deeply his thought was shaped by his life: his experience under the law, his conversion, his subsequent commission and his work.[2] These events stand out so vividly in those places where he *was* self-consciously autobiographical that they leave the impression of having shaped his thought more profoundly than even he had discerned.[3]

Paul's wonder at Christ was not simply intellectual. It was profoundly personal: Christ had inaugurated this new state of affairs *for him*. God's actions in history did not remain at a distance from him. Paul's wonder fueled his hunger to know Christ more. This knowledge included the intellect: he knew *about* Christ (1 Cor 15:1-8). But his outburst in Philippians 3:7-11 came from *memory* (Phil 3:4-6). An increased intellectual grasp of Christ would never match the emotion in recollecting his former piety, privilege and zeal. Turning his back on his past, he had turned toward Christ with passion. The knowledge for which Paul longed was experiential, emotional and personal. He wanted to *participate* with Christ in the power of his own resurrection. Paul had no slick triumphalism in mind. He knew too well that power came through "the fellowship of his sufferings."

Paul hungered for fuller fellowship with the one he only claimed to know in part.[4] In the meantime, the Spirit was tangibly present to Paul, sharing his groans and sighs over the brokenness of the present age.[5] In a particularly vivid yet everyday image that captures the interplay of his life and thought, Paul saw himself as

---

[1] Acts 14:2-3, 6-7; 16:25-34; 19:30-31; 21:40; 25:9-12; 26:24-29; 27:33-35; 28:17-31; cf. Phil 1:12-18.
[2] Rom 2:17—3:20; 5:10; 7:7-25; 9:30-33; 10:5-15; 12:1-3; 1 Cor 13; 2 Cor 1:3-7; Eph 2:1-11; 2:11-22; Col 1:9-14.
[3] E.g., Phil 3:4-11.
[4] Rom 8:22-25; 2 Cor 1:22; 5:5; Gal 5:15-21; Eph 1:14.
[5] E.g., Rom 7—8; 2 Cor 3:17; Gal 3:2; 5:18. While the language is too abstract for Paul, James Dunn captures the immediacy of the Spirit to the apostle: "The Spirit is that power which operates on the *heart* of man "the 'heart' being the centre of thought, feeling and willing, the centre of personal consciousness, what we might call 'the *experiencing* I'" (*Jesus and the Spirit: A Study of the Religious and Charismatic Experience of Jesus and the First Christians as Reflected in the New Testament* [Philadelphia: Westminster Press, 1975], p. 201, emphasis his).

walking with Christ.[6] The metaphor no doubt emerged from his own extensive experience traveling the roads of the eastern empire. Robert Banks captures the spirit of the image: "His actual walking became a parable of his walking with God."[7]

The Experience of Strength in Weakness

Paul's break with his past and with the traditions of his day tended to isolate him. He carried a sense of weighty accountability to God, setting him apart from others who seemed more concerned with the approval of their peers.[8] This sense of isolation may well have deepened his resolve to identify with the dying and rising Christ with such ruthless self-denial. It no doubt also arose from his perplexing experience of living between the ages. He felt acutely the perversity and brokenness of life on the one hand, and the wonder of grace and a new creation on the other. He carried the sense of one born "last of all," the apostle who had been "the chief of sinners" (1 Cor 25:8). He was buoyed by hope even as he sensed the immediacy of the end. He carried all this in his own suffering and joy, his dying and rising with Christ as one "put . . . on display at the end of the procession, like men condemned to die in the arena" (1 Cor 4:9).

There was a sharp edge to Paul's experience of strength in weakness (2 Cor 12:9).[9] He did not cease to be weak at the moment he realized the strength Christ made available to him. *He remained weak.* Paul expressed this fellowship with Christ as the experience of paradoxical circumstances and choices: weakness and

---

[6]Col 2:6; 1 Thess 4:1. I am indebted to Robert Banks for this suggestion in relation to Paul's walking. See his *Paul: The Experience Within the Theology* (Canberra: Zadok, 1986). A further study provides extensive citation of the relevant texts, along with discussions of the semantic field in the Old Testament, the LXX, Qumran and rabbinic sources. See " 'Walking' as a Metaphor of the Christian Life: The Origins of a Significant Pauline Usage," in *Perspectives on Language and Text*, ed. E. W. Conrad and E. G. Newing (Winona Lake, Ind.: Eisenbrauns, 1987), pp. 303–13. Banks notes the likely influence of the Old Testament on Paul's choice of metaphor but rightly insists that Paul's own experience of walking was formative.

[7]Banks, *Paul*, p. 7. While Paul never used *peripateō* of his own travels (he generally preferred *erchesthai* or *poreuesthai*), it seems he used *peripateō* when he wished to contrast the manner and hope of the new life (Rom 8:4; 2 Cor 10:2-4; Gal 5:16; Eph 4:1; Col 2:6) with the futility and destination of the old (Rom 8:4; Gal 5:16; Eph 2:1-2; 4:17; Col 3:5-7). On the everyday circumstances of travels and accommodation that Paul was likely to have encountered, see David French, "Acts and the Roman Roads of Asia Minor," in *The Book of Acts in Its First Century Setting*, vol. 2, *Graeco-Roman Setting*, ed. D. W. J. Gill and C. Gempf (Grand Rapids, Mich.: Eerdmans; and Carlisle: Paternoster, 1994), pp. 49–58.

[8]1 Cor 4:1-5; 2 Cor 3:1; Gal 1:10; 2:6, 14; 5:11; 6:12-14, 17; 1 Thess 2:4.

[9]Peter Marshall notes that Paul's use of the metaphor of strength in weakness "conformed to usage in the Graeco-Roman literary tradition" ("A Metaphor of Social Shame," *Novum Testamentum* 25 [1983]: 311). What is unique to Paul is the way he relates the metaphor to his relationship with others.

strength;[10] foolishness and wisdom;[11] poverty and riches;[12] shame and honor;[13] slave and free;[14] suffering and comfort;[15] and frustration and glory.[16] His most extended set of contrasting pairs occurs in 2 Corinthians 4. (Figure 13.1 highlights the contrasts.)

hard pressed on every side	. . . but not crushed
perplexed	. . . but not in despair
persecuted	. . . but not abandoned
struck down	. . . but not destroyed
always carrying . . . the death of Jesus	. . . so that the life of Jesus . . . may be revealed
always being given over to death	. . . so that his life may be revealed
death is at work in us	. . . but life is at work in you
outwardly wasting away	. . . inwardly renewed day by day
our light and momentary troubles	. . . an eternal glory

Figure 13.1. The paradoxical experience outlined in 2 Corinthians 4:7-17

The sting in the left-hand column of figure 13.1 must not be robbed of its force. There is no triumphant movement from "dying" to "rising." Rising did not remove the sting of dying. Paul worked, traveled, taught and related under the pressure and stigma of a suffering, humiliated man. At times he could not conceal his pain and indignation: "Let no one cause me trouble, for I bear on my body the marks of Jesus" (Gal 6:17).

If Paul bore his suffering and humiliation as the marks of dying, it was, he said, in order to bring life to others.[17] The power of God and the story of Christ were not chained by Paul's adverse circumstances but were made effective by them.[18] In prison he was at pains to comfort the free. Ostracized by the self-styled elite of an

[10]1 Cor 1:25; 2:1-5; 4:10; 2 Cor 11:21, 30; 12:5, 9-10; 13:3-4.
[11]1 Cor 1:18-25; 3:18-20; 4:10.
[12]1 Cor 4:8-13; 2 Cor 6:10; 8:9.
[13]1 Cor 4:10; 2 Cor 11:21.
[14]Rom 6:15-18; 1 Cor 9:19-23.
[15]2 Cor 1:3-11; 7:5-7.
[16]Rom 8:18-25.
[17]2 Cor 4:14-15; cf. 1:5-6; Phil 1:21-26.
[18]Phil 1:10-12; 1 Thess 2:1; 2 Tim 2:9.

ekklēsia, he endured further humiliation at their hands so they would not lose the privileges he had originally brought to them. Forsaking his own rights, he had fought for those who had been marginalized in the same *ekklēsia*.[19] He bore his sufferings with the mixed emotions of one who had no place left for boasting.[20]

In a strikingly strong metaphor, possibly unique among Graeco-Roman authors, Paul portrayed himself as a captive being led to his death in the arena by the victorious Christ (2 Cor 2:14; cf. 1 Cor 4:9). This metaphor has troubled commentators.[21] However, Peter Marshall has shown how aptly the image conveyed Paul's continuing experience of dying for the sake of the Corinthians. Paul's use of the image reinforced the social shame and strained relations with the Corinthians that resulted from his labor and his refusal of their patronage.[22] Few images could have conveyed so powerfully how Paul reframed the marks of leadership. As Marshall notes: "That Paul could be a shamed and powerless figure, being led captive, while in that very position be used by God to display the 'fragrance *(osmē)* of his knowledge' (2 Cor. 2:14) is thoroughly consistent with, and most vividly portrays, Paul's self-conception of his apostleship in Corinth. It indicates not just that he is the medium of the message but the kind of messenger he is."[23]

Paul's ruthless parade of "the things which Greeks and Romans would attempt to conceal at all costs" did not end there.[24] As noted before, the Corinthians insisted that Paul take up the stance of a leader with rhetorical skill and a refined public

---

[19]1 Cor 8:13; cf. Rom 14:1-4.

[20]1 Cor 1:26-31; 9:15-18; 11:16—12:13; Gal 6:14; Phil 3:3.

[21]Concerns have been raised about the meaning of *thriambeuein* and its cognates, about the precise character of the Roman triumph, and about how well known it was outside Rome. Commentators also balk at the obvious meaning—that Paul regarded himself as a disgraced and vanquished captive—and have sought to avoid this by suggesting that Paul regarded himself as *sharing* in the triumph. But this is to put Paul on the wrong side of the arena. Both Marshall ("Metaphor of Social Shame") and Scott Hafemann (*Suffering and Ministry in the Spirit: Paul's Defense of His Ministry in 2 Corinthians 2:14—3:3* [Grand Rapids, Mich.: Eerdmans, 1990]) demonstrate that Paul took up the image as a metaphor of his suffering. See also J. Fitzgerald, *Cracks in an Earthen Vessel: An Examination of the Catalogues of Hardships in the Corinthian Correspondence*, Society of Biblical Literature Dissertation Series 99 (Atlanta: Scholars Press, 1988). Marshall sees the image as "a metaphor of social shame." Hafemann regards it as a critical part of what he understands to be the interpretive crux of 2 Corinthians, namely, 2:14—3:3: the metaphor conveys the sense of being "led to death" and forms a key image of Paul's suffering, which Hafemann suggests was for Paul the proof of his apostleship and mediation of the Spirit.

[22]Peter Marshall notes the similarities in Latin authors of Paul's use of the triumph as a metaphor ("Metaphor of Social Shame," pp. 304–5, 312). In particular, Seneca noted the constant social shame felt by a man whose benefactor will not let him forget his indebtedness: "In a triumph I should have had to march but once" (*On Benefits* 2.11.1). Marshall notes that "Seneca's example of the humiliated beneficiary provided a contemporary and remarkably similar metaphorical use [to Paul's use of *thriambeuein* in 2 Cor 2:14]. Both are used to denote social shame" ("Metaphor of Social Shame," p. 317).

[23]Marshall, "Metaphor of Social Shame," p. 316.

[24]Ibid., p. 315.

presence. The more he sought to answer their charges and to reframe their under-standing of him, the worse his case became. Finally, Paul let fly just how intently he felt his humiliation. In the astonishing passage of 2 Corinthians 10:1—13:10, Paul's anguish "concentrated upon the point of whether or not he was going to engage in what he called 'boasting'; he said that what they were demanding of him was that he boast like the rest, of his achievements as a leader. In the end he does it. In a soul-searching passage, which obviously cost him a great deal and must have stunned his critics in spite of the fact that this was what they were demanding of him, he lets himself go suddenly with great violence into a full-blown display of boasting about himself."[25]

Paul actually *played up* his disgrace (2 Cor 12:9-10).[26] He spoke as though the message had laid him bare, as if it had forced upon him a startling self-knowledge. Yet he appears not to have been self-preoccupied. He seems neither awed by him-self nor defeated by what he saw within.

The Experience of Social Humiliation

Paul's engagement with his *ekklēsiai* came at great personal cost. He described his efforts as continuing or filling up the sacrifice of Christ on others' behalf.[27] In some quarters, this self-sacrifice provided the grounds for accusations of inconstancy and impure motives.[28] Understandably, he was deeply perplexed at times.[29]

Despite all the difficulties his labor caused him,[30] Paul prized his independence from financial support.[31] He maintained that he had a right to this support as did the other coworkers, but he refused to exercise it so as not to be a burden. He saw his refusal as an imitation of Christ's dying and rising. It proved that his labors were motivated by Christ, not by ambition. There is deep irony in how Paul carried this social humiliation. On the one hand, it weighed heavily on him. On the other

---

[25]Edwin Judge, "St. Paul and Socrates," *Interchange* 14 (1973): 108.

[26]In his study of the *peristasis* catalogs of Paul and his contemporaries, Fitzgerald *(Cracks in an Earthen Vessel)* has demonstrated the considerable degree to which suffering formed part of Paul's self-understanding. He particularly draws out the similarities between the apostle and the philosophers' portraits of the suffering sage.

[27]2 Cor 1:3-7; 4:7-15; Phil 2:18; Col 1:24; 2 Tim 4:6; cf. Phil 1:21.

[28]2 Cor 1:13, 16-17; 10:1-2, 10; 11:7-11; 12:13-18.

[29]2 Cor 11:23-29; Gal 4:12-20. Abraham Malherbe argues that Paul's fight with "beasts" at Ephesus (1 Cor 15:32) may refer to struggles against his opponents there (cf. 1 Cor 16:8-9). See his *Paul and the Popular Philosophers* (Minneapolis: Fortress, 1989), pp. 79–89.

[30]On the workshop and Paul's strategy, see R. F. Hock, *The Social Context of Paul's Ministry: Tent-making and Apostleship* (Philadelphia: Fortress, 1980), pp. 37–42, and Malherbe, *Paul and the Thessalonians: The Philosophic Tradition of Pastoral Care* (Philadelphia: Fortress, 1987), pp. 17–20. On the relation of Paul's manual labor to his self-understanding, see Hock, *Social Context*, pp. 47–49.

[31]1 Cor 9:1-8, 16-18; 2 Cor 2:17—3:1; 4:1-2; 1 Thess 2:10; 2 Thess 3:8.

hand, he guarded his shame jealously. He could parade his financial independence to press home the claim that his message was neither derived from man nor tainted with the desire to win approval. He coveted the freedom to engage fearlessly with others. His humiliation branded him with the reproach commonly directed by the honorable at the dishonorable, yet it enabled him to survive any accusation of self-interest or personal gain. He was no freeloader, and he could prove it.[32]

To the Corinthians, however, he appeared fickle. He had taken the Macedonians' support while making mileage out of his refusal of similar help from Corinth.[33] Two factors may account for Paul's choice at Corinth. First, he seemed to trust his discernment of the motives of givers. The Corinthian responses no doubt endorsed his initial suspicions. Second, he may have refused to take support from any group where he was actually working at the time. While he no doubt accepted individual patronage, such as that of Lydia while in Philippi (Acts 16:15; Rom 16:1-2), he may have only taken the support of an *ekklēsia* while he was operating at *another* location.[34] If so, he seemed to avoid becoming ensnared in the conventions of reciprocity and deference to patrons. His experience at Corinth would confirm this strategy.

In an extensive though not unchallenged study.[35] Hock has gone a long way toward capturing the social realities of Paul's labor and ministry. It is worth quoting at length:[36]

---

[32]Quite possibly, Paul was trying to cut off similar accusations when he commended the labors and integrity of Timothy, Titus, Epaphroditus and others (2 Cor 8:16-24; 12:18; Phil 2:18-30; Col 4:13).

[33]1 Cor 9:3-18; 2 Cor 11:7-12; 12:14-18.

[34]I offer this as a suggestion only. The available evidence is admittedly inconclusive. I *am* convinced that the usual scenario for Paul was not the standard evangelical assumption of "full-time paid ministry." For a full discussion of Paul's entourage and means of support, see Edwin Judge, "The Early Christians as a Scholastic Community: Part II," *Journal of Religious History* 1 (1960): 128–36.

[35]Hock's emphasis on the workshop as the site of Paul's ministry has been challenged by Bradley Blue, "Acts and the House Church," in Gill and Gempf, *Graeco-Roman Setting*, pp. 172–73. Blue notes that Acts portrays Paul as spending considerable time in synagogues or other public venues. We should also note that Paul often taught from private homes, as Blue points out in other contexts. It seems that Hock may have overstated Paul's proximity to the workshop. However, the heart of his argument still holds: (1) scholars have ignored this aspect of Paul's life, and especially its impact on his thought; (2) Paul spent large amounts of time working, enough for this to be a major aspect of his self-understanding; (3) his work was arduous; and (4) it was humiliating to him, at least insofar as he had to endure the judgments of those persons of means among his *ekklēsiai* who had no need to labor.

[36]Paul was not unique in making a point of his labors and financial independence (cf. Dio Chrysostom *Orations* 103-53). The philosophers debated the question of support but generally reasoned very differently than Paul. They were concerned to preserve individual superiority and dignity. For surveys of the evidence, see Hock *(Social Context)* and Malherbe *(Paul and the Thessalonians,* pp. 18–20). Hock makes the point that Paul's attitudes toward labor and his actual practice are

Far from being at the periphery of his life, Paul's tent-making was actually central to it. More than any of us has supposed, Paul was *Paul the Tentmaker*. His trade occupied much of his time—from the years of his apprenticeship through the years of his life as a missionary of Christ, from before daylight through most of the day. Consequently, his trade in large measure determined his daily experiences and his social status. His life was very much that of the workshop—of artisan-friends like Aquila, Barnabas, and perhaps Jason; of leather, knives, and awls; of wearying toil; of being bent over a work-bench like a slave and of working side by side with slaves; of thereby being perceived by others and by himself as slavish and humiliated; of suffering the artisans' lack of status and so being reviled and abused. Paul's trade also provided him with his principal means of livelihood though never with enough to make him anything but a poor man and sometimes not even with that much, so that hunger and thirst and cold were at times his lot. His trade also may have served directly in his missionary activities in the sense that workshop conversations with fellow workers, customers, or those who stopped by might easily have turned into occasions for informal evangelization. Finally, his trade was taken up into his apostolic self-understanding, so much so that, when criticized for plying his trade, he came to understand himself as the apostle who offered the message free of charge.[37]

These social realities made Paul's labor and teaching mutually explanatory. Those he taught in daylight hours were likely to have enough financial security to live without personal labor. In other words, he worked to teach those who didn't have to work.[38] This disparity formed part of the deep anguish in his lists of hardship.[39] Paul's labors supplied his financial needs but cost him dearly in the process. The impact of this social humiliation on his sense of self should not be overlooked. Chris Forbes relates this experience of social shame to his exercise of authority:

> That Paul should "boast of (his) weaknesses" is a quite extraordinary paradox. . . . Yet it is clear that in this paradox Paul is saying fundamental things about the nature of his understanding of both apostolic authority and life "in Christ" generally. For Paul apostolic authority is the authority of the Gospel itself, mediated through the apostle. Since the Gospel is the message of the "foolishness" and "weakness" of God himself (1 Cor 1:18-25), the apostle, if he is such at all, embodies that foolishness and weakness.[40]

This recalls some aspects of our earlier discussion of leadership. Paul understood that his message disallowed any elitist model of leadership. His experience of manual labor and social humiliation lay behind his choice of the laborer as his

---

illumined more by contemporary Graeco-Roman evidence than by the older scholarly opinion that his labor was an aspect of his Pharisaic self-understanding and practice.

[37]Hock, *Social Context,* pp. 67–68, his emphasis.

[38]Ibid., pp. 52–61.

[39]1 Cor 4:10-13; 2 Cor 6:5, 8-13; 11:27; 12:13.

[40]Chris Forbes, "Comparison, Self-praise and Irony: Paul's Boasting and Conventions in Hellenistic Rhetoric," *New Testament Studies* 32 (1986): 22.

most distinctive image for leadership. His own experience of giving up the marks of leadership had shaped this inversion of the normal marks of authority. For Paul, authority was a personally earned respect arising within relationships. Thus he would not encroach on another's work (Rom 15:20). At the same time, he refused to acknowledge the authority of those who had no claim to have walked with him or with his *ekklēsiai* for the sake of the gospel. It did not matter whether they carried the impressive credentials of Jerusalem or of the sophistic super-apostles.

The Freedom of Slavery to All

Paul was loath to tolerate any undue obligation to Jerusalem or to any of his *ekklēsiai*. He believed this would restrict his message and movements and hinder his mission. He guarded his freedom jealously. Yet freedom for Paul did not mean throwing off all obligation and authority. He felt obligated to make Christ known to all his hearers without partiality as to race or social position. This obligation and freedom forms part of his imitation of the dying and rising of Christ. He freely chose to "die" with Christ in order that those without hope might hear his message, believe, and so "rise" with Christ.

The dynamics of slavery-freedom and dying-rising were not academic for Paul. They took shape in his social experiences. Paul had laid aside his considerable Jewish prestige in order to know Christ. He often refused to trade on his social standing with potential benefactors and patrons as he traveled from city to city. He crossed traditional social boundaries. No longer accepting the scruples of Jewish and Graeco-Roman religious and cultural conventions, he believed he could operate in many contexts without raising questions of conscience. He would conform or innovate according to the circumstances. So he refused to act as a sophist, but he was open to eating with Gentiles. He could operate under the law or apart from it. He could live as a Jew or as a Gentile.

Paul summed this up as being free to "become all things to all men so that by all possible means I might save some" (1 Cor 9:22). Paul understood that "in Christ, one is free to become *as* anyone."[41] In other words, he was free to adopt the unnecessary and binding restrictions of others' scruples in order to make Christ known to them. He could also appear scandalously free to those of an opposing religious or cultural group. Beneath this vacillation between freedom and obligation, he accepted a basic social weakness as an ongoing and nonnegotiable obligation in imitation of the dying and rising of Christ. He refused to grasp at his own rights.[42]

---

[41]Barbara Hall, "All Things to All People: A Study of 1 Corinthians 9:19-23," in *The Conversation Continues*, ed. R. T. Fortna and B. R. Gaventa (Nashville: Abingdon, 1990), p. 152.

[42]Although not in every circumstance; cf. Acts 16:37; 25:10.

There is no formula to this paradox so central in all his labors. When his hearers responded in faith, he not only worked to assure them of their new freedom but also suggested that they imitate his own radical self-denial.

The Shape of Dying to Rise

Paul exposed himself as a man possessed. His dogged insistence on the centrality and sufficiency of Christ bore out the drama of his conversion. His previous confidence had been utterly dislodged, and in its place he worshiped Christ and placed his faith in the scandalous events of the Messiah's self-sacrifice. The law had run its course. He would not set aside grace to appease those who wished to retain and revive the law. At stake, he believed, was hard-won freedom.

What Paul offered was neither abstract nor idealized. He gave voice to a relationship. We watch a man gripped and transformed, a man engaged and passionate. He suffered and hoped. He walked the cities and country roads of the empire bearing the shame of a crucified Jewish messiah. He labored long hours for little pay, often to teach those who had no need or inclination to work. He worried, he wrote, and he prayed. He was constantly reflecting and learning, yet he had no time for abstraction. He was gripped by the possibilities of the present moment and of the next. He showed remarkable insight. He was capable both of subtle and perplexing paradox and of tight turns of argument. He gives the impression of working out his thought on the run with both remarkable clarity and surprisingly little formulae. He was admired, scorned and misunderstood.

Paul was determined to form the image of Christ in his converts, yet he formulated little by way of precept for them. He rejected the conventions of prestige and was ostracized as an embarrassment. He repudiated the reality of local idols and was run out of town. He proclaimed the impartial call of God to all people and styled himself a slave and a common laborer. He labored to present his *ekklēsiai* strong and mature, while he defended the weak. He proclaimed his message with authority as the words of God, not men, but he looked to his converts for mutual encouragement. He trumpeted the humiliated and exalted Christ, but he refused his own rights. This was the living shape of a new way.

14

FRAMES FOR
NEW COMMUNITY

PAUL'S MESSAGE HAD A PROFOUND SOCIAL IMPACT IN HIS OWN LIFETIME. NEW GROUPS formed without respect to the marks of rank and status. Paul strongly opposed both Jews and Gentiles who sought to maintain these conventions within the *ekklēsiai*. As noted earlier, Paul was savage on status, while conceding the pragmatic necessity of rank and its obligations. To be sure, Paul urged the *ekklēsiai* to uphold good order in the family and to obey the civil authority structures as in some sense God-given.[1] Yet though he had no agenda to transform Graeco-Roman society, he clearly sensed the broad social implications of his message. Whatever he could see at the time, his life and thought was to become "a paradigm of change, a source of social tensions both ancient and modern."[2]

Ancient Assemblies and New Communities
According to Paul, the message had created a new people of God gathered together in community. This was not unanticipated. In its simple household-based meetings, each *ekklēsia* expressed a tapestry of history, promise and hope. This included the great assemblies of Israel's past and the prophets' promises of an assembly of renewed people at the day of God. But the appeal was not all Jewish. The *ekklēsia* also fitted the hopes for community expressed

---

[1]Rom 13:1-7; Col 3:18—4:1; Tit 3:1-2.
[2]Peter Marshall, *The Enigmatic Apostle—Paul and Social Change: Did Paul Seek to Change Graeco-Roman Society?* (Melbourne: ITIM, 1993), p. 40.

in many Graeco-Roman clubs and in the common ideals of the city.

Paul's use of the term *ekklēsia* for the new communities linked to each of these themes. First, the term could apply to any gathering of people, including an assembly of citizens for some formal purpose.[3] It carried no religious connotations. Second, according to Judge, "great theoretical significance might be attached" to these assemblies.[4] As we will note later, the contemporary use of the term *ekklēsia* allowed an association between the actual gathering of Christians and the ideals of the Graeco-Roman *polis* (roughly, the city). Third, the Greek translation of the Old Testament, the Septuagint, occasionally used *ekklēsia* to translate the Hebrew term *qahal* used of some of Israel's most memorable mass assemblies. Those familiar with the Septuagint, therefore, could link their simple dinner parties to the great assemblies and feasts of God's ancient people.[5]

Whatever importance the *term* held for Paul, his understanding of the gathering drew deeply from his heritage in the Jewish Scriptures. He understood the new people of God as being drawn from all nations to fulfill the ancient promises made to Abraham (Gal 3:6—4:31). Paul framed these broad hopes for the people of God within a pattern of creation and re-creation. For Paul the *ekklēsia* was the model of the new humanity who wait to inherit a new creation. They are the people of the second Adam, the man from heaven who gives the Spirit.[6] Those "in Christ" had taken their place in heaven with him and thus belonged to the "Jerusalem above."[7]

Graeco-Roman Desires for Community and the Shape of the *ekklēsia*

Paul's innovations marked a decisive break with the patterns and conventions of Graeco-Roman and Jewish moral tradition. They also departed from contemporary social structures. At the same time, certain aspects of Paul's *ekklēsiai* fitted the desires of Graeco-Roman urban dwellers.

---

[3] E.g., Acts 19:39.

[4] Edwin Judge, "Contemporary Political Models for the Inter-relations of the New Testament Churches," *Reformed Theological Review* 22 (1963): 74.

[5] It is important to stress that this significance attached to the actual gathering or group who gathered, not to any ideal or abstracted entity such as a so-called universal church. Edwin Judge's caution in this regard remains valid: "The difficulty found by New Testament lexicographers in allotting the instances of the term to the two categories 'local church' and 'whole church' suggests that the categories are themselves false. . . . We must ask whether even the most all-embracing claims made by St. Paul for the church are not being made with nothing more in mind than the church he happens to be addressing, and, of course, each other of the multiplicity of churches in its turn. Or, to put the matter positively, we should expect quite plain verbal indications before accepting the view that he has at any point translated the term from its concrete sense to some supernal parallel" ("Contemporary Political Models," pp. 74–75).

[6] Rom 8:18-25; 1 Cor 15:20-57.

[7] Gal 4:25-27; Eph 2:5-6; 1:3; Phil 3:20; Col 1:13; 3:1-4; cf. Heb 12:18-24.

The social structure of the Hellenistic cities revolved around three overlapping institutions: household, club and citizenship. Each institution was very old. Aristotle had argued that man was a threefold being: political, familial and communal. By the Graeco-Roman era these had become three social spheres: the household, the small republican state and unofficial associations.[8] Much of the dynamic of first-century life came from the rivalry between these institutions: patriarchal household *versus* democratic ideals *versus* money and blood. The right to form clubs had been crucial in breaking the dominant place of the household in Greek society. These groups catered to a need for *koinōnia* (fellowship) that the households and republic could not meet.

Paul's *ekklēsiai* were simple gatherings of friends and acquaintances for a meal based on the patronage of one or more households.[9] While some *ekklēsiai* may have occurred in more public locations, they were mostly attached to households.[10] Several house *ekklēsiai* may have existed in the larger cities like Corinth. Many probably formed along occupational lines as did other associations.[11] Most likely, the *ekklēsiai* gathered in larger meetings from time to time.[12] The smaller home-based *ekklēsiai* remained the most frequent and influential meetings. These simple dinner parties became charged with the Jewish significance of the commonwealth of heaven and the new creation. Robert Banks believes this cluster of ideas was tailor-made for this context. His insights are worth quoting at length:

> Comparison of Paul's understanding of *ekklēsia* with the intellectual and social climate of his day emphasizes both the comprehensiveness of his idea and its appropriateness for his times. Attention has already been drawn to three aspects in the contemporary scene that were particularly significant: those aspirations for a universal fraternity which captivated the minds of educated Greeks and Romans and devout Jewish leaders; the significance of the household as a place in which personal identity and intimacy could be found; the quest for community and immortality pursued through membership in various voluntary and religious associations. In a quite

---

[8]Edwin Judge, *The Social Pattern of the Christian Groups in the First Century* (London: Tyndale Press, 1960). Judge's documentation of this schema as an interpretative model for Paul's groups subsequently became a benchmark for studies in the social history of Paul and his *ekklēsiai*.

[9]For the archaeological evidence for these house *ekklēsiai*, including the size of meeting areas, possible group numbers, socioeconomic position of the patrons/home owners, and the later rise of formalized sanctuaries, see Bradley Blue, "Acts and the House Church," in *The Book of Acts in Its First Century Setting*, vol. 2, *Graeco-Roman Setting*, ed. D. W. J. Gill and C. Gempf (Grand Rapids, Mich.: Eerdmans; and Carlisle: Paternoster, 1994), pp. 119–222.

[10]Acts 2:46; 1 Cor 16:19; Col 4:15; Philem 2.

[11]Robert Banks, *Paul's Idea of Community: The Early House Churches in their Historical Setting* (Sydney: Lancer; and Grand Rapids, Mich.: Eerdmans, 1980), pp. 37–40. See also Earle Ellis, *Pauline Theology: Ministry and Society* (Grand Rapids, Mich.: Eerdmans, 1989), pp. 135–38.

[12]Rom 16:23; 1 Cor 14:23.

remarkable way, Paul's idea of *ekklēsia* managed to encompass all three: 1. It is a voluntary association, with regular gatherings of a relatively small group of like-minded people. 2. It has its roots in, and takes some of the character of, the household unit. 3. These small local churches were invested with a supra-national and supra-temporal significance. They were taught to regard themselves as the visible manifestation of a universal and eternal commonwealth in which men could be citizens.[13]

Banks continues:

Only Paul's understanding of *ekklēsia* embraces all three ideas of community to which people gave their commitment in the ancient world at the time. This means that, psychologically speaking, Paul's approach had a decided advantage over its first century competitors, since it offered so much more than any of them and offered things which elsewhere could only be found by adhering to more than one religious group. Sociologically, the distinctive element in Paul's conception was its combination of all three models of community. I am not suggesting that Paul systematically related each of these models, or even consciously viewed his idea as the fulfillment of contemporary striving, merely that his view was conceptually richer and more socially relevant than others advanced in his day. In all this, by his use of the quite ordinary term for assembling in the ancient world (*ekklēsia*) and by his setting such gatherings in ordinary homes rather than cultic places, Paul shows that he does not wish to mark off his gatherings from the ordinary meetings in which others, including church members, were engaged. . . . Paul did not see such gatherings as more religious in character than any other activity in which Christians were involved.[14]

It is important to clarify how Paul's idea of *ekklēsia* related to the heavenly commonwealth and the somewhat parallel images in Graeco-Roman thought. When Paul spoke of the "people of God" (Rom 9:25-26), he undoubtedly had in mind a wider group of people than a specific gathering. But he did not use *ekklēsia* in this way. Nor were the local gatherings a "*part* of the heavenly one any more than they are a part of any alleged universal church."[15] All the significance that had become associated with the *ekklēsia* attached to *each individual group of believers as they gathered*. Paul did not move by analogy from the idea of common membership in the heavenly assembly to suggest that local assemblies should be bound together by an organizational framework. Their common loyalty to Christ and to one another led them to pray for each other; to exchange greetings, letters and gifts; and to commission others to join Paul's traveling circle.[16] But these intimate bonds were not formalized by any constitutional framework. Paul knew nothing of a so-called universal church.

---

[13]Banks, *Paul's Idea of Community*, p. 49.
[14]Ibid., pp. 49–50.
[15]Ibid., p. 47.
[16]Rom 16:1; 2 Cor 8:11-14; 4:16; 13:13.

The Centrality of the Meal and Conversation

A new humanity was understood by Paul to be emerging in the fledgling *ekklēsiai*. In these communities, the power of the Spirit transformed relationships, bringing new patterns of thought and behavior in keeping with the members' new identity and the new "law of love." Paul understood that the transforming power of Christ was most at work in the relationships of those who gathered. Their relationships proved the effectiveness of Christ's work on their behalf. Those in the *ekklēsia* ought to identify strongly with one another, support those who struggle, and ensure the strengthening of all. This was the acid test of love: to drop prestige and self-interest for the well-being of those for whom Christ had died.[17]

As we have often noted, Paul nowhere made this point more forcefully than to the factious Corinthians. In a careful study of 1 Corinthians 8—10, Barbara Hall brings out Paul's even-handedness toward the "strong" and the "weak."[18] The strong must recognize their responsibility to the weak. The weak must do likewise. Paul was not arguing for a balanced or middle position. According to Hall, he urged something far more demanding:

> Paul does not take the side of one group against the other, nor does he try to resolve the problem once and for all. Certainly, he does not enunciate a general principle and then apply it to this specific issue. He works instead on relationships. He asks something of both groups which he hopes will make it possible for all of them to move forward together. Paul does not ask or expect everyone to agree. What he asks, rather, is that those on each side identify with those on the other side, to become *as* the ones with whom they disagree. They are not initially required to change their convictions; they are to act on behalf of those with whom they disagree. Paul knows that this is a difficult and complicated thing to do. It is, however, necessary if the eschatological community is to exhibit and proclaim the new creation, even as its members take diverse paths of obedience.[19]

Unity took on a very different meaning for Paul than the prevailing mood of upholding social order. First, unity was an established reality founded on the work of Christ—they *were* united. Second, it was an ongoing influence of the Spirit—who *kept* them united. Third, it was a matter for diligence—they needed to value and protect this unity. Paul was conscious of the impact of discord on the *ekklēsia* and of its likely consequences should it spill over into the public

---

[17]Rom 15:1-3, Phil 2:1-5.
[18]Barbara Hall, "All Things to All People: A Study of 1 Corinthians 9:19-23," in *The Conversation Continues*, ed. R. T. Fortna and B. R. Gaventa (Nashville: Abingdon, 1990), pp. 137–57.
[19]Ibid., p. 153.

arena.[20] He was aware that each *ekklēsia* might uncritically mirror the conventions of Graeco-Roman urban life. It was therefore critical to help them see through these conventions. Hence Paul called for a deep knowledge and discernment about the purpose and character of the gathering.[21]

Why *did* the *ekklēsia* gather? Most evangelicals, and indeed Christians of nearly all persuasions, traditionally answer that churches meet for worship. Paul's consistent answer was "to build each other up."[22] The members met to use their personal endowments from the Spirit for the common good. They prayed, read Scripture, encouraged, sang, taught, and prophesied to one another as the Spirit enabled them.[23] Paul *never* defined *ekklēsia* in terms of a vertical relationship of worship. The meeting was for *one another*. The gathering was a *conversation*—a rich, diverse, extended conversation. Robert Banks writes:

> According to Paul's understanding, participation in the community centred primarily around *fellowship*, expressed in word and deed, of the members with God and one another. It demonstrates concretely the already-experienced reconciliation between the individual and God and the individual and his fellow-men: the gifts and fruit of the Spirit being the instruments through which this is expressed and deepened. This means that the focal point of reference was neither a book nor a rite but *a set of relationships*, and that God communicated himself to them not primarily through the written word and tradition, or mystical experience and cultic activity, but *through one another*.[24]

The meal at the heart of the gathering clearly expressed the centrality of relationships in the *ekklēsia* and the corresponding rejection of religious and social prestige. The meal was not a cultic ritual in terms recognizable to Greeks and Romans. It seems that the Christians adopted the standard Jewish practice of commencing their meal by sharing bread and ending it by drinking wine. They would also pray at both the beginning and the end of the meal. In this regard, no outsider familiar with Jewish custom would have noticed anything unusual. The proceedings also fell somewhat within the expectations of a non-Jewish outsider, though the whole affair would have seemed grossly inadequate from a religious point of view. The meeting would have failed the expectations of both Jewish and Gentile observers.[25]

---

[20]In this respect, Paul mirrored the concerns of the philosophers (e.g., Dio Chrysostom *Orations* 39.3). See Bruce Winter, *Seek the Welfare of the City: Christians as Benefactors and Citizens*, First Century Christians in the Graeco-Roman World 1 (Exeter: Paternoster; and Grand Rapids, Mich.: Eerdmans, 1994), pp. 85–96.

[21]E.g., 1 Cor 11—14; Eph 4.

[22]1 Cor 14:26; Eph 4:11-16; cf. Rom 15:2; 1 Cor 3:10-17.

[23]1 Cor 12:4-6; 14:26; Eph 4:11-16; Col 3:15-16.

[24]Banks, *Paul's Idea of Community*, p. 111, emphasis his.

[25]For an engaging reconstruction of these early home meetings, see Robert Banks, *Going to Church in the First Century: An Eyewitness Account* (Sydney: Hexagon, 1985).

Paul expected the *ekklēsia* to disregard social distinctions and to honor the less honorable.[26] This advice must not be intellectualized. It involved inverting the normal conventions of honor. Paul expected them to break with the normal convention of allocating food and seating according to status (1 Cor 11:17-22, 33-34). He expected Greeks and Jews, citizens and noncitizens, slaves, owners and freedmen to dine together without regard for positions of honor. A man of means might take a lowly place at the meal, perhaps even serve his slave or children. All of this was scandalous by normal community standards. There were prayers, singing and conversations about God and the world, but no priest presided. Hosts and regulars saw great significance in their eating and drinking. They spoke openly of the death and resurrection of Jesus, of how he had given his life for theirs and of how they would eat with him one day. The meal expressed the solidarity and intimacy of the group and formed a focus for their conversation.

This engagement with one another and the constant concern about compromise with the world's patterns partly explains the strong intellectual life among the communities. Participants in each *ekklēsia* had to grapple with ongoing challenges of making sense of their lives in the light of the story of Jesus Christ. Each community was an informal learning network.[27] Their well-being required them to remain open to the learning that the Spirit would bring to bear through their conversations and care for one another and their interactions within the wider society. Paul Sampley gives voice to the vitality of this arrangement:

> It is no wonder Paul's communities had such a liveliness: each individual counted, yet the community's well-being was always valued. The community is supposed to provide a vibrant, supportive, and corrective context for the maximum development of the individual, and the individual is supposed to contribute to and care for the common good. Little wonder that the pot almost boiled over from time to time. It is a delicate balance—maximizing individual expression and development on the one hand and community well-being on the other—but its power may lie precisely in its frailty and vulnerability.[28]

It is timely to reflect on this vitality for our own contexts. This description of Paul's communities bears little resemblance to what most of us have known as church. The conventions of preaching and church services effectively gag our conversations. There is no meal. Spontaneity is avoided, absent or slotted into five- or ten-minute "greeting" or "sharing" segments, small conversational digressions

---

[26]Rom 12:3-4, 16; 1 Cor 12:21; Gal 3:28.

[27]See Marshall (*Enigmatic Apostle*, p. 36), who built on the insight of Judge, "Contemporary Political Models."

[28]J. Paul Sampley, *Walking Between the Times: Paul's Moral Reasoning* (Philadelphia: Fortress, 1991), pp. 118–19.

from the main performance led from the front. We endorse the need for "sharing" but locate it away from "real church." In a sad irony of Paul's meals, we speak of coming to church to be "fed." In our case, the "meal" is usually a course of words prepared by one chef rather than the smorgasbord of rich conversation.

The Reframing of Human Relations

Paul's *ekklēsiai* included those of means and social standing. Those of lower position were included by their links to the extended households of the better off.[29] This social mixture brought vitality: "What set the Christians apart was their bringing together within the same fellowship people who were bound to see life differently."[30] When we add Paul's rejection of the marks of status to the unconventional diversity of the gatherings, we begin to see a living experiment in the reframing of human relations.

At times Paul was supported by patrons. He therefore had personal experience of the Graeco-Roman conventions of friendship and its obligations. Yet he avoided the notion and its terminology, and he placed no great value on patronal relations. Instead, his favorite social vocabulary came from the worlds of labor and subordination. He called himself a servant and his associates, including his patrons, fellow laborers, not friends.[31] Edwin Judge notes that Paul sought to "escape the traps of superiority and inferiority by a total subjection of all to a common master who stands above all." Each believer "was given some gift of the Spirit, some endowment by God."[32] This endowment bound the community together as each individual used his or her gifts for the development of the others.[33]

This creative social experiment reworked the conventions of beneficence, honor and reciprocity.[34] Members could still be honored for their labors and their position in society,[35] but not to imitate or reinforce the system of benefactions that maintained rank and social order. This system depended on three practices: (1) main-

---

[29]See Judge, *Social Pattern*, pp. 35–39. See also Wayne Meeks, *The First Urban Christians: The Social World of the Apostle Paul* (New Haven, Conn.: Yale University Press, 1983), pp. 29–31.

[30]R. M. Kidd, *Wealth and Beneficence in the Pastoral Epistles,* Society of Biblical Literature Dissertation Series 122 (Atlanta: Scholars Press, 1990), p. 68.

[31]E.g., Rom 1:1; 16:1, 3, 9, 12, 21.

[32]Edwin Judge, "St. Paul as a Radical Critic of Society," *Interchange* 16 (1975): 197.

[33]Rom 12:3-8; 1 Cor 12:1-31. Robert Banks notes that while the body metaphor was widely used, "Paul was apparently the first to apply it to a community *within* the larger community of the state, and to the *personal* responsibilities of people for one another rather than for more external duties" (*Paul's Idea of Community*, p. 70).

[34]See James Harrison, "Paul's Language of Grace *(charis)* in its Graeco-Roman Context" (Ph.D. diss., Macquarie University, Sydney, 1998), forthcoming from Tübingen in the Wissenschaftliche Untersuchungen zum Neuen Testament series.

[35]Rom 16:1-2; 1 Tim 5:1-8.

taining personal honor before peers, (2) promoting competition for honor between peers, and (3) maintaining the elite as ideals for imitation. Paul presented Christ as the benefactor who voluntarily impoverished himself without reserve, even to the loss of his own status and honors.[36] The *ekklēsiai* accordingly were taught to give the greater honor to those without (social) honor. Paul also exhorted the wealthy in the *ekklēsiai* to maintain their benefactions, and the less so to labor with their own hands rather than to stay dependent on charity: "As a result, they would be liberated from the tyranny of maintaining and reciprocating honour."[37] Paul's message attributed the common terms of honor found on the inscriptions (honor, glory, righteousness and faith) to *all* within the *ekklēsia*. This democratization of the system must have appealed to those of marginalized social status.[38] The hallmark of maturity, then, was to discern one's own gifting and to exercise this to the common good without thought for comparison or reciprocity. The only enduring debt now was to love (Rom 12:3-4).

Paul's rejection of social elitism was part of a strategy to ensure that life in the *ekklēsia* was not structured by the constraints of moral conventions or law, whether Jewish or Graeco-Roman.[39] While giving high regard to the law of Israel, he argued that its time had passed. The law itself was good, but the experience of living under it created self-righteousness and abject guilt (Rom 7:7-25). The immediacy of the Spirit now gave the believers what they could not have known through the law (Gal 3:1-5). Paul located all behavior as a response to the dying and rising of Christ arising from the inner person without external compulsion. This is the sense of the "law of Christ" (Gal 6:2); not a substitute for the law, but the replacement of the shadow of law by the immediacy of Christ and the Spirit (Gal 5:1-6). The *ekklēsia* must now walk in the new way of the Spirit, not along the old paths of the written code.[40]

This realignment of social behavior was critical. In Paul's estimation, the free-

---

[36]2 Cor 8:9; Phil 2:6-8.

[37]James Harrison, "Ethical Motivation and Reward in the Honorific Inscriptions and the New Testament" (unpublished manuscript, 1995), p. 24.

[38]Ibid., p. 22

[39]Paul's understanding of the Jewish law and its relationship to his message has long been a subject of controversy. The exchange has been particularly framed in the last two decades by the numerous publications of Paul Sanders and James Dunn. Sanders argued that Judaism's problem with Paul was not about the historical priority of grace but about Paul's emphasis on the primacy of Christ. Dunn locates Paul's problem about "justification by works of the law" in the context of his rejection of the nationalism inherent in Judaism. Both agree that first-century Judaism has been unfairly and unhistorically typecast as excessively legalistic. In the broadest terms, both perspectives are helpful: Paul *was* dogged in emphasizing Christ, and he *did* oppose all attempts to orient his message to Jewish mores.

[40]Rom 8:1-4; Gal 5:16-18; Phil 3:3.

dom of the message was hampered whenever elitism and law (whether Jewish or Graeco-Roman) remained at work in the *ekklēsia*. Paul desired for them an unhindered experience of their true freedom—freedom *from* deceptive paradigms, and freedom *to* forsake their own rights in service of one another.[41] This freedom went with the confidence and assurance of those who saw themselves through the merits of Jesus Christ. Here, Paul argued, there was freedom from fear and the drive for self-justification.[42] Here personal transformation could proceed without the constraints and agendas of self-interest, status-seeking and personal development.

The Reframing of Leadership

There was no longer any room for individual superiority where each believer found his or her righteousness in Christ. Nothing in the *ekklēsia* was the peculiar domain of any person. There were no cultic acts to be performed by any consecrated or appointed person. There was no ordination. There was no room for personal power or office. Edwin Judge's assessment goes further: "Nor surely is there any ideal or notion of leadership."[43] While the Corinthians pushed Paul to assume the role and social presence of a leader, he pushed in the opposite direction, making servile labor the dominant image for every expression of talent and role.[44]

Chris Forbes's study of prophecy in Paul and Graeco-Roman literature underscores this point. He argues that the shift of social context from Graeco-Roman divination and cult to Christian gathering fundamentally altered the role of the prophet: "No longer is he the independent figure of power. Now he is one member among many in a community in which all have the same Spirit—and potentially the same gifts—as he has. He has no specialist skills, and no particular privileges beyond a hearing—a critical one—in the gathering of the community. Thus is the power of the prophet/miracle-worker subordinated to the good of the community."[45]

---

[41]Gal 4:8-10; 5:1-11; 1 Cor 10:31—11:1.

[42]Wayne Meeks (*First Urban Christians*, pp. 180–92) provides a stimulating discussion of the interplay of several of Paul's metaphors for the accomplishments of Christ: bondage-liberation (redemption, adoption, inheritance); guilt-justification (righteousness); estrangement-reconciliation (peace, unity); deformity-transformation. He sets each within its social contexts and argues that these aspects of his message were not abstract axioms or so-called timeless truths but were provocative and enduring images of entering into a new life while ensconced within the social structures.

[43]Judge, "Contemporary Political Models," p. 197.

[44]On the broad topic of the contrast between leadership in the society and in the *ekklēsia* (at Corinth), see A. D. Clarke, *Secular and Christian Leadership in Corinth: A Socio-Historical and Exegetical Study of 1 Corinthians 1-6* (Leiden: E. J. Brill, 1993).

[45]Chris Forbes, "Prophecy and Inspired Speech in Early Christianity and Its Hellenistic Environment" (Ph.D. diss., Macquarie University, Sydney, 1987), p. 379.

The personnel of Paul's mission seem to fall into two overlapping circles. First, some remained more or less continually in one location, either as indigenous dwellers or as immigrants.[46] For the most part, "leadership" in the *ekklēsia* would simply be an extension of the role of patron exercised by the head of the household where they met.[47] At other times Paul ensured that some (additional?) believers would shoulder this responsibility.[48] Second, there was a smaller, more mobile group. Paul frequently referred to this group as his colaborers or "the brothers" to whom he attached considerable importance and affection.

Women played a significant role among both circles, apparently without restriction to the character or extent of their ministry.[49] Paul's only concern was that wives maintain the generally accepted decorum of marriage both in public life and within the *ekklēsia*. Thus a wife was not to judge her husband's prophecies nor publicly to admonish or exercise authority over him.[50] This presented no barrier to full verbal participation by wives in all manner of ministry and gifts, but only a call for social decorum.

In our own day Paul's instructions concerning women are fiercely debated among evangelical scholars and clergy. However, the whole debate is premised on notions of leadership and ordination that cannot be found in Paul or the rest of the New Testament. Given the ways Paul repudiated the conventions of leadership, the argument should not be about whether women should be ordained, but about why *anyone* should be. But as we will explore in later chapters, the debate is not and never has been about theology or exegesis. The whole debate is framed by men's need to maintain power and control within the systems of church and theological leadership. All of this simply perpetuates the Corinthians' desire for the marks of rank and prestige,

---

[46]Phil 1:1; 1 Thess 5:12; 1 Tim 5:17-20; see also Acts 20:17, 27-31.

[47]Rom 16:1-2, 3-5, 10; see also 1 Tim 3:4-5. On Phoebe's role as a patron *(prostatis)* of Paul and the *ekklēsia*, see Edwin Judge, "The Early Christians as a Scholastic Community: Part II," *Journal of Religious History* 1 (1960): 128–30, and "Cultural Conformity and Innovation in Paul: Some Clues from Contemporary Documents," *Tyndale Bulletin* 35 (1984): 16–23. Paul's description of Phoebe as a *diakonos* identified her as part of his retinue of co-workers. The modern ecclesiastical debates over women's ministry miss Paul's point in both directions: Phoebe certainly *was* the patron-leader of an *ekklēsia*, yet this did not warrant "ordination" to ecclesiastical office, a concept totally foreign to Paul.

[48]Tit 1:5; see also Acts 20:17-35.

[49]Ellis, *Pauline Theology*. On the importance of women colleagues to Paul in his imprisonments (2 Tim 1:16), see Brian Rapske, "The Importance of Helpers to the Imprisoned Paul in the Book of Acts," *Tyndale Bulletin* 42 (1991): 3–30. On their vital role in continuing his nurture of the *ekklēsiai*, see Abraham Malherbe, *Paul and the Thessalonians: The Philosophic Tradition of Pastoral Care* (Philadelphia: Fortress, 1987), pp. 62–68.

[50]1 Cor 14:29-35; 1 Tim 2:11-12. I understand the two most debated passages to refer to a husband and wife in their specific relationship, not to men and women generically (Ellis, *Pauline Theology*, pp. 65–86).

and it is a far cry from Paul's remarkable innovation and courage.

Paul's letters provide no model of church structure or lines of authority. He has no "doctrine" of church or leadership. A common evangelical response to church difficulties is to tighten leadership authority and permission, ironically often justified by an appeal to Paul. This is a serious misrepresentation of Paul, who did not appeal to leaders to solve the thorny and nearly intractable problems of the Galatians or Corinthians. Paul always maintained a high regard for the competence of each member of the respective *ekklēsiai* to work things out. He called them to live up to what they already possessed, and he spelled out at length God's gifting of them through the Spirit.[51] One might imagine a certain inclination on Paul's part—especially in the case of the Corinthians—to impose order by way of code or leadership. Instead, he trod the risky path of emphasizing their possession of the Spirit and personal gifting. What they lacked, Paul implied, was sensitivity to pursue the well-being of each other.[52]

Paul avoided the vocabulary of leadership, preferring to use metaphors of service and care from work and the household. At Corinth, an *ekklēsia* marked by a fascination with power and authority, there were some who belonged to the ruling classes (*sophia*, wisdom; *dynamis*, influence; *eugenos*, noble birth) (1 Cor 1:26). Their manner of leadership was to control others by virtue of their prestige and talent. Paul dismissed their marks and style of leadership in preference to his own: "We have become the scum of the world. . . . Therefore, I urge you to imitate me" (1 Cor 4:13, 16)! Paul claimed *not* to have lorded over the Corinthians but to have worked *with* them for their joy. As Clarke explains:

> Paul models a paradigm of leadership which he urges the Corinthians to imitate. . . . In distinction to the secular categories of leadership which had been so readily adopted, Paul defines the Christian practice of leadership for them: they are not to rely on boasting or social status to create reputation, not to establish a popular following by recourse to the law-courts, and not to rely on a reputation carved out by oratorical prowess or patronal respect. This constitutes an inverting of the world's views of leadership.[53]

The leadership that Paul endorsed *stopped* the body from centralizing ministry. A leader must ensure that the message and the *ekklēsia* were not taken captive to any special interest group or power base.[54] There must be no centralizing of any activity in the body. Those who fancy themselves as leaders must refuse to take control and must value and preserve the experience of equality that reflected God's

---

[51] 1 Cor 2:9-16; 12:1—14:40; 2 Cor 3:6-18; Gal 3:1-14; 5:13-26.
[52] 1 Cor 12:39—14:21; Gal 5:13-26; cf. Phil 2:1-5.
[53] Clarke, *Secular and Christian Leadership*, p. 125.
[54] 1 Cor 1:10-17; 1 Tim 1:3-4, 18-20; 4:1-6.

impartial kindness. Wayne Meeks links this style of leadership with a new paradigm of authority: "The impression is one of great fluidity, of a complex . . . open-ended process of mutual discipline. Perhaps this fluid structure of authority in some measure expressed the perception, at least for Paul himself, that the crucifixion of the Messiah marked the end of the time when 'the law' shaped the limits of God's people and the beginning of the new age that would yield soon to his Kingdom."[55]

Scholars often presume that 1 and 2 Timothy and Titus portray a later tightening of authority as the Pauline circle drifted from a more open and charismatic leadership. This reconstruction assumes that leadership operates by giving and withholding permission and by regulating decision making. To read the letters to Timothy and Titus alongside the letters of Ignatius of Antioch from the turn of the century is clearly to pull the former back on the side of the apostle. Paul wrote with conviction about the critical links between his coworkers' faithfulness and perseverance and that of the *ekklēsia*. He exhorted them to appoint others to continue this ministry. Neither practice exceeded what Paul had advised in relation to the gatherings at Philippi or Ephesus.[56] The letters to Timothy and Titus are private communications to close associates and coworkers. This alone accounts for many differences in style, tone and vocabulary from the undisputed letters. Paul's exhortations to pay close attention to their teaching came as a response to those who were undermining family and social relationships and the integrity of the message itself.[57] This does not represent a departure from Paul's practice as shown in the undisputed letters.

However we read the differences, real or apparent, between Paul's earlier letters and the so-called pastoral letters, conventional appeals by evangelicals to the latter in support of ordination are entirely out of keeping with Paul's intent and spirit. Like the Reformers, our sixteenth-century forebears, mainstream evangelical church life has never come to grips with the freedom and social radicalism at the heart of Paul's communities. We fear loss of control too greatly. In my own experience, this is as true of charismatic evangelicals as of those who oppose their distinctives. Notwithstanding the many laudable traits of participation and spontaneity, the style of leadership in charismatic churches often has become more hierarchical and manipulative than in mainstream churches. Evangelicalism of all kinds has always stressed the concept of the priesthood of all believers. But that is what it remains—a concept, idea or principle, not a lived reality of a robust grace that liberates and reframes us.

---

[55]Meeks, *First Urban Christians*, p. 139.
[56]Phil 2:19-30; Tit 1:5; Acts 20:17-35.
[57]1 Tim 4:12-16; 2 Tim 2:1; 3:11-12; Tit 2:1; 2:15; cf. 1 Tim 1:3-20; 4:6-7; 2 Tim 3:1-7; 4:3-5; Tit 1:10-16; 3:9-11.

15

THE RHYTHM
OF CONVERSATION

THE RHYTHM OF PAUL'S CHOICES—ALTERNATELY CONFORMING AND INNOVATING—WAS far from easy to pick up. The metaphor is deliberate. Paul was more akin to a jazz musician improvising than to a lawyer or theologian assembling a tight argument or system of thought. There were two aspects to his improvising. First, Paul creatively adapted his message and methods to match new challenges raised by new circumstances. His thinking and practice was *contextual*—shaped by and for each new context. Second, his improvisations were *coherent*—strong patterns and defining experiences linked all that he said and did. This coherence lay in his personal admiration and allegiance to Jesus Christ and in his preoccupation with Christ's dying and rising.

Coherence in Improvisation and Conversation
Paul's ideas, the patterns of his relationships, and his self-understanding form a coherent whole. Every contingency offered him new opportunity to articulate the coherence he saw in the dying and rising of Christ. Each new circumstance recrafted his understanding of Christ (see figure 15.1).

Theology and sermons are built on the distinction between theory and practice, interpretation and application. One interprets first, then applies. But simplistic formulas like these do not do justice to the ways people live and think. Paul is no exception. We must not reduce what he was doing to "applying" the gospel. *Paul*

| Paul's message was fluid but centered | Each circumstance brought opportunity | He improvised to match the message to the context | His understanding grew with each experience |

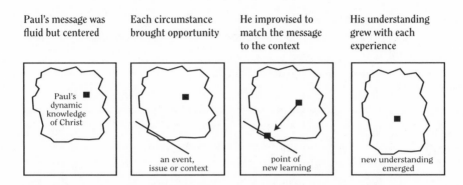

Figure 15.1. Paul recreated the coherence of the message for himself and his *ekklēsiai* in each new contingency

was generating new meaning. The richness of Paul's message—the coherence he found in the dying and rising of Christ—only emerged as Paul was open to the possibilities of changing circumstances.

This dynamic opens three theses regarding grace, improvisation and conversation. First, the dying and rising of Christ gave coherence to Paul's conversations. He taught and modeled the story of Christ as the content and the process of conversation. Each conversation brought grace to some aspect of everyday life, liberating identity, thought and practice from enslaving social conventions and expectations.

Second, the dying and rising of Christ enabled Paul to take significant personal and social risks in engaging fully with people in changing contexts. The conversation was open to all people and ranged across all the topics of everyday life. Grace meant Paul could let go of the need for self-justification, self-protection and the control of others. Grace enabled the vulnerability that opened up space for learning and creative improvisation.

Third, the dying and rising of Christ gave new and varied shape to social relations. Paul taught and personally modeled the freedom of Christ, not the tyranny of ideals and law. The conversation was the means of "coaching" one another in new understandings and expressions of grace and love.

Paul's sense of the coherence in Christ appears throughout his letters. On occasion, he offered explicit statements of Christ's rank and achievements that implied his priority and centrality.[1] These statements identify Christ as the source of Paul's inspiration and the focus of his personal wonder and loyalty. Most of his letters commence with some brief portrait of Christ.[2] These cameos

---

[1]E.g., Rom 5:12-21; 1 Cor 15:20-28; Phil 2:6-11.
[2]Rom 1:1-4; 1 Cor 1:1-9; 2 Cor 1:2-5, 21-22; Gal 1:3-5; Eph 1:3-14; Phil 1:6; Col 1:5, 11-20; 1 Thess 1:9-10; 2 Thess 1:7-10; 2 Tim 1:9-10; Tit 1:1-3.

set the scene in diverse ways for whatever followed.

At times Paul appealed to the coherence of Christ somewhat cryptically, as when he claimed that he had proclaimed "nothing but Christ and him crucified" at Corinth (1 Cor 2:2). Plainly, he did not intend his remark to be taken at face value. Rather, "Christ and him crucified" summarized a way of seeing and speaking which in that letter subverted the elitism and factionalism of the Corinthians. Christ was the unity within the diversity of Paul's thought. The breadth of Paul's thinking spans the character of God and the revelation of his purposes for humanity and history. Paul related every point on this spectrum to Christ, yet he remained for Paul the living Jesus of Nazareth whom he knew and adored, not the "Christ" of Christology.

Like the phrase "in Christ," Paul's image of the dying and rising of Christ linked the historical events of Christ with their loaded personal and social implications.[3] Paul had only to mention the original events to bring immediately into focus a whole range of new patterns of understanding and behavior. Likewise, the pairs that Paul associated with the dying and rising of Christ—weak-strong, suffering-joy, poor-rich, slave-free, clay-treasure, dishonorable-honorable, foolish-wise—were so loaded with the meaning of those events as to call them to mind even where they were not stated explicitly. None of this amounts to a formula.

Improvising and Conversing from the Old Testament

Prior to his conversion, Jerusalem and the law were the chief symbols of coherence in Paul's life and thought. This coherence was fractured irrecoverably by his encounter with Christ on the Damascus road. Paul subsequently relearned his Old Testament. He came to reframe the old cohering symbols in terms of the story of Christ. He did not discard his heritage, but he reframed it in the light of Christ's appearance to him.

This reframing created new patterns for his understanding of the Old Testament. First, the Old Testament remained Paul's primary source for framing the story of Christ. The more he looked at the Old Testament, the more he understood Christ. Second, the coherence he saw in Christ, and which he understood to be grounded in the Old Testament, allowed him to reframe the old themes and texts in different and sometimes surprising directions. The more he understood Christ, the more he reframed his understanding of the Old Testament. Drawing on a wide

---

[3]Peter Marshall calls the dying and rising of Christ "the most pivotal and integral theological idea in Paul's writings." See his *The Enigmatic Apostle—Paul and Social Change: Did Paul Seek to Change Graeco-Roman Society?* (Melbourne: ITIM, 1993), p. 16.

selection of the Hebrew Scriptures, he retold Israel's history as leading to Christ.[4]

Paul believed he remained true to the Scriptures when he saw meanings in them beyond what the original writers had foreseen. A clear example is his view of the end of the law.[5] He could also use Old Testament passages and themes to support varying perspectives. For example, he used the story of Abraham for different purposes. On the one hand, he appealed to Abraham as a means of affirming the pedigree of his message that righteousness comes through faith in the promises of God.[6] On another tack, he argued for Christ's place as the *one* seed of Abraham.[7] Even more novel, in Galatians 4:21-31 he asserted the supremacy of Sarah (the heavenly Jerusalem) over Hagar (the contemporary city). In each case, Paul used the Old Testament to place himself beyond the claims of its two central symbols, Jerusalem and the law.

The same coherent improvisation surfaced in Paul's handling of textual detail. The coherence he saw in Christ did not require a set method for translation, citation or exegesis. Again, Paul appears uninterested in methodological precision. He varied his citations between the Septuagint and Hebrew (or of unknown/his own translations). His style of using texts to support his case sometimes fitted contemporary Jewish models and sometimes did not. Paul used the Old Testament creatively, coherently and flexibly. No single method framed his reading of text, except that he believed he was always mindful of Christ. The Old Testament stories and promises were like mines yielding rich understanding of the mysteries now revealed in Christ (1 Tim 3:15-16).

Improvising and Conversing Within Graeco-Roman Culture

It is a mistake to tie Paul to Graeco-Roman intellectual and social patterns. Paul showed no conscious dependence on any one school of thought. Rather, as an independent thinker, he simply built on whatever was to hand, as Edwin Judge has remarked, creatively "exploiting the material rather than subjecting [him]self to it."[8] Paul's conversations were peppered with the phrases and thought of Hellenistic education and of popular philosophy and morality. Yet though he largely accepted the civil order of life in the cities, he promoted a distinctive set of social relations in the *ekklēsiai*. No simple formula can account for his choices.

Paul engaged with the world rather than retreating into an intellectual or reli-

---

[4]E.g., Rom 9:1—10:4; Ps 18:49; 2 Sam 22:50; Deut 32:43; Ps 117:1; Is 11:10.
[5]Rom 7:6; 10:4; Gal 3:19-25.
[6]Gen 12:1-3; 15:6; Rom 4:1-25; Gal 3:6-9.
[7]Gen 12:7; 13:5; 24:7; Gal 3:16.
[8]Edwin Judge, "St. Paul and Socrates," *Interchange* 14 (1973): 110.

gious ghetto. He was a thoroughly urban man. He had no difficulty in employing his audiences' vocabulary, literary techniques, intellectual models and even social conventions. All the more so wherever these enabled him to improvise his approach to converse with an audience, entering into their needs and worldviews. He used clichés from contemporary letter writing, including his remembrance of friends and letters of recommendation. As we have noted frequently, he was conscious of the conventions of friendship. Indeed, he deliberately exploited the theme, reframing it in the light of his message. When Paul described himself as a debtor *(opheiletes)* to those with whom he had no prior relationship (Rom 1:14), he reversed the normal expectations of Graeco-Roman friendship. His opinion on reciprocal rights and obligations in marriage was thoroughly conventional. His approval of celibacy (1 Cor 7:3-7) ran contrary to the classical ideals for a man and society.[9]

Paul's use of contemporary vocabulary and themes was at times simply matter-of-fact; in other contexts, it appears clever and innovative, even startling. He played on known imperial, religious and honorific contexts in using the words we commonly translate "gospel," "mystery," "righteousness" and "grace." He recast the common honorific and moral term *philotimia* ("love of honor, ambition") to advertise his choice *not* to compete with others (Rom 15:20). He avoided religious terminology except where he could empty it of religious meaning.[10] He used the building as a metaphor for social relations in a remarkable innovation that enabled him to dismantle the traditional indicators and expectations of status.[11]

While Paul freely used aspects of the Graeco-Roman patterns, he kept his distance wherever these confused his appeal for an alternative mindset. His personal experience of social humiliation and of the paradoxes of joy in suffering and strength in weakness ran against the prevailing models of the moral man. This is perhaps clearest in relation to the moralists' portraits of the ideal life as progress in virtue toward the perfect man.[12] Figure 15.2 summarizes the differences.[13]

---

[9]For a discussion of the shifts in Greek, Roman, Jewish and Egyptian law and custom regarding marriage, divorce and dowries, see Stephen Llewelyn, *New Documents Illustrating Early Christianity* (Sydney: Macquarie University Press, 1992), 6:1–18.

[10]For example, *latpeiav* (Rom 12:2) in Llewelyn, *New Documents*, 7:105–11. See also *leitourgia* (Phil 2:17) in Horsley, *New Documents*, 1:14.

[11]1 Cor 3:10-15; 8:2; 10:23; 14:5, 21; Eph 4:16.

[12]On the parallels and departures between Paul and the moralists regarding the development of character, see Wayne Meeks, *The Moral World of the First Christians,* Library of Early Christianity 6 (Philadelphia: Westminster Press, 1986), pp. 45–52.

[13]See also the matrix of moral traditions at the end of chapter twelve.

Graeco-Roman emphases	Paul's emphases
pursue knowledge by abstraction	base understanding on the stories of Israel and Christ, and on the Spirit
create precision through reason	create coherence and unity by the Spirit, the message and love
give priority to abstracted reality	ground all truth in relationships
play down the everyday	focus on the everyday
pursue ideals	pursue relations of love, not ideals
educate to reinforce social conventions	critique conventions where they undercut identification with Christ
broadcast rank	equivocate about rank
pursue status	remove all ground for status
preserve social order by leadership	trust the Spirit and believers to build the community in love and the truth
maintain balance and constancy	abandon serenity and stability for extremes of dying-rising with Christ
applaud individual ambition	promote well-being of community
censure change	promote transformation
model virtue	identify with dying and rising of Christ

Figure 15.2. Discrepancies between Paul and Graeco-Roman patterns of reason and moral purpose

Paul sensed how these contemporary patterns framed his friends' understanding. He also believed passionately that the dying and rising of Christ had radically *reframed* their identities and that if they chose to believe this, it would lead to a similarly radical reframing of their social relations. He conversed with them in order to shift their sense of their place in the world.

Two short case studies will allow us to draw together the threads of Paul's remarkably fluid and coherent message and methodology. Both chronicle conversations framed by tension. In Galatians it was the tension between law and Spirit. In 1 Corinthians it was the tension between prestige and love.

Galatians: The Freedom of the Spirit Versus the Tyranny of Law
Galatians provides a case study in Paul's reframing of behavior away from law and

morality. At the heart of his troubled relationship with this *ekklēsia* was his dispute with certain apostles and leaders either from Jerusalem or sympathetic to the Jerusalem cause who, as he saw it, had deceived the *ekklēsia* and distorted his message. He did not mince his words: "Mark my words! I, Paul, tell you that if you let yourselves be circumcised, Christ will be of no value to you at all" (Gal 5:2).[14] Traditional theological arguments about the possibility of "losing salvation" miss Paul's point here. His message was starkly realistic: the one who chases the law will so bind himself under its obligations as to be unable to see grace (Gal 5:4).[15] The war is fought and lost in the heart, the mind and the will. A person cannot live by grace with a conscience fixed on law.

Now that the Christ had come, any mindset fixed on circumcision, sabbath observance, dietary regulations and other obligations under the law would rob believers from experiencing the personal and social benefits of grace. Those captivated by grace must refuse to focus on law (Gal 5:5-6). Only the Spirit could make clear the significance of the dying and rising of Christ—only the Spirit, not the dead letter of the law (5:16-26). This same confidence in the Spirit and his people also underscores his exasperation that the Galatians and certain of the apostles had chosen to return to the law (2:11-14; 3:23-25). Paul was amazed that Gentile believers had been bewitched to place themselves under a superseded law to which they had never been obligated (3:1-5).

Paul understood his way of contrasting the law with the Spirit not as an innovation, but as in keeping with the prophets. This is critical to understanding how Paul worked with the specific circumstances of the Galatians. The old arrangement, through no fault of its own, had only brought death (3:10, 21).[16] The new had brought life (3:13-14). The law could not guide this new life (5:13-18). This provides a vantage point on the force and logic of Paul's pleas in the final chapters of Galatians.

As Lategan notes, if Paul were still tied to (a modified) law as the pattern of the new way, then we would expect him to have responded to the Galatians with a "comprehensive set of rules for ethical conduct."[17] Yet there is no hint of such a move. He made no attempt to lay down the law in any form. Rather, he set before them the contrasting ways of death and life as something self-evident to

---

[14]Cf. Gal 5:7; 2 Cor 6:1.

[15]This point is similar to my earlier comments about the "I" of Romans 7. There is no need to nail down the identity of the "I": it is anyone who chooses to live by law, or by any other religious or moral standard.

[16]Cf. Rom 7:7-13.

[17]B. C. Lategan, "Is Paul Developing a Specifically Christian Ethics in Galatians?" in *Greeks, Romans and Christians: Essays in Honor of Abraham J. Malherbe*, ed. D. L. Balch, E. Ferguson and W. A. Meeks (Minneapolis: Fortress, 1990), p. 320.

those who have the Spirit (5:19-23). Regarding the fruits of life in the Spirit, Paul only stated that "no law is against these things." The cryptic character of this remark was integral to his strategy. It reinforced that the fruits of the Spirit were not in any way a new law: "There is no new system to be learned or to be played."[18]

Responsibility is left with the readers to discern what they must choose if they are to live by the Spirit. In this sense, Hans Dieter Betz is right when he insists that "Paul does not provide the Galatians with a specifically Christian ethic . . . [but] his goal is to induce self-examination and self-criticism, in order to keep the level of ethical awareness high."[19] At the same time, Paul did not encourage self-examination in the sense of the moral philosophers since, according to Paul, self-examination does not lead to a changed life. The new point of reference was the dying and rising of Christ, not the individual conscience.

The overlap between Paul's list of the Spirit's fruits and certain attitudes and behaviors commonly found in the lists of virtues put forward by Graeco-Roman moralists is also suggestive. It seems that Paul understood several impacts of the dying and rising of Christ on behavior. First, it spelled the end of the law. Second, it spelled the comprehensiveness of the new way of the Spirit. Third, Paul believed himself free to mirror or draw from the Hellenistic traditions even as he criticized and reframed them. Paul assumed that the Galatians were capable of seeing the startling significance of the dying and rising of Christ. He assumed that they could address normal Hellenistic mores with new eyes and hearts. Fourth, the Galatians' choice to enslave themselves to the old order forced Paul to speak as though they had no part in Christ (Gal 4:11, 16),[20] yet he did not dismiss them summarily. Paul appealed to the Galatians to understand their new identity and to act in the liberated and responsible manner befitting those who no longer needed the external stimulus of a codified manner of life.[21]

1 Corinthians: The Priority of Love over Prestige

Speaking of the struggles between the strong and the weak at Corinth, Wayne Meeks notes that "Paul uses the mediating symbol of Jesus crucified, not to achieve a theoretical synthesis of these opposing positions, but to signify a way in which the persons who occupied the position could understand their engagement with one another."[22]

In Paul's conversations, the "knowledge which builds up" first tore down (1 Cor 8:3).

---

[18]Ibid., p. 324.

[19]Hans Dieter Betz, *Galatians*, Hermeneia (Philadelphia: Fortress, 1979), p. 292.

[20]Cf. 1 Cor 3:1-4, 19; 6:7.

[21]Gal 5:24; cf. 5:1-6; 6:14-15.

[22]Meeks, *Moral World of the First Christians*, p. 136.

This surprising knowledge, founded on the strength and wisdom of the weak and the foolish story of the cross, reversed the ideals of those who drew near to Christ. Those who think they are wise *(sophos)* must become foolish *(mōros)* in order to know true wisdom.[23] They must endure the indignity of a reversal in status in order to know the startling reinstatement of "all things" (1 Cor 3:22-23). Paul's choice to identify with Christ's death placed him in stark contrast to the elitists at Corinth: they were rich, he was poor; they were kings, he was the scum of the earth. Paul and his coworkers were mere servants who stewarded God's mysteries, without comparison for praise and in self-humiliation. This is the manner of those possessed by the Spirit and his mysteries.[24] Those transformed in these ways "do not exceed what is written"; they do not boast beyond what Christ has done, nor make comparisons between men.[25]

Paul staked a great deal on bringing the Corinthians to a new understanding. The cross obviously implied reversal of status and convention. He now urged the Corinthians to take these reversals to heart in the ways they saw themselves, each other and him. In his estimation, they ought to have understood this from the manner in which God had worked among them.[26] But their insistence on the marks of conventional social honor had reinforced elitist boundaries within the group (1 Cor 1:13-17). So long as they remained tied to the social system of honor and the prestigious place of education within that system, they would not see the system for what it was, nor grasp the mysteries of the Spirit.[27] The debacles over the immoral brother (1 Cor 5:1-13) and lawsuits within the *ekklēsia* (1 Cor 6:1-11) only highlighted for Paul the need to loosen the grip of their conventional mindset. Paul and Apollo modeled the new way. As colaborers for Christ (1 Cor 3:5-17), they too had wisdom, but they did not boast of their own achievements. They had been held up as fools and outcasts as they labored to build up the new people of God (1 Cor 3:5—4:13). The contrast was stark.

At this point, Paul moved his critique from what, to him at least, was *self-evidently wrong* in the Corinthians' mindset, to what was *right but equally mistaken*. In the first place, Paul largely affirmed the slogans of the strong: "Everything is permissible" and "Food for the stomach and the stomach for food." Yet they had failed entirely to reframe these according to the message Paul had delivered to them. Where God is building community, Paul argued, what matters is not the permissible, but the benefi-

---

[23] 1 Cor 1:18-25; 3:18-23; cf. Job 5:13; Ps 94:11.

[24] 1 Cor 4:1-17; cf. 2:5—3:23; 4:6, 18, 19; 5:2; 8:1; 13:4.

[25] 1 Cor 4:6-7; cf. 1:10-17, 26-31; 3:1—4:5.

[26] 1 Cor 1:13-17; 1:22—2:5; 3:5—4:13.

[27] 1 Cor 1:18-20; 2:3—3:1. For a discussion of Paul's relation to contemporary education practice, see Edwin Judge, "The Reaction Against Classical Education in the New Testament," *Journal of Christian Education* 77 (1986): 11–12.

cial *(sympherei)*: "Everything is permissible"? Yes, but not expedient. "Everything is permissible"? Yes, but better not to be mastered by it. "Food for the stomach and the stomach for the food"? Yes, but God will destroy both. "The body for immorality"? No, the body is for the Lord, and the Lord is for the body (1 Cor 6:12-13).

In the following conversation Paul offered answers to explicit concerns raised by the Corinthians themselves. He encouraged a new mindset in much the same spirit as Romans 12:1-2. He called the Corinthians to new conversation and reflection. They must critique the conventions of society and act out the radical perspectives of the new era in the light of the impending destruction of the old.[28] Walking in the new way was not bound to any one path of choices. By grounding choice in the believer's identity and allegiance—"The body . . . for the Lord, and the Lord for the body"—Paul could not only prescribe certain actions but also provide a platform for choice and flexibility.[29] He left many choices open, though not totally so. He established certain boundaries but placed the onus on personal discernment and responsibility. He cast all choices as issues of faithfulness to Christ, and he frequently restrained from prescribing an exclusive option.

The way Paul unfolded this new way of "making up one's mind" in the light of Christ is apparent in the "grammar" of 1 Corinthians 7. Note how the language alternates between prescribing and remaining open-ended:[30]

> It is good . . . but since there is . . .
> I say this as a concession, not a command . . .
> I wish that . . . but each has his own gift from God . . .
> One has this . . . another has that . . .
> I give this command (not I, but the Lord) . . .
> She must not . . . but if she does . . . she must . . . or else . . .
> To the rest, I say this (I, not the Lord) . . .
> If . . . and she/he is willing . . . he must not . . .
> Otherwise . . . but as it is . . .
> But if . . . let him do so . . . he or she is not bound in such circumstances
> God has called us to peace
> How do you know, wife/husband, whether . . .
> If circumcised/uncircumcised, stay so . . .
> Neither is anything . . . just keep God's commands . . .
> Each one should remain where he or she is . . .

---

[28]On the recurring interplay in 1 Corinthians between message and response, note the proximity of the following "message" statements to Paul's exhortations to change thought and behavior: 1 Cor 1:18-25, 30-31; 2:6-16; 3:10-23; 4:6-7; 5:6-8; 6:2-3, 9-11, 12-20; 7:29-30; 8:1-6, 11-13; 9:1-27; 10:11; 10:23—11:1; cf. Rom 12:1; 13:11-14; 14:5-12; 15:1-13.

[29]1 Cor 6:12-20; 7:17-24.

[30]Meeks describes this as Paul's "grammar of moral process" in a succinct and fascinating discussion of 1 Thessalonians and 1 Corinthians (*Moral World of the First Christians*, pp. 124–36).

If a slave, stay so . . . don't be troubled . . . although if you can get free, do so . . .

A slave is the Lord's freeman . . . a freeman is the Lord's slave . . .

Each man, as responsible to God, should stay where he was when . . .

Now about . . . I have no command . . .

Because of your present circumstances, I think that it is good . . .

Are you married/unmarried. . . . stay so . . .

But if you do marry, you have not sinned

But those who do face many troubles . . . I want to spare you this . . .

What I mean is . . . the time is short . . .

From now on . . .

If "A" . . . live as if "B" . . . If "B" . . . live as if "A" . . . (etc.)

For this world in its present form is passing away

I would like you to be free from concern . . . with interests undivided . . .

I say this for your own good, not to restrict you . . .

If anyone . . . and if . . . he should . . . he is not sinning . . .

But if another has settled the matter in his own mind (the other way) . . .

So then, he who . . . is right . . . but he who . . . does better

A woman is bound . . . but if . . . she is free . . . so long as . . .

In my judgment, she is happier . . . and I think that I too have the Spirit . . .

Paul extended the spirit of this grammar to the conflict of the strong and the weak (1 Cor 8–10). Christ's dying and rising had abolished the sacred-profane dichotomies of Jewish and Graeco-Roman religion and morality.[31] This held far-reaching implications for the Corinthian factions. First, the weak must face what they still did not know but the strong did know: that "an idol is nothing"; that there are no real gods other than the one God and his Christ; and that one is free to mix with unbelievers without raising matters of conscience (1 Cor 8:4-10). Second, the strong must face the responsibilities Christ had placed on them for the well-being of those who "do not yet know" (1 Cor 8:9-13). Third, the strong must face the real dangers that the weak rightly discern in idolatry (1 Cor 10:1-22).

In other words, true perception counts for nothing without love, since "knowledge puffs up, but love builds up" (1 Cor 8:1).[32] The one who loves God is the one

---

[31]Wayne Meeks helpfully captures the social impact of this desacralization: "The Pauline school had self-consciously abandoned the rules of purity that helped to maintain the social boundaries of the Jewish communities, for in a community composed largely of former gentiles these rules were dysfunctional—and, for Paul, they appeared to deny the newness of the message of the crucified and risen Messiah" (*The First Urban Christians: The Social World of the Apostle Paul* [New Haven, Conn.: Yale University Press, 1983], p. 103).

[32]It is important to recall at this point that the conflict at Corinth was fundamentally social, not narrowly ideological (ibid., pp. 69–70, 97–100). Chris Forbes's comment on 2 Corinthians would seem to hold for the earlier stages of the conflict and correspondence: "We need not . . . assume any real theological coherency within this group, though it is conceivable. We may rather see an

whom God acknowledges, not necessarily the one with complete knowledge. Likewise, love of "the one for whom Christ died" must shape the imitation of Christ.[33] The whole section is bracketed by Paul's remarks on the priority of love and its exposition in the self-sacrifice of Christ.[34] This suggests that he regarded the imitation of Christ's self-giving love as the controlling pattern for matters of conscience and social relations.[35] This pattern led Paul away from the Graeco-Roman moral ideal of consistency to adapt his manner of life freely to the concerns and circumstances of his hearers (1 Cor 9:19-23).

Paul epitomized this new way in his own refusal of personal rights (1 Cor 9:1-27). This seeming shift of focus actually continues his counsel to the strong and the weak. While the passage was crucial to Paul's self-defense, it also offered the Corinthians an extended analogy to their own concerns. It was as if Paul said, "This is how I imitate Christ in *my* circumstances; consider now how you make *your* choices." The point of Paul's defense was twofold. First, while those who preached had a right to financial support, Paul refused this right for himself (1 Cor 9:7-18). Second, this refusal was a poignant expression of his determination to place himself under "slavery" to those whom he served. The analogy cut deeply. Just as Paul refused his own rights (*exousia*) in order to place himself at the service of all (including the Corinthians), so the strong ought also to surrender their authority (*exousia*) to serve the weak (1 Cor 9:12; 8:9). As Wayne Meeks puts it, "The apostle exercises his liberty by choosing not to use it; so ought the 'strong.'"[36] At the same time, Paul moved to protect the strong from the tyranny of the weak.

Meeks helpfully distinguishes Paul's process in 1 Corinthians 8—10 from its intended outcome.[37] The immediate goal was compromise; both the strong and the weak were to accommodate one another. The blandness of such an outcome, however, does little justice to the profundity of the process. What Paul effected, Meeks argues, was "a dialectic of affirmation and reversal." Paul *affirmed the beliefs and concerns of both groups* at the same time as he *reversed the claims of both groups* to any superiority. He affirmed certain of their premises yet undermined their conclusions. What he sought to achieve, then, was not "theoretical synthesis" but "engagement." As Meeks understands it: "In that process meet three different but overlapping perceptions of the world—that of 'the weak,' that of 'the strong,' and

---

ad-hoc alliance, for diverse social and theological purposes" ("Comparison, Self-praise and Irony: Paul's Boasting and Conventions in Hellenistic Rhetoric," *NTS* 32 [1986]: 15).

[33]1 Cor 8:11; 10:31—11:1; cf. 4:16.

[34]1 Cor 8:1; 10:33—11:1.

[35]1 Cor 8:6, 11-12; 9:19-23; 10:16.

[36]Meeks, *Moral World of the First Christians*, p. 134.

[37]Ibid., pp. 134–36.

Paul's—each informed by the distinctive experiences, history, and social location of the different parties, but each transformed in its own special way by the novel Christian teachings as those persons appropriated them."[38]

It is clear that Paul led his communities into a new process of framing their identities and purposes. It was a profoundly relational strategy, crafted in the moment to demonstrate what it meant to choose the well-being of others in imitation of the dying and rising of Christ. Paul left the Corinthians having to work and learn together. He left them to experience the meaning of that "love which builds up." Barbara Hall portrays the risks and riches of this arrangement:

> Paul does not take the side of one group against the other, nor does he try to resolve the problems once and for all. Certainly, he does not enunciate a general principle and then apply it to this specific issue. He works instead on relationships. He asks something of both groups which he hopes will make it possible for all of them to move forward together. Paul does not ask or expect everyone to agree. What he asks, rather, is that those on each side identify with those on the other side, to become *as* the ones with whom they disagree. They are not initially required to change their convictions; they are to act on behalf of those with whom they disagree. Paul knows that this is a difficult and complicated thing to do. It is, however, necessary if the eschatological community is to exhibit and proclaim the new creation, even as its members take diverse paths of obedience.[39]

Similar affirmations and reversals frame the remainder of the letter. Paul did not offer a "manual" for the Corinthian gatherings, but he continued to provoke a radical reorientation of their expectations and experience. The Spirit, Paul affirmed, was among them to manifest his power (1 Cor 12:1-11). At the same time, Paul reversed the arrogant claims and expectations of some. Paul took up the hallmarks so prized by the haves—and perhaps envied by the have-nots—wisdom *(sophia)*, knowledge *(gnōsis)*, reason or eloquence *(logos)*, power *(dynamis)*, and spirit *(pneuma)*. He then reframed them as unmerited gifts *(charismata)* and areas of service *(diakonia)*. In this way he undercut all grounds for boasting.[40] The strong did not have more of the Spirit than others. Indeed, their boasting suggested that they were devoid of the Spirit and in league with the old era of the flesh *(sarkinois)*.[41]

Paul used the common political metaphor of the body to drive home the rever-

---

[38]Ibid., p. 136.

[39]Barbara Hall, "All Things to All People: A Study of 1 Corinthians 9:19-23," in *The Conversation Continues*, ed. R. T. Fortna and B. R. Gaventa (Nashville: Abingdon, 1990), p. 153.

[40]1 Cor 12:4-11; 13:1-13; 14:6-9, 20; 15:34, 58; cf. 1:18-21, 31; 2:1, 5, 6-16; 3:18-21; 4:10; 5:6; 8:1-3; 9:16; 10:1.

[41]1 Cor 3:1; cf. *psychikon*, 15:44-47.

sal of status (1 Cor 12:12-26). The image was normally used to reinforce the greater necessity and worth of the head over the lesser parts. But once again Paul has reframed convention. No member (the weak?) was inferior to any other. Nor was any member (the strong?) superior to any other. All were vital to the body's well-being. Honor must go to those judged less honorable by the Corinthians' standards. The Spirit granted gifts to build up the community, not for individual display and prestige.[42]

The centerpiece of Paul's new way of living and conversing *(kath hyperbolen hodon)* was love *(agapē)*.[43] Paul seems to have used the word *agapē,* which was little used in the papyri and literary sources, as a substitute for many of the Graeco-Roman virtues and moral conventions. Perhaps substitute is too weak: *agapē* summed up many of Paul's vivid images and desires of social relations transformed by the dying and rising of Christ. The way of love required service, partnership and edification. It eclipsed every gift, including prophecy, languages and knowledge. It was the antithesis of boasting, self-interest and factionalism. It was *the* mark of maturity *(to teleion)*. Love was the way of those who refused their personal rights, ideological precision and rectitude for the welfare of those for whom Christ died. It was *the* mark of imitating Christ.[44] Love held no regard for the marks of power and prestige. Love did not offer formulas for behavior and thought. Those who love do not wall themselves within fortresses of unassailable reason, but they remain exposed to the risks of relationships.

Finally, 2 Corinthians suggests that Paul failed. It seems that his own example, first put forward in 1 Corinthians 9:1-27, had not endeared him to the powerbrokers at Corinth. Rather, he had become the focus of the Corinthians' disapproval, scorn and enmity.[45] Such, Paul would have argued, were the risks of love.

The Cutting Edge of Conversation

The coherence Paul saw in Christ did not single out any one exegetical procedure for using the Old Testament. Nor did it predispose him to any one way of dealing with Graeco-Roman cultures. Nor again did it imply any single path of Christian experience. The imitation of the dying and rising of Christ was not an alternative moral code. Imitation required new wisdom about one's actions and choices. There was no single formula for working out the implications of weakness-strength, foolishness-wisdom, poor-rich, slave-free and suffering-joy in any new context. Paul framed each pair to provoke conversations about what it might mean to imitate

---

[42]1 Cor 12:15-27; cf. 1:10-17; 10:33.
[43]1 Cor 12:31b—13:13; cf. 8:1b.
[44]1 Cor 4:14-17; 8:3; 10:32—11:1.
[45]2 Cor 1:12—2:11; 10:1—13:10.

Christ. They were not a means of securing conformity to new ideals for behavior.

This point is crucial to understanding the rhythm of Paul's conversation. He was not interested in uniformity of behavior. Paul's own life embodied the dynamic transformations that he believed the Spirit sought to bring about within the *ekklēsiai*. His teaching was provocative, not legislative. It avoided the pettiness of religious and legal controversies.[46] Nor did he prescribe any single pattern for the gathering. His advice left room for spontaneity and diversity (1 Cor 14:26-33). Clearly, Paul did not proceed from the coherence of Christ to reduce experience, relationship and learning to intellectual abstractions and formulas. There remained an open-endedness about "walking worthily of one's calling."[47] His message offered no formula to settle in advance which way to respond to contemporary intellectual and social patterns.

New understanding for new circumstances emerged within the communities through conversation. Indeed, the power of the story of Christ only came to its fullness in the contingencies of social life. Paul, his colleagues, and the communities were each working out the message as they went. Yet even as his thought matured, Paul continued to show no interest in formulating final statements in the sense of the doctrinal debates and creeds of subsequent generations. He remained focused on specific people and contexts. New contexts continued to prompt new responses as Paul sought to remain open to the Spirit and to his own experiences and relationships to guide his thought. As Sampley notes, there was nothing dispassionate or removed about Paul's thought:

> Paul has no gospel that fails to intercept flesh-and-blood life or the real happenings in people's lives. . . . We may be tempted to distil Paul's gospel out of the particularity of letters to real people . . . [but] Paul's thought world, his moral deliberations, and life in the world are so intricately intertwined as to be ultimately inseparable. That is Paul's genius. . . . Paul's moral reasoning functions around the categories of the "fitting" or "appropriate.". . . Paul's view of the life of faith, when lived as it should be, requires vigorous involvement of the mind and heart. . . . It is a delicate balance . . . but its power may lie precisely in its frailty and vulnerability.[48]

The rigor accompanying this frailty did not lie in any artificial rule of precision. The truth Paul pursued and communicated was not narrowly propositional. It came to expression in a deep congruence of faith, hope and love in the lives of his *ekklēsiai*. His means of retelling the dying and rising of Christ and of urging imitation were often cryptic, suggestive and provocative. His style was to draw out hearts

---

[46]2 Tim 2:14-26; Tit 3:9.
[47]Gal 5:13, 16; Eph 4:1; Phil 1:27; Col 1:10; 3:1-5, 17; 1 Thess 4:1; 2 Thess 1:11-12; 2:15.
[48]J. Paul Sampley, *Walking Between the Times* (Philadelphia: Fortress, 1991), pp. 117-19.

and minds to engage with Christ, not to create an intellectual system to be memorized and canonized. We misrepresent Paul to the extent that our representations suppress the enigmatic and cryptic character of his thought.

In a short excursus on philosophy in Ephesians 4:17-32, Paul contrasts its fruits—insensitivity and hard-heartedness toward God and the concerns of others—with "the truth that is in Jesus." This truth renewed life and brought compassion to social relations. Paul located this truth in *Jesus*. The personal name on its own is rare in Paul's writings. He normally affixed the messianic title—Christ Jesus, Jesus Christ—or simply referred to him as Christ. In another place (Gal 6:17), Paul's reference to Jesus plainly calls to mind his suffering and humiliation before the crucifixion. It may be that Paul was making a similar allusion in Ephesians: the sophistication of philosophical and moral abstraction was now eclipsed and silenced by the ruddy simplicity and personal suffering of a Jewish messiah.

Paul's conversations bore the marks of his personality: pleading, strident, exasperated, affectionate, urgent, reflective, passionate and at times impatient. They bore the marks of his close knowledge of the popular intellectualism of his day and of the social systems of status and honor. If Paul had had his way, his *ekklēsiai* would have remained creatively messy. But his opponents wanted neatness—and they won. Twenty centuries later, we may look back amazed that we have drifted so far. Then again, perhaps we still don't get it. It remains profoundly difficult for leaders to let go of their need to control people. It is easier to impose order and conformity through prescribing belief and practice than to acknowledge the dignity and gifting of Christ's people. It is easier to disallow the conversation than to hear the hard questions. For many, it is easier to disallow the conversation than to join it.

PART 5

NOW & THEN

Reframing Grace-full Conversation

16

LIVING IN THE SYSTEM

THE CITIES IN WHICH PAUL LIVED AND WROTE WERE HIGHLY STRUCTURED AND EFFECTIVE social systems. People knew the importance of keeping their places. When road-work was needed or new seating at the theater or any other investment in city infrastructure, the project would likely depend entirely on the beneficence of a wealthy citizen. According to their personal ebb and flow of honor and cash, lead-ing citizens would either compete for the most flamboyant city projects needing a patron or duck for cover. Everyone had an interest in keeping the wealthy and influential in their places and the less so in theirs.

Security and economy turned on rank and status. Religious and moral custom reinforced the honors and duties of the great and the duties of the less so. Like our own worlds, life in a Graeco-Roman city was shaped by vast webs of formal and informal convention that had evolved and solidified to mark the boundaries of acceptable and unacceptable relationship, ambition and behavior. Persons of extremes, those who disregarded rank and convention, were a threat to social and moral order. Progress within one's allotted place was applauded; change was cen-sured.

The System Is What the System Does
The power of a system lies in its invisibility. When we see the system as system, we may question it; when we see nothing but normality, we raise no query. When Paul stepped out of line with the expectations of those at Corinth and Thessalonica, his

behavior bewildered his hosts. It was entirely proper and morally upright for a man of learning to advertise (discreetly) his attainments and to adopt a posture befitting his rhetorical and social progress. Paul's refusal of patronage and the marks of eloquence seemed entirely churlish to them. What possible point could he be making? He said he wished to uphold the reputation of Christ and his message, but surely *he* was the one who brought it into disrepute by his own pigheaded insistence on doing menial labor and disavowing rhetoric.

Jesus' life, death and resurrection sparked a radical restructuring of human relations. Paul added fuel to the fire by deliberately framing the life of the early *ekklēsiai* around a radical break with rank and status. These early groups thus began one of the most radical social experiments of all time. Yet even the most radical social change never simply exchanges one system for another, much less moves from having a system to having no system. The early gatherings had their own social systems. It was the growth of these systems that absorbed so much of Paul's efforts. His push for the social radicalism of grace was always against the tide.

Sir Geoffrey Vickers, the eminent British systems theorist and government adviser, once described "living" systems this way:

> The form of a society is determined partly by external pressures and opportunities and partly by internal cultural structures ranging from explicit laws to countless subtle conventions which deter or control the spread of deviance. Systems, then, are bundles of inter-acting relations, internal and external. The internal ones enable each to maintain coherence even through change. The external ones regulate the system's relation as a whole with its milieu including all the other systems of which it forms a part. This is as true of a city government as of a cat.[1]

It is equally true of churches and other Christian organizations. In a myriad of formal and informal ways, we are caught up in endless framing and reframing of the system to maximize internal conformity and external security. But there is a twist in any tale of evangelical systems.[2] We choose to define ourselves by reference beyond ourselves to the Bible and its grand account of God working in the world. This is crucial and proper, but herein lies the twist. We think of the Bible as both inside and outside the system. And the Bible and the system clash—or they *don't* when they *should!*

An unavoidable double standard pervades church life and theology. We preach reform according to the patterns of the Bible while we maintain systems that mitigate

---

[1] Sir Geoffrey Vickers, "The Poverty of Problem Solving," *Journal of Applied Systems Analysis* 8 (1981): 16.

[2] I am working with a fairly broad understanding of who is an evangelical, framed more by who identifies themselves that way than by the debates about who is "entitled" to do so. My experience is that church conventions and ideals remain fairly constant no matter how groups may disagree theologically.

reform. We preach and theologize the radicalness of grace from positions of rank and status. What I want to understand and convey is *how* this happens. How does the system work *as a system*? Whatever we *say* about the gospel reforming us, a system *is* what a system *does*. If the system supports the preaching of grace *and* the practice of law, then the system *is* inimical to grace. In what follows I want to sketch the workings of present-day church systems in order to frame the conversation over whether our heritage reflects the spirit of Paul—or that of his Graeco-Roman contemporaries.

The Priority of Preaching in the System

At the heart of evangelical faith stands the person of Christ and his death and resurrection for sinners. Thus we stand or fall by the trustworthiness of the Bible and by the integrity of our proclamation of its message. The strength of these beliefs has made the sermon the central event of evangelical life and faith, and the preacher/pastor its central figure:

Preaching is indispensable to Christianity.[3]

Preaching is the primary task of the Church and therefore of the minister of the Church . . . everything else is subsidiary. . . . Far from being controlled by the congregation, the preacher is in charge and in control of the congregation.[4]

The one thing that the pastor can do, and must do because nobody else can do it, is to preach the Word. . . . Preaching is the single most effective thing in equipping the Church for its mission.[5]

Denominations and seminaries exist to ensure that only men[6] of suitable calling, training and outlook are ordained to preach. Their role in the system is to maintain uniformity of content, culture and process in the pulpit:

Doctrinal orthodoxy is thus necessary to the authority of preaching.[7]

Those with the very best minds and training belong in the pulpit. . . . The pulpit will never have the power it once had (and ought to have) until this happens.[8]

---

[3]John Stott, *I Believe in Preaching* (London: Hodder & Stoughton, 1982), p. 15.

[4]Martin Lloyd-Jones, *Preaching and Preachers* (London: Hodder & Stoughton, 1971), pp. 26, 83.

[5]Peter Hastie, interview with James Boice, in *The Briefing* 56 (1990): 9.

[6]I adopt the traditional convention of using the masculine voice throughout part five. My sincere apology to those who find this offensive and insensitive. In many respects it *is* insensitive, but that is my point. The world I am describing is overwhelmingly male centered. No matter how much I might wish otherwise, inclusive language would misrepresent the system.

[7]Samuel Logan Jr., "The Phenomenology of Preaching," in *The Preacher and Preaching: Reviving the Art in the Twentieth Century*, ed. S. T. Logan Jr. (Philadelphia: Presbyterian & Reformed, 1986), pp. 151–52.

[8]James Boice, "The Preacher and Scholarship," in *The Preacher and Preaching*, ed. S. T. Logan Jr. (Philadelphia: Presbyterian & Reformed, 1986), p. 91.

This task is made more urgent by the sense of hostile forces external to the system. The pressures of modern worldviews and the enticement of intellectually provocative but unorthodox theologies, it is argued, require an armory of exegetical skills and theological discernment. The trainee preacher must master Greek (though hardly ever Hebrew, and not in every seminary) and absorb the whole system of denominational theology. Intellectual acumen is a key indicator of a man's call to preach. Ordination is the safeguard of the church:

> If a person cannot handle [seminary], we should assume that he is not being called to the work of the gospel ministry.[9]

> It is to the *church* that kingdom authority has been granted; individual preachers possess it as they speak on behalf of the church (which is, of course, what the ordination process is supposed to mean—it is the church's recognition that the individual being ordained has the kingdom authority to speak to and for the church).[10]

The seminary prepares a man to be ordained to preach. Preaching therefore must stand, it is argued, at the beginning, the middle and the end of theological curricula and method. The seminary reinforces the ideals of theology, ministry and piety, passing them on through biblical, historical, systematic and practical curricula and methodologies. Preaching classes teach the ideals of eloquence and a leader's persona. Powerful conventions of voice, manner, appearance and style frame the ideals. Young preachers model themselves upon accomplished preachers like young sports stars imitate their own heroes.

The Absoluteness of Theology and Preaching

Seminaries, by and large, teach methods that fragment and reorder the ancient texts into systems of theology. This has an impact on students that few recognize. While theologians are unlikely to claim that a course in the doctrine of God actually gives a more pristine knowledge of God than, say, reading Isaiah, students are likely to *feel* that this is the case. The seemingly timeless and universal patterns of systematic theology *function* in conversation and preaching as more exact and exhaustive than the text.

The whole experience of seminary study is colored by ideals of objectivity and precision. In the name of becoming "biblical" thinkers and preachers, students learn how to work within, and pass on, an intellectual and social system. In the name of rigorous understanding of the text, the student actually absorbs an entire intellectual and social system.

---

[9]Joel Nederhood, "The Minister's Call," in *Preacher and Preaching*, pp. 50–51.
[10]Logan, "Phenomenology of Preaching," p. 151, emphasis his.

Seminaries have a long history of being oriented toward systematic theology, a point acknowledged by advocates and critics alike. The discipline aims to draw together into one place the fruits of the biblical and historical disciplines. It then orders these insights into rigorous classifications of theological truths yielding precise, objective definitions of topics and subtopics making up the total system of biblical truth:

> Systematic theology is more comprehensive. . . . It is final and normative in a way that its sister disciplines are not. It seeks the final view of Scripture, rather than the transitional one of the Old Testament or even the Book of Acts.[11]

> To the extent that our interpretation of Scripture (i.e., the system of doctrine) corresponds to God's revelation in nature and Scripture, it provides a metaphysically ultimate and true analysis of the world.[12]

Theologians stress that the drive to systematize truth must not overwhelm the particulars of the text and audience. Nevertheless, they argue, preachers must be trained in the art of ordering the fruits of their theological labors into precisely structured sermons. This systematizing of the message, students are told, helps clarify the needs of the congregation and the critical role of preaching. It is central to the process of extracting, distilling, applying and communicating. Indeed, systematizing is central to the very heart of evangelicalism—the ministry of the pulpit:

> Systematic theology . . . is *normative*. It regards its own conclusions as representing not what a particular biblical author thought or what certain theologians believe or what it may be inspiring for the church to accept, but the truth. . . . First [this] system of truth elucidates each text. . . . Second, the system of doctrine *exercises control* over the exposition of a particular passage. Precisely because there is a system, and because truth is one, dogmatics lays down parameters that exegesis must never trespass.[13]

For all its supposed rigor and precision, theological and exegetical method is often remarkably sloppy. More to the point, theological methodology surrenders rigor to the higher goal of validating the system.

I once took a seminary class titled "Ministry of the Word" where we were taught the supposed biblical basis of preaching. We were given a list of Greek words for various speech acts used in the New Testament. Our group task was to study preaching from these words: preaching as *keryxo*; preaching as *euangelizomai*, and so forth. We looked up the references and synthesized our findings as "A New Testa-

---

[11]Donald Macleod, "Preaching and Systematic Theology," in *Preacher and Preaching*, pp. 247–48.
[12]Mark Karlberg, "On the Theological Correlation of Divine and Human Language: A Review Article," *Journal of the Evangelical Theological Society* 32 (1990): 104.
[13]Macleod, "Preaching and Systematic Theology," pp. 248–49, emphasis his.

ment Theology of Preaching." It occurred to a friend and me that the exercise was flawed because we had assumed the conventions of preaching, then sought to validate these conventions with texts. But the group would hear no detraction. Apart from our failure to grasp Paul's repudiation of sophistry with the Corinthians, it never occurred to the group that there is absolutely no evidence for anything like our conventions of preaching in the New Testament—no expository talks, no pulpits, no ordination, no teaching of eloquence. The evidence does not point to the centrality of a monologue in the early gatherings, let alone the conventions of preaching as we have known them for two millennia.

Back in the main group, the professor defended the method. The centerpiece of his argument was the need for authority: "The Word must be ministered with authority," and this implied the conventions of preaching. My friend and I asked if the Word was *always* to be delivered with authority. "Yes," came the ready answer. "Even in Bible study groups?" we asked. "Emphatically yes," our professor replied. "Then why don't we insist on the same conventions on Tuesday nights as we do on Sunday mornings?" we responded. "Because Sunday is church," the professor replied, somewhat less enthusiastically. The rejoinder was obvious: "And what in the New Testament leads us to distinguish Sunday mornings from Tuesday nights as though one were 'real church' and the other something else? If the distinction is simply our construct, why do we persist with it? If the conventions of preaching are unnecessary on Tuesdays, and if the Bible study leader still ministers the Word with authority, then why do we insist on the conventions for Sundays?"

The argument was coming full circle. The case for preaching starts and finishes by presuming preaching, ordination and church as we know them. Without them control, prestige and power lose their footing. The sermon and the service prop up the conventions of eloquence and authority. No sermon, no church service. No church service, no demarcations of authority and control. But church in the evangelical system *is* about order and control. Leaders must retain the "central" ministries. At the very center is preaching. Therefore preaching must remain the domain of the ordained and those whom they acknowledge. Eloquence and erudition must demarcate sermon from conversation, ordained from laity, truth from mere opinion.

Two years later the conversation resumed with the same professor, this time on the second fairway. "You were right." he admitted. "Church and preaching as we know it is very little like what happened in the New Testament."

"Why then," I asked, "do we keep teaching this stuff? Most of your students do not see the discrepancy. How will this ever change?"

His answer was as telling as it was unconvincing: "It was my generation's work to lay out the biblical theology. It is yours to change the system."

Preaching as Therapy of the Soul

Many scholars and preachers speak of the evangelical faith as a beacon shining absolute truth on a world lost in relativistic ignorance and idolatry. For them the sermon is a *saving* event. Any challenge to the centrality of preaching or any diminution of its authority will supposedly condemn the preacher and his congregation to a malaise of relativity and doubt. Many sense subtle pressures at work *within* evangelicalism to white-ant the priority of preaching. The need of the hour, we are told, is not *less* preaching but *more*.

Preachers must call down a vision of God and his redemption. This vision must be timeless, universal and absolute. Here, it is claimed, is the true meeting point of interpretation and proclamation—the preacher labors at the text to uncover the absolute and universal truths that his congregation need most:

> If what the preacher says is meaningful at all, it is so because and to the degree that it conveys analytic, objective information. Thus, from this perspective, the primary function of the preacher's language shall be to communicate propositional (shall we say orthodox?) truth.[14]

Bridging ancient and modern worlds, the preacher must preserve the historic faith as he charts a contemporary vision that the congregation can make their own. He must translate biblical truths and principles into clear ideals of faith, and in so doing, he must shape the commitments and behavior of his hearers. The preacher must convey the persuasion and conviction of his message. It is unabashedly his role to move the congregation "so that the full impact of drama and emotion can take place."[15] Paul should have taken the sophists' eloquence more to heart!

> The preacher learns from Cicero that the genuine orator has a goal, persuasion; he has a means, language; and he has a technique, delivery. The measure of his expertise is how well he molds an audience to his purpose.[16]

> The conclusion of the sermon . . . is the decisive conflict. Humanly speaking, eternity hinges on the effectiveness of the preacher's conclusion. He must give it his all. Here his proposition is clearly in mind—it is the one great luminous truth that must be mounted high for all to see in its most comprehensive statement.[17]

Preaching thus functions in the system as "the primary means of pastoral care."[18] The health of the people of God is understood to depend primarily on the truth, clarity and power of preaching. The congregants are, as it were, spiritually infirm:

---

[14]Logan, "Phenomenology of Preaching," p. 135.
[15]R. C. Sproul, "The Whole Man," in *Preacher and Preaching*, pp. 119–20.
[16]L. de Koster, "The Preacher as Rhetorician," in *Preacher and Preaching*, p. 310.
[17]D. C. Knecht, "Sermon Structure and Flow," in *Preacher and Preaching*, p. 295.
[18]Macleod, "Preaching and Systematic Theology," p. 262.

The pastor should come to terms with his calling to be a physician of souls. . . . The local church is a stone quarry, not the finished temple. Innumerable aches and pains will have to be treated in the Lord's infirmary, which we call the local church. A hospital for the infirm is not an inappropriate analogy.[19]

[The preacher must tell them] they have been served notice what the Holy Spirit expects of them.[20]

The preacher enters the ear that he may gain entrance to the most important gate of them all—the gate of the heart, leading to the emotions, the conscience, and finally the will, where the inner spring is, where life is bent and changed and directed to the will of God.[21]

In this preaching-centered system, every malady of faith derives ultimately from a failure to grasp and apply the word of the preacher. This reinforces the need for rhetorical power to move an audience. If, the argument goes, the great classical orators conveyed the power to release captive minds, preachers should all the more so, since they have the real truth:

Nothing of the passion and finesse of classical rhetoric need be lost, but all is refocused. The commitment and power of a Demosthenes, the analytic of an Aristotle, the poise and urbanity of a Cicero, and the scope of a Quintilian are indeed, like the jewels of Egypt, placed rhetorically by Augustine in the service of the people of God. The power of the spoken word surges into the world now from a pulpit as well as a podium; moral as well as political behaviour comes under the sway of eloquence, requiring no less rhetorical training than commanded by the classic treatises.[22]

These are the ideals of seminary, pulpit and congregation. What the sources do not admit is the elitism, power games and abusiveness that so often accompany the ideals. What they do not admit is that the system no longer works for many people. What they can not admit is that their own principles and system are often a parody of their rhetoric of grace. The links between evangelicalism and the ideals and conventions of the classical and Graeco-Roman eras are all too obvious. The emphases on ideals, universal principles, abstract systems, intellectual capacity, eloquence, preaching as therapy, elegance as a mark of leadership, professionalism—Paul fought against them all. The great irony is that evangelicals appeal to Paul as they enshrine the ideals and system of the Graeco-Roman sophists.

But what happens when a student cannot attain the ideal? I vividly recall the stories of two peers. One friend was (and is) a remarkably gifted teacher. But he was

---

[19]Errol Hulse, "The Preacher and Piety," in *Preacher and Preaching*, p. 75.
[20]John Bettler, "Application," in *Preacher and Preaching*, p. 340.
[21]Knecht, "Sermon Structure and Flow," pp. 300–301.
[22]De Koster, "The Preacher as Rhetorician," p. 319.

unconventional and unpolished. His talks broke all the rules. Another friend tried to conform to the paradigms of preaching, but his style was stiff and awkward. Both men had big hearts for God and his people. The seminary instructors in preaching made it clear that neither would make it as preachers. My unconventional friend was unfazed and went about doing what he had always done, ignoring any need for membership in the denominational clubs. My conventional friend was crushed. The implication was clear: no eloquence, no pastoral ministry. I am left incredulous at how these professors dared appeal to Paul to justify this.

Idealism and Authority in the System

No matter how important theology is to evangelicalism, it is not simply a set of beliefs. Nor is preaching simply a matter of communication. Beliefs involve far more than what the words seem to convey. They are not spoken or accepted in a vacuum. They live in social settings expressing a complex of assumptions, values and commitments. The audience "hears" part or all of these. While both preacher and audience may have clear *ideas* of where doctrine finishes and application begins, those boundaries are themselves part of the vagueness and complexity of what the text or doctrine ends up meaning to someone.

Any doctrine means far more than its formal expression. It *means* the cluster of conventions, ideals and expectations that surround the private and public utterances of those beliefs. The doctrine includes all the goes-without-saying roles, expectations and experiences of church and seminary life. In short, both the words of the sermon and the responses of the hearers convey far more meaning than is apparent. Thus, the preacher unavoidably seeks conformity and uniformity through rules and ideals while uttering the words of grace and freedom.

No preacher *thinks* he is a legalist or moralist. Yet even those preachers most attuned to the rhetoric of grace can damn and defraud those who respond to it. It is not only the more overtly legalistic or moralistic preachers who bring their personal backgrounds and prejudices to the text and the congregation. What the preacher of grace understands as preaching grace, and what he expects as true, uncoerced responses of the heart to grace, are shaped by the expectations he lays upon himself—or avoids. The spontaneous changes he seeks in the heart are *those he has already determined*.

The ideals of evangelical experience, coupled with the weight of responsibility attached to preaching and the service, spiritualize the need for control. This need is externalized as others' need to submit to authority. The call to submission is objectified as a response to the authority of Scripture rather than to that of the preacher. The *words* revolve around the doctrine of Scripture. The *words* uphold grace and the equality of all believers. But the words *mean* what the system allows. What *does* the authority of Scripture mean to those who sit silently through sermons listening to Greek quoted as a key to deeper understanding? What *does* it mean when someone grows up experiencing the admiration and criticism of preachers' oratory skills, hearing comparisons between successful and struggling ministers and churches, and noting the deference shown to pastors and professors? What *does* the doctrine mean when one grows up having to request permission from pastors for "lay" ministries? What *does* it mean in a system where qualification, ordination and salary are the marks of those who dispense permission?

These experiences form the interpretive grid for preaching and theology. The sermon and the service are the centerpiece of a system that regulates conformity and uniformity. Every sermon and service proclaims not only beliefs but an entire culture. To accept the sermon is to accept the culture, and vice versa. To question one is to question the other. In this sense, the culture and its systems *are* evangelical reality. Its ideals and conventions are *the* patterns of evangelical experience. Every sermon conveys ideals. Every service reinforces control, rectitude and the boundaries of acceptable meaning and behavior.

It is critical for evangelical theologians and preachers to feel that they are right. Think of how the vocabulary of *certainty* works in evangelical conversations. The following terms and expressions (and their antonyms) occur commonly and convey a sense of self-evident rectitude: right, correct, evangelical, truly evangelical, proper, perfect, full-on, godly, solid, true, absolute, strong, objective, sound, reliable, inerrant, robust, complete, infallible, inspired, assured, biblical, spiritual, reformed, truly reformed, powerful, holy, confessional, mature, orthodox, rigorous, exegetical, convicted, committed, the original meaning, the Greek means, ordained, licensed, authoritative, submissive, theological, doctrinal, loyal, called, sanctified, covenantal, authorized, ideal, faithful, pure. These terms occur in conversations covering every facet of evangelical life and underscore the pervasive ideals of rectitude and certainty.

I once spent a weekend with a class of ordinands. The experience has remained with me as a vivid portrait of the system. The graduates and their families had become close friends through four years of studying and living together. Now they gathered for perhaps the last time in a beautiful setting in the woods. I expected conversation, laughter and tears. What I found was a church service. Forty close friends sitting in rows with one standing at the front leading us. This was the fruit of four years of conversations with one another and Paul! One man had left an executive position. "At college I was treated as inferior by people I would never have hired. Ask the guys here and their wives about the games of control to ensure that we conformed."

The next morning I wondered whether I had pushed them too far. Their retort was sharp: "The system is *far* worse than you imagine. You don't know the games we have been a part of to get our first appointments. 'Mike' is heading to (name) church. We all know what that means. Next will be (name) church or (name) church, then a professorship and Ph.D. 'Gavin' got (name) church. That's a dead end. 'Phil' drew the shortest straw." Phil's wife, "Christine," wept as he told his story. Years before, he had suffered depression. Christine discovered supportive charismatic friends. Late in his studies, professors probed about his illness and Christine's beliefs. "Intern placements became harder to get. Now they say I won't be ordained. No explanation. I've had no relapse, and Christine doesn't push her beliefs. Why won't anyone speak with me honestly?"

Perhaps this all sounds like preacher bashing. Not so. Preachers too languish in the system. "Roger," the pastor of a rural evangelical congregation, had refused to stay quiet about the adultery of an influential and wealthy deacon. Denominational authorities were called in. Privately, the denominational secretary assured Roger that they would back him. If necessary, they would find him a new church. The same man told the deacons that *Roger* was the problem. Roger was left high and dry. After the public meeting, the denominational secretary sought to soothe Roger: "I knew it would be better to get you out of here. We will bring you back to the city and find you a good church." When Roger returned to the city, he was left with his own removal costs, and his salary was suspended. No real explanation was given. Preaching invitations evaporated. Whenever Roger asked about his future, the official line remained, "We're still looking for a suitable church for you." No church was ever found. Roger's own personality may have contributed to the crisis, but this can never excuse such shabby treatment.

Professionalism in the System

Evangelical conventions of authority and control presume the professionalism of ministry. This is the norm. Preaching and ministry must be a full-time, paid vocation. The minister is the "indispensable professional."[23] We have already noted the pivotal role of ordination to ensure conformity and uniformity within the system:

> In the church, says Ward, status is earned by knowing; what is required for leadership is the possession of a "magic bag of merits." "These magic bags of merit are systematically dealt out only to a relatively few players in the game. The dealers are the theological seminaries. Once a magic bag of merit is in one's possession, it can be traded for

---

[23]Harvie Conn, "Theological Education and the Search for Excellence," *Westminster Theological Journal* 41 (1979): 330.

honor and prestige (plus a salary) at the friendly local church, and thus one maintains oneself, career and salary, more in terms of what one knows than what one *is*.[24]

Theological inquiry comes embedded in the social patterns of expertise and authority. The categories and definitions of theology create both the questions that drive inquiry and the parameters for legitimate answers. The products are couched in terms of timeless and objective absolutes. Convention is placed beyond conversation. Harvie Conn takes us to the heart of the system:

> Coordinate with the rise of the schooling, abstractionist model of excellence has grown a concept of theology as the academically disciplined, thematic ordering of biblical data, "the scientific presentation of all the facts that are known concerning God and his relations." . . . The legitimate place for a teacher as one in whom those gifts of edification are heightened has been transposed into an acculturated model of the professional. And theology has become his job, not the task of the church. . . . Does [then] the structure of a theological seminary, isolated from community with the body of Christ, and from the world which it observes, *not teach more about theology than it intends?*[25]

Theology creates a web of abstraction validating the need for professional expertise and authority. It is a closed system:

☐ Preaching is central to evangelical life.

☐ A preacher must be ordained (or licensed) to preach.

☐ An ordinand must complete an approved seminary's prescribed course of theological and ministerial training.

☐ The seminary faculty is likewise ordained.

☐ The denomination directs the seminary.

☐ The denomination oversees the placement of clergy.

☐ The denomination and the seminary offer career prospects (larger churches or managerial or academic posts) to those suitably qualified, successful and respected.

Denomination, seminary, church structure and church service form a closed system centered on the preaching profession and the key controls of calling, qualification and ordination. In more recent years, the system has been altered in line with alternative strategies for growth. Large ministries based around university students and church planting, often created in reaction to the stifling nature of the traditional system, have in effect created alternative denominational structures. But for all their innovation, the shape of the system remains.

---

[24]Harvie Conn, *Evangelism: Doing Justice and Preaching Grace* (Grand Rapids, Mich.: Zondervan, 1982), p. 93. Conn quotes from T. Ward, "Servants, Leaders and Tyrants," a lecture delivered at Calvin Theological Seminary, Grand Rapids, Michigan, March 29, 1978.

[25]Conn, "Theological Education," pp. 350, 353, 359; emphasis mine. Conn quotes from B. B. Warfield, *Studies in Theology* (New York: Oxford University Press, 1932), p. 68.

To the faithful, the system reinforces the mystique of evangelicalism as self-evidently right. To the disaffected, the system looms as closed, fearful and irrelevant. To both, the system is only as viable as its ongoing ability to demarcate the acceptable from the unacceptable. Central to the dynamics of maintaining these boundaries is what I call the "biblical-unbiblical" game.

Maintaining System Boundaries: The Biblical-Unbiblical Game

My portrait of the system behind the sermon and the service suggests that while we may *think* of evangelicalism as simply a set of theological beliefs, we nonetheless *experience* it as a complex network of cultural events and involvement. The young theological student does not know the doctrine of church independently of his experience of church structures and meetings. He knows that the doctrine *means* a church service designed and led by a pastor, an order of service, an ordained ministry, and the ways the denomination conducts its affairs. He is sure that the tasks and conventions he associates with becoming an ordained professional *are* what Paul did and wrote about. When evangelicals speak of being true to Paul (and the other authors of the Bible), they refer to someone or something as "biblical." What they judge as out of step is "unbiblical." Exegesis, theology, church practice and experience are audited by a single question: Is it biblical or unbiblical?

This question is a key driver of the system. No doubt it springs in part from a sincere desire for the Bible to judge the issue at hand. But the tags *biblical* and *unbiblical* indicate more than faithfulness to the Bible. They reinforce the rectitude of evangelicalism and mark a person as acceptable or otherwise within the system.

The perennial debate over the ordination of women is a prime example of the biblical-unbiblical game. A handful of evangelicals have noted that ordination itself is the unspoken presupposition of the debate and that a fresh examination of its validity could shift the debate:

> Perhaps there is a more deep-seated reason for our division. *Perhaps we need to question the whole nature of ordination*, rather than the gender of the ordinand. Many people have made this point, but it has not greatly affected the debate. Evangelicals have not sorted out what they mean by "ordination" and have not questioned our existing structures from a Biblical perspective. We find ourselves arguing bitterly about a power structure that has little or no New Testament warrant. Our failure may not lie in our attitude to the Bible, so much as in our compromise and double-mindedness over the whole subject of ordination. Before we engage in the next round . . . are we ready to face this issue?[26]

---

[26]Tony Payne, "The Evangelical Double Standard," *The Briefing* 14 (1988): 2; emphasis his. In the following decade the editors and contributors to *The Briefing* took an increasingly hard line on women's ordination and their ministering to men. The spirit of Payne's remark resurfaced from time to time, but it was overwhelmed by assumptions of the traditional conventions of preaching.

Evangelicals who oppose the ordination of women face a double bind (so too do many of those in favor of ordaining women). It is unpalatable either to pursue or to ignore examining the status quo in the light of the Bible. It is equally uncomfortable to abandon or to defend the status quo. While discrepancies between text and convention trouble evangelicals, the games of theology and churchmanship rationalize each discrepancy and tame each objection. If one acknowledges, for example, that ordination is itself an "unbiblical" notion and practice, then what integrity is there in arguing "biblically" to preserve its historical and current expression against those who seek to bring "unbiblical" changes to the practice? Yet this double standard does not soften those who hunt for "unbiblical" evangelicals. There is more at stake here than correct interpretation.

The issues surrounding the debates are not simply about believing or disbelieving the Bible, but about the sacrosanct nature of the system. Professional ministry is basic to the system. The seminary, the denomination and the pulpit form a self-referential loop centered on the unquestionable conventions and values of ordination and the clerical career. The model must not change. Most of those who argue for the otherwise radical change of ordaining women are equally committed to preserving the model. It is a closed loop, admitting no breach and shaping most aspects of evangelical life. Everything comes from this circle: the literature, the conferences, the publishing agendas, the orders of service, the Bible study aids, the translations, the building programs, the shape of the gathering, the denominational debates, the guest speakers, the permission for lay ministries, the weekend retreats, the educational programs, the reforms, and so forth. It also deeply influences most so-called parachurch agencies. It even facilitates the "liberation" of the laity. Debates and decisions over women's ministry allow evangelicals to *rethink* their scruples about authoritarianism, clericalism and sacramentalism—but they are unlikely to *act* upon them. Change means breaking rank.

I once had lunch with a denominational leader. Despite a few fast-growing churches, membership was steadily declining. Settling into the café, "George" had a question waiting: "Mark, if you were in my position what would you do?"

I had anticipated the question. "I would initiate diverse new groups and learn from them. You have millions of dollars in assets and hundreds of experienced people. Resources are not a problem—so long as you count this more important than retaining real estate. I would start with ten diverse teams working in a variety of socioeconomic and cultural contexts. Mix paid and unpaid, ordained and unordained, old and young. Then give them a free hand. Some will grow; some will fail. Get them together regularly to learn from one another."

He liked what he heard. "But one thing, George," I said, "You must cover for these people. Protect them from your zealous and jealous colleagues. Don't lose your nerve. Back them and patiently harvest the learning."

George's face fell. "I do not doubt what exciting things could come from this. But I know the resistance I would face."

A couple of ventures did get off the ground. Communities of unchurched people grew around the wonder of new-found grace. But then George's colleagues pounced. The groups were inadequate. People must be moved into "real" churches. Families whose faith had been restored withdrew—disillusioned, hurt and angry. George lost his nerve and withdrew support.

My stories may have prompted recall of your own stories of the *system as system*. If we sense the need for radical change, then we will need to start telling our stories. Theological inquiry and discussion will only create more abstraction and mollify our sense of unease. We need conversations full of stories. We need to hear where meaning has broken down in the system. We need to hear where pastors and people are squeezed out for daring to speak and feel the truth. We need grace-full conversations in order to face the truth, bring justice, forgive, heal and grow.

17

WHEN MEANING
BREAKS DOWN

ANY GROUP THAT IS DEEPLY COMMITTED TO ABSOLUTES AND AUTHORITY WILL STRUGGLE with the gap between ideals and lived experience. Churches are no exception. Many suppress this dissonance, reassuring themselves that God is on their side. Many lose hope. Many others find new heart away from the system.

The Burden of Being Right
The ideals confronting preachers are formidable. We have only skimmed the prescriptions of senior preachers and scholars such as those cited in the last chapter. What is the impact on a young or a "dry" preacher as he tries to emulate them? As a "man of God," he is expected to live an exemplary life so that he "is ready for any challenge as he ministers to the needs of God's congregation."[1] He must act with composure befitting his dignified office. He must convey divine power and be an eminent man, full of assurance and faith. His position and pulpit presence must reinforce the image of the ideal Christian. He must also measure up to the expectations of the congregation. From the start he must meet the approval of those who hire him:

---

[1]John Bettler, "Application," in *The Preacher and Preaching: Reviving the Art in the Twentieth Century*, ed. S. T. Logan Jr. (Philadelphia: Presbyterian & Reformed, 1986), p. 334.

Knowing that everything rises or falls depending on the quality of leadership in the parish, the work of the incumbency committee is therefore vital in selecting the best possible leader. . . . Thoroughly research the track record (the specific achievements and failures) as well as the reputation of your top 3 candidates. . . . Ask tough questions (e.g., tell us specifically about your daily devotions, recent answers to prayer, when you last led someone to Christian commitment, how many hours a week do you work; what recent changes have you made, etc.).[2]

What takes place in the heart and mind of a man who feels the fate of his congregation resting on him? What happens when the sermon fails—when the ideal is *not* reached? What conclusion is the preacher likely to draw? He *may* attribute failure to the congregation, as one mentor suggests: "When the preaching of the Word fails, there is only one place where blame can be placed—on the condition of the listener's heart."[3] There *are* preachers whose first thought is to blame the hearers. But there are many others who will judge themselves against the ideals of piety and preaching. Older mentors stand ready to add to his guilt:

One of the reasons why poor preaching is dull is that the preacher himself fails to experience what he is talking about as he speaks—there is no joy, sense of awe, tingling down his spine, or whatever. When *he* fails to relive the event, it is almost axiomatic that his congregation will "experience" that failure.[4]

The young pastor is urged to preach with authority and power. But such power eludes, and the path to it has many dead ends:

The problem is universal. There is not a denomination or fellowship of pastors that does not designate powerlessness in the pulpit as its greatest weakness, and there is no shortage of homiletical literature that suggests to preachers the source of power and a revolution in their ministry. . . . Where, then, is power for preaching to be found? For some the answer is *glossolalia*. . . . For others the answer is intimidatingly austere and almost frighteningly monastic in its tone—agonizing in prayer, fasting, mortification, and self-denial are all absolutized as the only answer to our powerlessness. How it intimidates the young pastor![5]

The author goes on to substitute one burden for another:

Every sermon is to be accompanied by divine power if it is to be true proclamation of the Word of God. Is it not as sinful to preach the Scriptures powerlessly as it is to misrepresent them by false exegesis? The only way that the New Testament knows of preaching the gospel is with the Holy Ghost sent down from heaven. . . . Where may

---

[2]P. Crawford, "How to Present Your Parish When Looking for a New Leader," *Essentials* 9 (1993): 8–9.
[3]W. L. Hogan, "Take Care How You Listen," *Reformed Theological Review* 53 (1994): 9.
[4]Jay Adams, "Sense Appeal and Story-Telling," in *Preacher and Preaching*, p. 355; emphasis his.
[5]G. Thomas, "Powerful Preaching," in *Preacher and Preaching*, pp. 369–70.

such power be found? . . . Clearly its own explanation is the life of God in the soul of the preacher.[6]

The ideal looms. The preacher fears that his piety and consequently his power in preaching will break down. According to the mentors, such breakdowns indicate a "lack of self-denial," "nervous tension," "moral failure," "pride and selfish ambition," and "deviation from the truth and from reliance on the instituted means of grace." Ultimately each "ministerial breakdown . . . may be traced to a lack of proper biblical piety."[7] So pastors must guard the time to prepare themselves in heart and mind. They must draw back from their congregations and maintain the aloof discernment of those who will address the flock with the authority and power of preaching:

> Ministers touch conscience all the time . . . [thus] it is absolutely essential that a minister possess the gift of judgement, the gift of wisdom. He must have the ability to understand what is really happening among the people he is most closely related to. . . . Such judgement can only be exercised if a minister is able to maintain a certain degree of emotional distance from other people and from the circumstances in which he finds himself.[8]

Folding under the feeling of poor performance in the face of impossible ideals and desperately in need of truthful conversation, the ailing preacher can actually be driven *away* from the place of grace by advice like this. What he needs is candid grace-full conversation with peers and friends. But the ideals reinforce his sense of weakness in not being able to go it alone. *Surely,* he thinks, *a true man of God would lean only on God and not look for support from people.* The mounting pressure may hasten his resignation. When this happens, what is at stake in the eyes of his peers and the denomination?

For most ex-pastors, the emotional and spiritual strain associated with their transition out of parish ministry is considerable. One writes, "My denomination and colleagues treat me as if I were a leper." Another: "The only contact from the Superintendent of my denomination when I left the pastorate was a terse request for the keys to the manse!"[9]

In the end, isolation may engulf the "failing" pastor. I know what this is. Very

---

[6]Ibid., pp. 370–71.

[7]Errol Hulse, "The Preacher and Piety," in *Preacher and Preaching,* pp. 70–79.

[8]Joel Nederhood, "The Minister's Call," in *Preacher and Preaching,* pp. 52–53.

[9]Taken from the information brochure of Rowland Croucher, John-Mark Ministries, Melbourne. Croucher researches the sociology of pastoral resignations and offers a counseling service to ex-pastors and their spouses. He estimates that approximately fifty percent of Australian clergy retire prematurely. Many of these become deeply disaffected by their experiences of ministry and resignation.

often there is no one to listen. To admit the struggle is to lose face with peers and superiors, the very "ones who will give advice to others about job places both now and in the future."[10] The ideals of preaching and ministry consign thousands to silence and a gnawing sense of unreality.

The Power of Ideals and Rectitude

So far we have looked mostly from the preacher's side of the pulpit at the institutional and personal capital invested in preaching by ministers, seminaries and denominational authorities. But this is only one view of the system. The sermon is a *social* event in which its form is as much the message as the words. The sermon is a cultural experience. This leads us to ask new questions: What is the sermon to a congregation? What images, expectations and ideals does it convey? What parity or disparity lies between the timeless principles and ideals of the pulpit and the realities of experience? What happens when meaning breaks down?

The preacher himself may sense that a congregation has not experienced the event as relevant to life. For some this signals the need to preach *more*. Others recognize that blaming the congregation may only disguise and compound the problem. The ambiguity of life makes the ideals seem less than clear even to the preacher. He aims to enrich his congregation in the truth. But no matter how he engages with them, he cannot know their worlds as they do. Ironically, this may actually lead the preacher to push further down the path of preaching those principles that he believes apply *universally* to any congregation. Community increasingly comes to mean *conformity*.

Paul sensed this risk in his relations with the Corinthians. His disavowal of rhetoric was part of his strategy to free this *ekklēsia* from being dominated by certain members and their social rank and ideals. Ironically, incredulously, some evangelical scholars and preachers laud the same rhetorical tradition for its ability to suppress diversity and create conformity:

> The rhetorically artistic journey begins, for the Ciceronian, with narration [for the preacher, with doctrine]—bringing the audience to one mind with both speaker and itself . . . [to create the] *one audience-personality out of many audience-persons.*[11]

A circular dynamic sustains the system: Conformity requires ideals, ideals require persuasive oratory, the orator needs to feel he knows the truth; persuading others of the truth is the basis of conformity. The conventions of preaching establish boundaries for the congregation's thoughts, feelings and behavior. The effect is

---

[10]Robert Doyle, "Ministers Who Resign," *The Briefing* 135 (1994): 8.

[11]L. de Koster, "The Preacher as Rhetorician," in *Preacher and Preaching*, pp. 310–11, emphasis mine.

to make the whole system seem self-evidently true and to pull people back from the storms of their questions and doubts into the shelters of authorized explanations and ideals. They must be calmed before they find grief, anger and freedom.

For many the system just slips into sheer irrelevance. Unable to find grace-full conversation in the church, many spin new webs of conversation on the Net, waiting to start or find something better "in the flesh." For some time now, I have had conversations, like the following, with disaffected evangelicals around the world.

> I might, at best, be described as living on the fringes of the church, though even this would grossly overstate my actual involvement. Despite many years of effort in teens/ 20s, "church" hasn't ever worked for me. My chosen career eventually ended any notion of regularly attending anything. Hence, my nomadic existence neatly solved my early struggles of guilt vs. boredom over whether to persevere with this Ancient Institution. On my journey, the more distance I gained between myself and my church roots, the less I could comprehend the worth of propping up the institution—not through any malice or bitterness, but just through realizing its sheer irrelevance to me getting on with life. It confused me that so many bright people spend so much time dealing with centuries of associated baggage, defending institutional inevitabilities that simply make no sense. But for those who feel this way or find themselves in a similar position, what exists to help sustain Christian spirituality? It helped me to read a book like Dave Tomlinson's *The Post-Evangelical* to be reminded that experiencing such feelings did not place me outside the fold. Brian McLaren and Mike Riddell's books are also written for people outside the Christian faith or struggling with it, and their themes and approach might prove sustaining. Ultimately it's very difficult to pursue the Christian journey totally alone. The fact is that the Christian faith is about community. It is only in the presence of other believers that much of Jesus' story makes sense and can be appropriated.

Seeds of Disaffection

The shelters are collapsing. Even conservative evangelicals sense the denial in much preaching:

> When we reflect deeply on how life is, both inside our soul and outside in our world, a quiet terror threatens to overwhelm us. . . . In those moments, retreat into denial does not seem cowardly, it seems necessary and smart. Just keep going, get your act together, stop feeling sorry for yourself, renew your commitment to trust God, get more serious about obedience. Things really aren't as bad as you intuitively sense they are.
>
> Many more [preachers] communicate the same [false] hope by neither sharing honestly their own current struggles nor addressing realistically the struggles of others. It's tempting to stay removed from the problems for which we have no ready answers. . . . We end up unprepared to live but strengthened in our denial.[12]

---

[12]Larry Crabb, *Inside Out* (Colorado Springs: NavPress, 1988), pp. 15, 17.

Conformity no longer makes sense for a rising tide of ex- and disaffected evangelicals. The tensions between faith and life have become too acute in the face of deepening ambiguity, pain and the taste of freedom outside the system. They may try to conform, only to end up refusing to play the game. For some this *is* the shape of evangelical experience. There is no room for seeing things differently. The hearers must bow before the overwhelming verdict that the *system* defines relationship with God. The preacher *must* believe this and must never stop telling them so.

Church as sermon-plus-extras fuels this tension. Evangelicals have always emphasized the Reformation principle of "the priesthood of all believers." This principle acknowledges the equality of the congregation before God, both leaders and led. In recent decades the principle has been taken to imply a wider participation of nonclergy in the gathering. But little has changed.[13] The gathering remains the job of the pastor who must learn to perform with the timing of a talk show host:

> Lay participation in the Church services needs to be encouraged, after adequate preparation through well-run training classes. . . . Effective communication is more important than participation for its own sake. The laity's job is not primarily to help the clergy do their job in the church.[14]

> That jerkiness [in worship] can be prevented if . . . worship leaders plan to move toward the pulpit during the end of the hymn. For me that means timing the last few bars of the hymn with my walk from my seat to the pulpit. When I first began ministry, I actually practiced this on Saturday nights.[15]

The gathering remains a set of proceedings led from the front. More informal interactions happen before or after "real" church. It is striking how evangelicals routinely refer to the formal proceedings in which they are almost entirely passive as church and to their interactions with one another before and after as something

---

[13]Many books by evangelicals have explored themes such as "body life," "one-anothering," community and the house church. See Robert Banks, *Paul's Idea of Community: The Early House Churches in their Historical Setting* (Sydney: Lancer; Grand Rapids, Mich.: Eerdmans; and Exeter: Paternoster, 1980); *Going to Church in the First Century: An Eyewitness Account* (Sydney; Hexagon, 1985); Robert and Julia Banks, *The Church Comes Home: A New Base for Community and Mission* (Peabody, Mass.: Hendrickson, 1998); Howard Snyder, *The Problem of Wineskins: Church Structure in a Technological Age* (Downers Grove, Ill.: InterVarsity Press, 1975); *The Community of the King* (Downers Grove, Ill.: InterVarsity Press, 1977); *Liberating the Church: The Ecology of Church and Kingdom* (Downers Grove, Ill.: InterVarsity Press, 1983); R. P. Stevens, *Liberating the Laity: Equipping All the Saints for Ministry* (Downers Grove, Ill.: InterVarsity Press, 1985); and Frank Tillapaugh, *Unleashing the Church: Getting People out of the Fortress and into Ministry* (Ventura, Calif.: Regal, 1982). Each contributed something vital. Each created initial interest. But there has been little lasting impact on mainstream evangelicalism.

[14]Lance Shilton, "A Plan of Action for the Local Congregation," *Essentials* 9 (1993): 6.

[15]Jack Hayford et al., *Mastering Worship* (Portland: Multnomah, 1990), p. 61.

other than church. According to one mentor, there should be more interaction. But when and of what kind?

> The sermon should be the greatest period of participation in the church's assemblies. During a thirty-minute period a Christian should be moved to inward thankfulness and praise, conviction of sin and repentance, determination to love and obey God, new concern for his fellow-believers and his fellow men. The sermon is not for balconeers, but for travelers, for those who are most involved with God; it is the climactic aspect of worship.[16]

That response is audible and physical in some traditions: "When a Black congregation's heart and mind are gripped by the sermon, 'the ensuing dialogue between preacher and people is the epitome of creative worship.'"[17] But this is hollow rhetoric for most of us. The "participation" and "dialogue" in view is a game played in the mind of the preacher: he preempts the congregation's questions; he proclaims; they think over what he has said; and he responds to their *silent* questions:

> The kind of dialogical preaching I am recommending . . . refers to the *silent* dialogue which should be developing between the preacher and his hearers. . . . Preaching is rather like playing chess, in that the expert chess player keeps several moves ahead of his opponent, and is always ready to respond, whatever piece *he* decides to move next.[18]

Whatever the priesthood of all believers is supposed to mean, it does *not* mean that the gathering can be a genuine interaction between people. Except for some groups at the fringes, church has never meant genuine conversation and interaction to Reformed and evangelical churchmen. On this point, the Reformation never left Rome. Real conversation is kept outside "real church." For some evangelicals, this passive, silent, fragmenting system has become intolerable:

> Some manage to hold on at the edges of congregational life. Some find a temporary resting place in parachurch activities of one kind or another. Some withdraw into a private life to find a home there again. What binds these people together is a deep sense of desperation. They literally ache to belong to an informal, compassionate community. For them this is no general desire or optional extra. It is a life-and-death matter, a case of spiritual integrity and survival.[19]

The story below captures the angst of many I continue to meet. The group to which "Rebecca" belonged is a high-profile evangelical ministry renowned for its

---

[16]Thomas, "Powerful Preaching," p. 380.

[17]John Stott, *I Believe in Preaching* (London: Hodder & Stoughton, 1982), p. 61. Stott quotes from H. Mitchell, *Black Preaching* (New York: Harper, 1979), p. 98.

[18]Stott, *I Believe in Preaching*, p. 61, emphasis mine.

[19]Robert Banks and Julia Banks, *Church Comes Home*, p. 101.

solid Bible teaching, evangelism and strong emphasis on grace. But even the strongest advocates of the gospel may wittingly or otherwise package the message of grace in a system of ideals and performance. When "grace" comes with the expectation of conformity, there is little place left for those who question.

I worked for a large evangelical church for two years. I was assured that I was doing the best thing by working in ministry with this group as I would be supported and trained as a leader. However, I had difficulty and was uncomfortable with the way we practiced ministry—I could see that it alienated people and made them feel manipulated and judged. I would ask why there was no platform to challenge or question or change the system, but our leaders would not see that there could be anything wrong with the ministry philosophy and strategy as we practiced it. Generally the answer was that if people didn't fit in or feel comfortable then they needed to change and that if they wouldn't then they were immature or disobedient. Conformity was espoused as the virtue of "like-mindedness" and was interpreted as similarity instead of unity in diversity.

The solutions offered to problems and the style of ministry practiced disregarded who people were as individuals. If I didn't fit in with the ministry, if who I was wasn't "right," then the problem was mine and I just needed to change more and try harder. I was forcing myself to try to become some ideal person imagined by them. As hard as I tried to conform and to resolve the tensions I felt, I couldn't, and I did myself a lot of damage trying to be someone I wasn't.

A friend showed me an unpublished paper about abusiveness within evangelical church life. I read and reread that paper, gradually understanding more and more how Christian groups can be destructive to their members. Then the year after I left the ministry team—and cut off nearly all my ties with that church—I realised that I was living out the paper as I struggled with pain and anger and confusion and depression. I moved through the stages of processing abuse—torn between blaming the structure or people or myself or God or Christianity. I have forgiven now—and learnt to love and have compassion for all of our inadequacies and sin . . . though I still carry the scars. I still find church meetings and structures stifling and oppressive and boring and have a strong aversion to much I encounter in Christian subcultures.

I wrote a short play that I performed with a friend at a day devoted to the connection between postmodernism and Christianity. The play critiqued traditional "follow-up" ministry philosophy and contrasted it with a lot of the ideas I gleaned from the paper. I was very apprehensive about performing it and was blown away when everyone in the room broke into applause (including some staff from my old church who were there).

The paper gave me an intellectual framework for understanding how the inherent power relationships within social structures can be abusive. It helped me to process the pain and grief I felt over those relationships. It also gave me something to grasp onto—a way of understanding what went wrong, for people in my church (including myself) were so obviously trying their hardest to do the right thing and to help—but were still causing one another harm.

I'm now trying to live out Christianity in a way that is true to who I am and the relationships I have with God and other people. A few friends and I are starting to meet together—a group for people who don't like church—feels like a last ditch effort for me. I don't really know where to go from here. My subculture and community these days are made up of alternatives and artists—and there seems to be nowhere for people like that to feel comfortable. I am hoping that we can create a space for that.

Piety, Idealism and Rectitude

The need to keep up an appearance of strength and rectitude lies at the heart of much evangelical piety—and pain. Those who ultimately do not measure up may be ruined. Few issues expose the destructiveness of church ideals like the responses of some churches to women who have suffered at the hands of abusive (and often evangelical) husbands. The following story is sadly all too common.

> I despised his attendance and eager participation at church because it underlined the contrast to his behavior at home. Those who did believe me offered no solace; only sympathy and empty platitudes. They affirmed my submissive reaction to my husband's abusive tyranny. No one at any time went to talk to my husband about his behavior in loving correction. I was always left empty-handed to return to my living hell.[20]

After eight years of extensive research and interviews with battered Christian women in North America, James and Phyllis Alsdurf came to a disturbing conclusion. They claim that when evangelical leaders were made aware of abuse in their churches, many sought to maintain at all cost the semblance of an ordered family and congregation.

> Almost without exception women report that their pastors focused on getting them—not their abusive husbands—to change. Comments by pastors in our sample confirmed that stance. One minister said that his approach with abused women is to involve them in Bible studies because "the studies take their mind out of the home situation for a while," implying that his goal is to keep the wife preoccupied rather than to work for change. What this technique communicates to the battered woman is that the responsibility for change is hers; it becomes a spiritual strategy for blaming the victim.[21]

Some typical patterns emerge in the stories they relate:

> "All three pastors said a man was 'head of the family' and I must endure whatever he did," one woman wrote. . . . Since filing for divorce, that woman added, only two older women in her church talk to her. "I'm an outcast, being a victim of 'church discipline' for divorce, although my husband's behavior is well known."

---

[20]Survey respondent in James Alsdurf and Phyllis Alsdurf, *Battered into Submission: The Tragedy of Wife Abuse in the Christian Home* (Downers Grove, Ill.: InterVarsity Press, 1989), p. 14.
[21]Ibid.

Many have felt that leaving an abusive spouse also means leaving the church. One woman said she is "totally disillusioned" with the church after being told she was in the wrong for wanting to leave her abusive husband. "I finally decided that I didn't have to answer to the ministers, but to God," she concluded. "It was my neck being squeezed, not theirs."[22]

The same pattern is played out across the world:

People placed more importance on keeping the family together than excising the cancer. . . . Rather than believing my daughter and the inescapable evidence, rather than safeguarding the other children, I was expected to sacrifice the lot for the sake of "family" and "marriage."[23]

When Meaning Breaks Down

The ways some leaders and churches disregard the victims of violence and sexual abuse presents a poignant image of how ideals can tyrannize evangelical believers. But the problem is not confined to sexual abuse. Evangelical pulpits routinely reinforce conservative cultural standards and ideals in the name of being "biblical."

But what happens when the hearers sense that they are falling behind? Many work harder to comply rather than question the ideals. Some internalize the unreality of the ideals as their own personal inadequacy to live up to them. Every effort to attain the ideals only reinforces self-condemnation. The tension becomes intolerable in the face of a growing inability to see the world as the preacher does.

A preacher describes what he calls a "burnt-out Evangelical," typical of what he calls the "half-converted" to whom he ministers:

I think April (not her name) felt that because she was a Christian she had to "measure up" to a subconscious, unspoken standard—at least externally. The growing reality was that internally she wasn't measuring up. Now understand, no one does! But everyone is going around holding up some facade that they are measuring up to this unspoken standard. April went on for 15 years like this. . . . Her bad experience of church coupled with her growing disappointment with the realities of life kind of crowded in on her, and she dropped out. In talking to her it became obvious that she was simply burnt out. Her beliefs hadn't changed. But she had a growing skepticism about what she was experiencing in her life under the heading of "being a Christian."

It's interesting that the "burnt-out Evangelicals" that I've been corresponding with . . . seem to have four choices . . . they drop out altogether . . . they go the total emotional route . . . [they] go high church . . . [or] The only other option is to become

---

[22]Ibid., pp. 19–20.

[23]Client's story in H. McClelland, *The Almond Tree: Child Sexual Abuse and the Church* (Melbourne: private publication, n.d.), p. 103. See also Peter Horsfield, "Is the Dam of Sexual Assault Breaking on the Church?" *Australian Ministry*, May 1992, pp. 1–10.

Reformed, and at the church where I work . . . it seems that we're not only trying to reach the unconverted, but also the half-converted![24]

Supposedly "April" (and those like her) dropped out because of her compulsion to comply with the expectations and ideals of preachers and churches whose theology is inadequate. Second, her "spiritual exhaustion" is supposedly "self-induced."[25] Such explanations comfort those who need to believe that everything is fine, but they bear little resemblance to what is actually happening. Many "Aprils" are leaving churches whose theology *is* Reformed. The "performance mentality" operates as easily and pervasively within these churches as within those of a more fundamentalist or charismatic emphasis. Moreover, the exhaustion is at least as often *imposed* as self-induced.

Many people are indeed burned out. In response to the dryness of church life, some attend weekend "relational" workshops. Evangelical gatekeepers warn that such movements may offer immediate emotional benefits but that they ultimately undermine the objectivity of the gospel. One critical article drew this reply:

> I have felt for a while, and your article confirms it, that there can be such an obsession with doctrinal truth that we can't be touched by God unless everything is 100% correct. As much as I value my background, with its strong emphasis on correct scriptural interpretation, I find in myself and others almost a cynicism to anything emotional and experiential. I don't like it. I understand why people end up in the charismatic movement.
>
> The main impact for me [of the weekend] was not great spiritual growth, but the experience of *real*, open communication—people being real with one another. That's truth too. We can go away on a [retreat-style] weekend and have everything doctrinally correct but little depth of relating. I feel as though you are fighting those who are on your side.[26]

The need to be correct overrules the need for real open communication. While the correspondent remains committed to evangelical beliefs, the associated conventions leave her little room for important personal and relational dimensions of her faith. She is not alone.

It seems clear that many evangelicals are losing their loyalties. They will no longer play the games and believe the pat answers. The experiences and questions that drive them away begin as simple questioning. They end in disbelief, grief and anger. Here is a selection of those I hear frequently. Perhaps you have heard the same or similar. Perhaps you have spoken them:

☐ Why do I need to ask permission?

---

[24]P. Miles, interview of C. Heuss, "Carl's Coming Out," *The Briefing* 68 (1991): 6.
[25]Tony Payne, "Lessons from America," *The Briefing* 68 (1991): 2.
[26]Letter to the editor, *The Briefing* 146 (1994): 5, author's emphasis.

☐ Why won't they let me question?

☐ Why won't they let me be real?

☐ I wish they'd stop telling me to pray and read and participate more—don't they understand it doesn't work? Can't they see that I'm too tired and disillusioned for that?

☐ I can't stand to be with Christians!

☐ (Abuse) happened to me—can't you see why I can't cope with the idea of God being sovereign? Can't you see why I hate calling God "Father"?

☐ I feel physically ill if I go to church!

This is reality for those caught in a system they feel they cannot change.

At the end of the last chapter, we noted the impact of those who seek to demarcate the "biblical" from the "unbiblical." This quest for conformity can depersonalize and disaffect even those within the same fraternity:

> Another group of women have been totally disaffected by the whole public debate, because it's very painful to sit and hear yourself spoken of as a "something"—a "something" that in some cases is seen as right and good and in some cases seems to be the worst evil that could befall the church. It's very painful, when you know that you're a Bible-believing, God-loving person who is searching out the truth as much as anyone.[27]

We have examined how preaching is steeped in ideals and expectations. We have noted how conventions and assumptions of precision, truth, authority and rectitude shape the self-image and role of the preacher. The sermon and the service proclaim and justify the system. The service itself conveys the control of the clergy over congregational life:

> Worship preparation *is* basically my responsibility as pastor. Oh, congregations are responsible too. They make an enormous difference with their prayers and enthusiasm and healthy participation. But they aren't the leaders and can hardly be expected to provide the thrust toward more spiritual services. According to biblical warrant, that is *my* venue.[28]

These themes form a disturbing impression. What the pastor expects as his rightful and "biblical" role may be little more than control and insecurity overlaid with sentiment.

Two friends of mine, "Jennifer" and "Malcolm," were not alone in their frustration about where their church was heading. They were exasperated at the heavy-handed control of every aspect of church life by the pastor and elders and the dead-

---

[27]Tony Payne, interview with Narelle Jarrett, *The Briefing* 54 (1990): 8.

[28]J. Killinger, in Hayford, *Mastering Worship*, p. 19, emphasis his.

ening effect this had upon community. Although he professed a more collaborative style, the pastor had made himself the center of all church decision making, even to small administrative matters. Malcolm was the lone voice among the elders calling for conversation and the freeing up of control. He succeeded in getting sanction for a weekend church retreat to look at "Relationships Inside and Outside the Church." The retreat was to be an unanticipated watershed for Malcolm and Jenny and many others.

Such was the widespread frustration that over ninety percent of the congregation came to the retreat. Jenny recalls the enthusiasm of the small group sessions: "All the groups came up with wonderful ideas. Very practical and meaningful to people. The common threads to the conversations were remarkable. We had these big sheets of paper full of suggestions stuck up all around the walls. We all believed that at last we were getting somewhere. The feeling of community, joy and goodwill was palpable."

At coffee break, Jenny overheard the pastor and a couple of the "inner circle" elders discussing the morning's outcomes. She sensed their cynicism and was moved to speak with them. "What's happening here," she said, "is so important to us all. Please take this seriously." The pastor's response chilled her: "Ah, yes, but you have to remember that the elders must think of everybody."

In the year that followed, Malcolm attended every elders' session. What happened that weekend was never discussed. Not one suggestion was ever acted upon. Most people slipped back into frustrated silence. A few, like Jenny and Malcolm, had endured the gagging of the conversation long enough. And the pastor? He went on to speak at conferences and lecture at seminary—on grace!

Some pastors sense the deep dissonance between the elitism inherent in their position and the catch-cry of impartial grace: "This is an uncomfortable thought. . . . We're very good at making exactly the same mistakes as those made by the teachers of the law. . . . We've painted ourselves into a corner."[29] Changing the status quo away from professional ministry would trigger massive upheavals in the system. This is why it will never happen. The conflict of interest is too great.

Pastoral rank and control are loaded with the theological and cultural weight of truth, authority and godliness. Any challenge to the system may be taken as an encroaching liberalism or subjectivism, as a personal attack against the pastor or as an act of rebellion against God. As we have frequently noted, the system may blind the preacher to his living contradictions of his own preaching. He may preach the priesthood of all believers, then close down Bible studies that he or another authorized leader cannot attend. He may preach the impartiality of grace, then place

---

[29]P. Campbell, "That the Widows Mite Not," *The Briefing* 103 (1992): 8.

fences around public ministries to discourage all but a preselected few. He may preach the gifts of the Spirit, then subtly white-ant those who may be more effective in pastoral ministry than he is. He may preach against performance games, then insist on doing all preaching and pastoral ministry even in the face of palpable evidence of his own ineptitude or inexperience. And he is likely to cite Paul in support of each decision: "Command and teach these things. Don't let anyone look down on you. . . . Do not neglect your gift. . . . Be diligent in these matters . . . because if you do, you will save both yourself and your hearers" (1 Tim 4:11–16). The pastor cannot afford to face his own immaturity and insecurity. As Alistair Mant notes of leadership more generically, too many would-be leaders "can't hack . . . their jobs, and can't hack the fact that they can't hack it."[30]

Abstract theology, pastoral ideals and professionalism are bound up with pride and fear. They are inseparable for many who seek to be "biblical." It is easy enough to bolster insecurity by manipulating and controlling others in the name of "biblical" leadership. Love can seem like lack of conviction, being peaceable like an admission of being "unbiblical." Expressions of immediacy and intimacy toward God may seem like "unbiblical" subjectivism or sloppy sentimentalism. Pietistic and charismatic pastors and congregations who challenge the supposed prophecies and wise guidance of their leaders may be rebuked as unspiritual and told to "touch not the Lord's anointed." The drive to be radically biblical, Reformed, evangelical or Spirit-filled becomes a game to escape dissonance and hypocrisy. What drives a system where peers and friends audit one another's performance and have the power to make or break one another with a single word?

The noted North American scholar and preacher Don Carson had been invited to address evangelical Anglicans in Sydney on the then-current state of play in the debates over the ministry of women. In closing, Carson put aside erudition and spoke passionately against what he discerned as the myopic preoccupation of many in the audience. His theme echoes our impressions of the social force of the epithets *biblical* and *unbiblical*. His words go to the heart of the matter:

> Are you going to conduct the debate in a manner in which the whole watching world says, "My—those Christians love one another"? Or, in your passion to defend your view of the Word of God, will you—God help us—deny that very Word's injunction to love the brothers, to love the sisters? . . . I have heard already . . . that there are some of you on both sides of this issue who find it difficult even to be civil to the other side because you disagree on this issue. Isn't that sin? There is a want of godliness in this discussion. . . . Do not partition yourself off into holier-than-thou huddles which communicate with the other side only in the printed word but never over

---

[30]Alistair Mant, *Intelligent Leadership* (Sydney: Allen & Unwin, 1997), p. 101.

a cup of coffee. . . . You have so many strengths. Do not sacrifice them on this loss [of fellowship].[31]

An Invitation to Conversation at the Crossroads

Men and women of all evangelical persuasions, have we considered how we are going to manage in the face of the growing breakdown in evangelical meanings? What shall we do as the system loses the clarity of past boundaries? Reflect on the changed situation toward which this new state of understanding, disaffection and experimentation is tending. Where will we be left?

For many decades everything we have done has been dictated by the assured conviction that our conventions were demonstrably biblical, that people understood this clearly (or at least acquiesced), and that all dissent lay clearly with those who had or would soon abandon the evangelical faith once received. There was clarity for the most part about who may and may not own the name evangelical. Mostly we accepted the rules of engagement. We had unanimity on the need for periodical self-review and reaffirmation of evangelicalism as Christianity at its straightforward best. The line was clear between us and the rest.

All this has now changed. Our growing understanding of the New Testament era makes our assumptions of biblical warrant for the conventions of preaching, church and theology untenable. Scholar and rank-and-file alike clearly see the discrepancies. Our calls to return to an older, more stable era and practice elicit only incredulity. For decades people sensed something incongruous in our conventions and theological justifications. In the past we quieted these musings with assurances that we knew best. Our rationalizations no longer cut ice. We succeeded in equipping enquiry across the evangelical fraternity. We did not realize where this would lead. Now the conversations proceed apace away from all sanction and control. Here and there we point out pockets of remarkable growth. But the heart is dying. We will simply take longer to die than the liberals. For every success, there are many in the throes of demise. The system will always exist—but at what price?

So much of what we hold dear makes no impression. There is no interest in our reviews. "What is an evangelical?" we ask. "Who cares?" they respond. "Revive preaching!" we cry. "No one's listening!" they respond. "Reinforce the theological foundations of authority and objectivity," we write to one another. "You confuse the authority of the Bible and the gospel with your own needs for control and prestige," they accuse. "Tell them they will die without church and the preaching of the Word," we intone. "But church and preaching killed us!" they cry back. "But we

---

[31]From tape 2, side A of "Women's Ministry: Equal but Different," a lecture given at St. Barnabas Anglican Church, Sydney, Australia, on September 8, 1995.

know the Bible and can teach you," we plead. "We are no longer in awe of you," they calmly reply. "Many of us are better educated and more well-read than you; we are no longer mystified by the canons and subtleties of exegesis and hermeneutic; we occupy positions of far greater professional and social responsibility; we have far greater experience of the world; we can teach as well or better than you; our conversations have life and meaning that your erudition and eloquence never match— so tell us, why do we need you?" "Your postmodern and therapeutic themes will cut you loose from the Bible and the gospel," we warn. "Maybe, maybe not," they muse. "We choose that risk, for we simply cannot go back; we have not turned our backs on Jesus or the Bible, only on your constraint of our lives; we look for new places where the Bible and the gospel may ring true again."

The conclusions are obvious. The world is changing, and many of us will be left behind. The relations that matter now are no longer between ourselves but with a growing, disparate mass of disaffected and adventurous believers for whom "being evangelical" is less than no issue. The time has come to cease reassuring ourselves that at least we are right. The time has come to cease our perennial and futile debates about who or what is evangelical. We may as well be talking to the air. The time has come for new conversation with new partners—in our own backyards and beyond. We will not own these conversations. The agendas will be fluid. The venues will be open to all. The rules of engagement will frighten and perplex us. The experiments will trouble us. The realignment of boundaries will unsettle us. The accusations will be too accurate and too unjust to bear. The transparency and hypocrisy will confuse. None of us will be all victim or all perpetrator, all right or all wrong.

Conversation like this first unnerves, then exposes, then maybe—and only maybe, for there are no guarantees—brings understanding and grace and love. We are in a transient situation that will last the rest of our lives and our children's lives. The time has come for us to choose: will we continue to chatter safely among ourselves; or will we engage in risky grace-full conversation with brothers and sisters who defy our expectations? I make this call to all evangelicals of whatever club—Reformed, Arminian, charismatic, pietist, liturgical, dispensational. I make it to traditionalists and alternates alike. I make it to myself.

18

FRAMES FOR GRACE-FULL CONVERSATION

GRACE-FULL CONVERSATION DOES NOT MEAN AN END TO FORMAL TEACHING OR LARGE gatherings. Monologue had its place with Paul as it does now. But monologue needs to be framed by dialogue, not the reverse. Those gifted to teach need to do so in ways that (re)open places for conversation. We converse to know the God we serve and to know how best to realize all it means for us to be his created and redeemed image. We explore freedom within the bounds of wisdom and grace. We seek to create and sustain the conversations in which we work out what it means to wear Christ's name in all of life.

The Spirit urges us to improvise around the gospel of Jesus Christ. We do not know each path of wisdom and grace in advance. We cannot know in advance where grace-full conversations will lead or how they will reframe our understanding and experiences of leadership and the gathering. We cannot know where our lives will be challenged and changed. We will only know as we converse and improvise.

Grace-full conversations return again and again to the grand themes of Scripture and life, but they never move entirely away from specific contexts. Consciously or otherwise, we test and retest with one another how we see the unfolding drama of the Bible, the dying and rising of Jesus, and the myriad implications for our own circumstances. We liberally draw and model the metaphors framing our engagement with text and Savior and world.

Journey into Conversation

Earlier I mentioned my professional work in strategic conversation and leadership formation within corporations and government agencies. This is far from incidental to my purposes here. It is, in fact, deeply intertwined with my own journey into grace-full conversation. During my time studying in the United States, Sue and I were privileged to have the company of old and new friends from home and abroad. Bill, David and I in particular, coconspirators in conversation at the edges, kept pushing the boundaries of church and theological convention, and teasing out the implications of what it could look like to engage with the world with the confidence that the gospel had much more to say than theologians generally allowed. David's and my subsequent consultancy work grew from this conviction.

When I began to consult, I had no background in corporate life beyond a few years as editor of a small publishing firm. Tony, my new coconspirator, and I began business with three hunches. First, communications were poor in corporate life and were the outcome of upstream confusion of thought and relationships. Second, the gospel gave us rich perspectives on the complexities of how speech and word frames life and the processes of making meaning. Third, somehow we would learn to translate these insights from gospel to corporate life. Along the way we were joined by Rob, Anne, Jim, David, Joan, Neville, Rodney and a dozen or two more.

Within a few years we were being invited to participate at the sharper end of organizational strategy and design. The further we pushed our exploration of the Bible and the gospel, the further our thinking evolved about corporate strategy, design and leadership. At times we wondered if we had strayed out of our depth—and usually we had. In my story that follows, I chronicle this period from another perspective, that of my involvement in planting an "unchurchy" church and several other "alternate" ministries, of my later breakdown and of my doctoral research into Paul and the Graeco-Roman world. These threads—consultancy, church, "alternate" ministries, breakdown and Ph.D.—formed one tight band. Each part of my life conversed with the others. Each conversation linked partners from different worlds.

My breakdown and eventual recovery led me to desire more earnestly than ever to pursue and build the kind of work I really wanted to do. During my "black years," the time of my research, I maintained the conversation with my colleagues as best I could manage. Slowly the themes became richer. David and I explored how we name and rename our worlds as image of the Creator. We began to see corporate life and church life mirroring one another. Churches languish for lack of reality, and theology too often parodies grace-full conversation. Corporate leaders too struggle for lack of vital conversation and often inadvertently gag themselves on the verge of it. Many leaders remain caught in patterns of permission and control—unable to discern, create and sustain those conversations that would bring intent, strategy and design to life. The formulas of strategy and organizational change can be as abstract and lifeless as theology. My colleagues and I pushed to reframe strategy as a process of strategic conversation. I shared the substance of my thinking on the classical heritage, Paul, and the Graeco-Roman world with my colleagues and clients. Today I draw deeply from the wisdom traditions of the Bible (plus classical, ancient Near East and oriental traditions) to help build greater wisdom into the heart of leadership.

None of this journey has been purely intellectual or professional. Heady at times, the conversations remain grounded in living contexts. More importantly, there has been joy in these conversations—the joy of discovery and making. The joy of throwing off those traditions of evangelicalism that can only see limitation, liability and corruption in being human. The joy of wondering at what it means to be image of God—of tasting what it means to create a world, name it, declare it good and bless others with it.

Finding a Rhythm for Grace-full Conversation

Grace-full conversation aligns the Bible, the gospel and people with their needs for insight, integrity and improvisation. The desired outcomes are grace and truth to bless the world as redeemed images of God.

No two grace-full conversations are identical, yet much is held in common. At heart is a kind of rhythm between ancient narrative and modern story; between insight, healing and challenge to live boldly. The agenda is as broad as life. The mood may be analytical and incisive, light and irreverent, deep and therapeutic; or maybe all, some or none of the above. We are talking about people, engaging with one another around common concern and desire, not the neutral posturing of traditional exegesis and theology or the pseudo-interaction of preaching and church service. We are talking about people, wrestling with the Spirit and with one another to know the truth, grace and freedom of Christ in all the particulars of who we are and what fills our lives. Conversations full of grace. Conversations that bring grace. Conversations marked by grace. That is as close as I will come to defining grace-full conversation.

Scan your own fond memories of conversations that brought you reality and joy, the sense of truly engaging with God, with his word, with his creation and with one another. That is the raw data of your definition. Certain questions seem to hover in the conversations, framing and reframing our engagement of heart and mind:

☐ If grace, why do we revert to law?

☐ If grace, who am I, and who are you?

☐ If grace, what is the world to me?

☐ If grace, what is growth?

☐ If grace, what does it mean to have influence in the world?

☐ If grace, how can we use the Bible?

☐ If grace, what are the boundaries and possibilities for improvisation?

Each question (and many more) is loaded for me and my friends, but two stand out.

First, *if grace, what is growth*? Over a decade ago my friend and colleague Tony and I articulated this question in one of those magical extended conversations. Ours scanned Ephesians, our personal stories, and the challenges of serving our professional clients. There are two assumptions behind the question: (1) we struggle to grasp just how radical grace is; and (2) much (most?) teaching on Christian experience is really about performance (law)—even from those who style themselves as the restorers of preaching true grace. It's performance all the way down. Grace *is* radical. So radical that it threatens to overthrow growth: Why change when I stay in grace anyway? Most evangelical answers to this question lose the plot on grace. We end up back with performance and guilt. For us the journey led to some significant reframing of what it means to be human (perhaps the subject for another conversation) and to the other question.

Second, *if grace, what does it mean to have influence in the world?* Decades ago Cornelius Van Til and his more famous pupil Francis Schaeffer popularized the notion of a Christian worldview among evangelical students. Along with many other apologists, they spawned a whole new evangelical curiosity with the idea of an integrated view of faith and life. The bottom line was a call to reject dualism in all its forms and to embrace a holistic understanding and practice of "the lordship of Jesus Christ over all of life." Much good has come from this. Yet in an ironic twist to Schaeffer's intent, this preoccupation has tended toward the creation of a parallel universe of evangelical equivalents to "secular" institutions. Whatever the merits of these institutions, they have generally *not* promoted deep, sustained interaction between faith and the world.

My friends and I did not build a "Christian" consulting firm, nor would we. Affixing "Christian" and "Christianly" to one's activities easily degenerates into a silly game and usually leaves one talking to the converted, not to the world. Our heart was for playing in the world for the good of the world with the best thought and practice we could derive from the best sources of wisdom we could tap. We mined the wisdom of the gospel for life—all of life lived by all people. We did not Christianize consulting, strategy formation or leadership. We sought to influence the world as common people playing in common worlds by others' invitation. Learning how to influence the world deliberately yet naturally has led us on a journey of discovering afresh the wonder and brokenness of being the image of God on this side of the Fall.

Whatever the focusing question, storytelling pervades grace-full conversation. We tell and retell the story of Jesus. We play with the story, using images like those of Max Lucado and Calvin Miller, the poetry of Dave Andrews, the color of Eugene Petersen's *The Message*, Don Francisco's songs of Jesus' life and delightful cameos like Robert Banks's *Going to Church in the First Century*. Biblical characters like Abraham, Moses, Joseph, Daniel, Peter, Paul, Aquila and Priscilla, Barnabas and many others feature again and again. From Genesis to Revelation we string the story together around the grand themes like creation, wisdom and redemption. Time and again we tell what we know of the stories of Jesus and Paul and their friends. We raid the primary sources of everyday life in their times. We ask about what the early believers faced, how they conversed and what they chose.

It doesn't matter where we start or finish. We don't waste our time on methodological pedantry. We talk and draw and map and model our way as our thoughts and feelings diverge and converge. We allow for agendas. We allow for aimlessness. We do require integrity of one another as we work with primary sources—there is no place for twisting texts. We go from big picture to small picture and back to big picture again. The stories of our own lives are woven in as we find the humility and courage to tell them. We resist turning the concerns of our lives into topics, our joys and sorrows into subjects. We work to *know* Jesus and his grace, not just to know *about* him. We wrestle with what we and others have done to bring guilt and fear to our own lives and to others, and we ask what choices will bring grace and freedom. We ask ourselves what we need in order to change. We seek to move beyond a split experience of faith and life. We learn to trust the Spirit of grace in the conversation. This is something of the rhythm of *my* conversations.

Recently I have joined new worlds of conversation on the Internet. Many people are troubled by the proliferation of "virtual" relationships. Me too. Web romances have gone horribly wrong (so do "real" romances). Some evangelical gatekeepers criticize those who find fellowship on the Web. But this is to miss the blessing. The Web is not a sustainable substitute for flesh and blood conversation and love. Almost everyone I have "met" on the Web acknowledges this. But it *is* a meeting place for many who otherwise would disappear from any word of grace. It *is* a realm in which people test out what it might mean to move from guilt and fear to grace and freedom. And it *is* a halfway house for many to reframe what it means to believe.

A lot of what I read on the Internet bothered me deeply at first. It still does at times. It's too loose, too disconnected from the Bible and the gospel. And yet it's not. The Lord holds onto his own. I am learning to trust where the conversation may go—and to realize how much *I* need to learn and change. If church is no longer an option for thousands of disaffected evangelicals who hunger for reality and grace-full conversation, then perhaps the Web is a godsend.

What I am suggesting about grace-full conversation is no game. It has reframed my expectations and experiences of leadership and the gathering. Grace-full conversation is never abstract. Never impersonal. Never objectified. Grace-full conversation is the domain of the Spirit of God. He inhabits every conversation. He does not play games. He frames growth from grace, freedom from fear. He cements grace and freedom with the responsibilities of love. I cannot spectate on these conversations. I cannot draw aside from God or my friends. Both draw me into change that frightens and liberates me. I am called to grow up, to be an adult image. Yet the Spirit also leaves me with the joy of childlikeness. Grace-full conversation is not my invention; it is his and ours. It is as old as the image of God. I cannot prescribe the conversation to you. I would not dare. You already know it. What I offer in conclusion is two pieces of my own story: one sweet, one bittersweet.

The Group with No Name

From the mid to late 1980s I had the privilege of participating in a reframing of theology and church. It occurred in my lounge room, and my friends and I called it CLAG. The genesis of the group was some university students enrolled in an experiential agricultural degree program who invited me to join their conversations about faith, philosophy and their futures. The university course was structured around various "learning groups," so we formed a Christian learning group, hence CLAG (which sounded better than CLIG, CLUG or CLOG). I look back on those years of meeting together every Tuesday night as one of the most satisfying experiences of community in my life.

No one could label us. Was it an "official" ministry? I set out with high ambitions of establishing an alternative quasi-qualification in theology. With good grace we came to abandon such expectations and find our own natural momentum. Was there a curriculum? My friend Bill and I had an idea of where we were going. So did others. Occasionally we got somewhere near our goals; always we reached somewhere better. Were we academic? Sometimes we researched weighty issues, read secondary literature and debated topics for hours. Were we a practical skills course? Sometimes we spent months working together on a common project. Were we a leadership group? Many who joined us over the years moved on to other parts of the city, the country and the globe, planting, teaching and innovating wherever they found themselves. Were we a personal support group? Sometimes we threw out any sense of agenda, spending the night praying and weeping with someone who wept. Were we change agents? We never set out to change anything, not even ourselves. Yet little by little our lives and those of others beyond the group were touched by renewing conversations and acts of compassion.

What Bill and I remember best are the people and our conversations—rich, provocative, soft, tough, robust, thoughtful, sensitive, bombastic, groundbreaking—conversations grounded in everyday life, Jesus and the Bible. There were few demarcations between conversation with one another and with God. Dialogue and prayer followed seamlessly. Exegesis, biblical theology and the concerns of employment, relationships and society wove together in one unfolding conversation of mind and heart, hands and feet. Conversation led to compassion, compassion to action and action to conversation. At the heart of it all beat a vibrant adoration of Father, Son and Spirit for the magnificence of their creation and salvation.

When the World Fell Apart

My fascination with Paul and his world has always been energized by my deep concern over what happens within evangelical circles. When I think of our birthright in Jesus and our heritage in Paul's writings, our practice so often seems impoverished. Unlike Jesus and Paul, we shrink back from reality. We do not like theology to get personal. We do not want our leaders to be human. We are embarrassed at weakness and failure. Our conversations pull back from truth that would set us free. We do not want church services to become real conversations. We do not want grace to step out from behind the pulpit and enter the marketplace of heartache and joy.

In the early 1980s Sue and I and our first child, Miriam, arrived back in Australia after three years studying at a seminary in the United States. We look back with affection on our many friends there and upon the radical seminary within the conservative seminary that we discovered in a few professors. One in particular encouraged us to see ministry as wider than "the clubs" (official church organizations). We returned home and discovered a dozen or so people with a heart for reaching others in a university and air-force town on the rural fringe of the city.

Another couple, Brian and Julie, invited us to share their large house in the woods for a few weeks while we looked for a place to stay. A year later (don't ever invite us to stay!) we moved into our own home in the town. By this time the dozen had become more than fifty meeting in homes and in the local elementary school. We named ourselves a community church. Four years later there were more than one hundred fifty. Most had no church background or had been alienated by former church experiences.

The local pastors' fraternal group feared we would steal their sheep. With the exception of good friends at one mainstream church, local church leaders spread innuendo about us. We had anticipated as such and let it go. We had no desire to steal sheep from other congregations. Our whole intent was to reach those who would not normally go anywhere near church. We often joked, more than half-seriously, that we were "the church you have when you're not having a church."

The group acknowledged Brian's and my gifts for leading, yet we retained our separate employment and business interests. There were no salaries to work in the church. No church buildings. Minimal programs. No constitution. No doctrinal statement. No membership. No ministry was fenced. No two meetings ever looked the same. Brian and I did lots of teaching, but Sunday meetings were led by children or families or small study groups or groups of friends. It continued to grow like this well into the early 1990s. In the end over two hundred gathered each Sunday. Yet the real impact was far greater than this. The population of the town had a fifty percent turnover every four years (the period between each population census). The transient nature of often marginally employed public housing tenants, Air Force personnel and university students, together with the irregular participation of people who lived on the social fringe, meant that the group probably had a direct influence on many hundreds of people over the decade.

None of this was smooth sailing. Brian and I carried a heavy load. I was involved in an unusual honorary chaplaincy ministry at the local university to students and staff in an innovative experiential education program. I positioned my ministry in the faculty around dialogue with students and professors. Many students came to Christ—a professor too. I taught six or seven times a week, and our house always seemed full of students and people in distress. On top of that, I was helping build a consultancy business that would become unique in the world for its approaches to strategy and design. Somewhere in there was my family. Not surprisingly, early in 1990 I burnt out. Then in late 1992 the wheels fell off the group in a big way. But I am getting ahead of myself.

Early in 1988 I left for five weeks of teaching leaders in the foothills of the Indian Himalayas (as I recall, this somewhat anticharismatic teacher was taught far more by these beautiful Pentecostal folk than I ever taught them). Three days after I left, Brian collapsed at home, falling back onto his head on the concrete floor. The fall fractured his skull and caused massive frontal lobe bruising to the brain. The blackout had been triggered by a large acoustic neuroma at the base and side of his skull. When word reached me in India that Brian was fighting for his life, my Australian companion in India was likewise struggling with typhoid. When I arrived home, I found the group dispirited and somewhat confused. Brian went through a series of major surgical interventions to remove the tumor and address the life-threatening hydrocephalus. God brought him through his ordeal remarkably unscathed in comparison to many others with acquired brain injuries. But he did not get off free. For over four years we had worked closely together. People inside and outside of the group had often remarked on how well our partnership worked. But all this was changing.

The timing of Brian's accident roughly coincided with a growing unease about where we were heading as a group. For the first few years very few churched people had joined us. Brian and I had wanted to move in more radical directions. Then somehow we became *the* group to join. We were growing faster than any other local church, and the open style of leadership and participation was increasingly attractive to disillusioned local Christians. But churched folk bring church expectations. Some more traditional Christians began to agitate for the conventions of "real church." They wanted leadership with a capital L, control, paid staff, a "real church service," and more programs. The nature of the conversation began to shift. People wanted me to act like a "real pastor." They wanted me to refrain from any mention of my own inadequacies. To preach "proper sermons." To take a salary.

We began an ill-fated conversation to reframe and extend the leadership base. The conversation meandered for want of the truth. One Sunday I tried to clear the air. What was the real reason we needed to address leadership in the group? It was because Brian's and my friendship was crumbling. No one wanted to hear this. People rushed to reassure us of their support. Their love and fear condemned us to further weaken our already fragile friendship. We remained locked in the mystique and idealism of our former remarkable partnership. The group could not admit that neither Brian nor I nor our partnership was what it once had been.

Ironically, tragically, we began to centralize decision making. For years I had rejected any notion of leadership as being about permission. But now, locked into a dysfunctional, fragmented pattern of *ad hoc* leadership, we began to trip over one another. We vacillated between leading from behind as before and taking a heavy hand. People began to approach each of us about the other's leadership failings. People noticed but said little to our faces. Factional seeds fell into the soil of discontent.

Then came the bombshell. A man in the group was arrested on charges of having sexually molested a young girl some years before at another church. The first I knew of this was an allegation made to me some time before by a couple from a third church regarding their son. They suggested other children may have been involved. I tried to find out what had happened, but wherever I turned I hit a wall of silence: "The Lord has forgiven him and that it is the end of it." I could get nowhere. Finally I shared this with Brian, and we spoke with the man and a family in the group whose children spent large amounts of time with him. We took bad legal advice and believed we could not speak about any of this. Until this time neither of us had any real understanding of the issues of child sexual abuse. Within a few months I was working closely with many survivors of sexual abuse and was immersed in their worlds of depressive illness, therapy and legal action. But it was all too late for the group.

The morning after the arrest, I broke the news to them. People imagined the worst for their own children and were outraged that we had sat on this knowledge. Night after night I went from home to home apologizing and offering to do whatever I could to bring justice, truth and healing. I threw myself into the case. In the thick of it all, my world began to fall apart. My dad died suddenly and unexpectedly. The night after his funeral my mom told me I had had an unborn twin. Two close friends were descending fast into emotional breakdowns and leaning heavily on me for support. One attempted suicide four times. The rawness of all these experiences and much more resurfaced painful aspects of my own childhood. Former friends and colleagues implied I was a failure as a teacher, a leader, a husband and a father.

I descended into a pit of guilt and despair that lasted over three years. I avoided answering telephones or the door. If I was home alone, I would often hide in the garage outside. I resigned from leadership. A few friends in the church stayed close and tried to help, but I was past consoling. Only a handful ever spoke to me about my resignation or anything else. It was like I no longer existed for most people in the church. On Sundays Sue and the children would still go to church. Many times I would hide behind the hedge in our front yard and watch the church folk drive past, then go inside and cry.

I struggled on for another year with the Sunday evening university group I led. Several times I walked out when I was supposed to begin teaching. On the whole, these young people showed far more grace and understanding than the older congregation. But despite their care and prayer, I felt empty, broken and desperately lonely. My mind comprehended grace, but my heart only condemned me. Though I generally withdrew from people, I ached for conversation about Jesus. A few persisted and broke through my isolation. Those conversations are etched on my heart. Most found in my isolation justification for never speaking to me. I withdrew from all formal Christian fellowship for almost three years. My doctoral research into Paul and the Graeco-Roman world provided a glimmer of purpose and meaning. I snatched whatever opportunities for grace-full conversation I found among my corporate clients, former professional colleagues and friends. At times I wanted to die.

Although I had not been a member of any denominational club or parachurch agency for over fifteen years, I was nonetheless relatively well known to other leaders for my book on biblical theology[1] and was respected as a Bible teacher. I now

---

[1]*Days Are Coming: Exploring Biblical Patterns* (Sydney: Hodder & Stoughton, 1989), released in the United States as *The Symphony of Scripture: Making Sense of the Bible's Many Themes* (Downers Grove, Ill.: InterVarsity Press, 1992) and translated into Korean by InterVarsity.

became an embarrassment. One of these leaders was wonderfully supportive and remains a dear friend. Others could not cope with my breakdown, depression and withdrawal from church. I learned that there is no place for weakness in those who should be evangelical leaders. Weakness is unseemly, unbecoming and messy. They wanted me tidied up and back at a "real church." I would hear their verdicts second-hand: "What a shame . . . He had so much potential . . . He always had this weakness . . . He brought it on himself . . . His theology predisposed him to this. . . . These individual churches can never last . . . " Innuendo grew among some. Rarely did anyone speak to me personally. A few would phone from time to time to set me straight. I would listen to them preach to me. Their words of grace piled guilt upon me. Not once did they ask to hear my story.

I meekly acquiesced before this rebuke and guilt for over two years. And then the light slowly came on. Faithful are the conversations of true friends. I wasn't to blame for everything that had happened in the church or in any of my other contexts of ministry. Many others had contributed to the mess and heartache of those years. Foolishness, immaturity and denial had marked the behavior of many who stood back feigning wisdom, maturity and piety. Many marvelous things had happened since the group began. Many people had (re)discovered Jesus and a richness of reality in grace-full conversation and love they have not found anywhere since.

As grace began to grip my heart again, I wrestled with what it meant for those relationships that remained fractured and seemingly irrecoverable. I longed for conversations that would redress the past. I wanted conversations that would put everything right. This happened with some. Slowly, painfully, we began to face the past and extend grace to one another. But with some, this kind of conversation remains seemingly impossible. Grace gripped me with a question: "Which matters most—the desire for others to acknowledge my pain, or my grief at lost friendship? Where does grace lead me? Can I renew fellowship without self-justification?" I learned that healing can coexist with pain. I found the joy of renewed friendship and grace-full conversation.

Nine years later I look back on my "black years" through the lenses of what I have seen in Paul. Likewise, I have seen Paul through the lenses of my experiences in those black years. For many this will discredit my reading of Paul: "He has only seen Paul that way because of what he experienced himself." I make no apologies. Scholars pretend neutrality. I have not offered a neutral, detached reading of Paul, but a living conversation between two worlds.

Paul's knowledge of grace in the dying and rising of Christ took shape in the experiences of his life. Imprisonment, slander, vilification, hunger, sleeplessness and, above all, social embarrassment at not conforming to the expectations of others—each experience gave shape and poignancy to his dying with Christ. The joy of lives transformed gave profound, immediate sensation to rising with Christ. Paul's bewilderment at those who turned back to Jerusalem and the law and his frustration at those who retained the emptiness of Graeco-Roman conventions beckoned the Spirit to lift his heart, to bring peace surpassing knowledge and fellowship in suffering. His deep love for his coworkers and *ekklēsiai* energized their conversations and fueled their hope.

Richer conversation has emerged for many from those black years. A softer spirit, quicker to listen, slower to speak, more open, less judgmental. Sometimes. Sometimes not. Sometimes it is as if I and my friends have learned little. Pride grows in having survived. We may look to the legalists and deserters of the past and thank God that we are not so devoid of grace as they are. We may pride ourselves on our new-found openness to grace, our acceptance of the weak, the abused, the hurting and the depressed. We may shut out those who have hurt us. "They" are unsafe. "They" do not respect our space. We may lounge in our grace-talk, never letting grace push us beyond self-justification. We may sustain a conversation about Jesus that doesn't need him. Yet his Spirit will not leave us here. His grace pushes into our lives. He reframes our conversation. The joy of new life returns. The wonder of the Father's love reframes our hearts and minds. Strength comes. Weakness remains.

Grace is subversive. It undermines the ideals and standards of those of us who cannot tolerate weakness in others (or in ourselves). It undermines the pride of those of us who search out every vestige of unbiblical belief and practice. It undermines the presumption of those of us who preach the pure gospel to cure all ills. It undermines the safety of those of us who throw off the shackles of abusive and codependent relationships only to exclude grace from those who have hurt us. It undermines our need to find the ideal, the answer, the method, the cure. We are left with the weakness of grace-full conversation.

Grace leaves us with Jesus. Jesus leaves us with his Spirit. His Spirit draws us into conversation. The conversation opens us to the wonder and fragility of life. The Father who gave us life bids us live and converse in grace.

Select Bibliography

Works on Paul and the Graeco-Roman World
Penguin Classics provide easy access to good translations of early Greek and Roman authors. New readers might start with the volume on the pre-Socratics titled *Early Greek Philosophy*, then see Plato *Timaeus, Protagoras* and *Meno*; Aristotle *Ethics*; Seneca *Letters from a Stoic*; and Plutarch *Essays*.

Banks, Robert. *Paul's Idea of Community: The Early House Churches in Their Historical Setting*. Sydney: Lancer, 1980.

Clarke, Andrew. *Secular and Christian Leadership in Corinth: A Socio-Historical and Exegetical Study of 1 Corinthians 1–6*. Leiden: E. J. Brill, 1993.

Clarke, Andrew, and Bruce Winter, eds. *The Book of Acts in Its First Century Setting*. Vol. 1, *The Book of Acts in Its Ancient Literary Setting*. Grand Rapids, Mich.: Eerdmans; Carlisle: Paternoster, 1993.

Dihle, Albrecht. *The Theory of Will in Classical Antiquity*. Berkeley: University of California Press, 1982.

Ellis, Earle. *Pauline Theology: Ministry and Society*. Grand Rapids, Mich.: Eerdmans; Carlisle: Paternoster, 1989.

Forbes, Chris. "Comparison, Self-Praise and Irony: Paul's Boasting and Conventions in Hellenistic Rhetoric." *New Testament Studies* 32 (1986): 1–30.

Fox, Robin. *Pagans and Christians in the Mediterranean World from the Second Century AD to the Conversion of Constantine*. London: Penguin, 1988.

Gill, David, and Conrad Gempf, eds. *The Book of Acts in Its First Century Setting*. Vol. 2, *Graeco-Roman Setting*. Grand Rapids, Mich.: Eerdmans; Carlisle: Paternoster, 1994.

Grant, Robert. *Gods and the One God*. Library of Early Christianity 1. Philadelphia: Westminster Press, 1986.

Hafemann, Scott. *Suffering and Ministry in the Spirit: Paul's Defense of His Ministry in 2 Corinthians 2:14—3:3*. Grand Rapids, Mich.: Eerdmans, 1990.

Hall, Barbara. "All Things to All People: A Study of 1 Corinthians 9:19-23." In *The Conversation Continues*, ed. R. T. Fortna and B. R. Gaventa, pp. 137–57. Nashville: Abingdon, 1990.

Hemer, Colin. *The Book of Acts in the Setting of Hellenistic History*. Wissenschaftliche Untersuchungen zum Neuen Testament 49. Tübingen: J.C.B. Mohr, 1989.

Hengel, Martin. *The "Hellenization" of Judaea in the First Century After Christ*. London: SCM Press, 1989.

Hock, Ronald. *The Social Context of Paul's Ministry: Tentmaking and Apostleship*. Philadelphia: Fortress, 1980.

Horsley, Greg, ed. *New Documents Illustrating Early Christianity*, Vols. 1–5. Sydney: Macquarie University Press, 1981–1989.

Judge, Edwin. *The Social Pattern of the Christian Groups in the First Century*. London: Tyndale Press, 1960.

———. *Rank and Status in the World of the Caesars and St. Paul: The Broadhead Memorial Lecture 1981*. Christchurch: University of Canterbury Press, 1982.

———. "Cultural Conformity and Innovation in Paul: Some Clues from Contemporary Documents." *Tyndale Bulletin* 35 (1984): 3–24.

Lefkowitz, Mary, and Maureen Fant, *Women's Life in Greece and Rome: A Source Book in Translation*. London: Duckworth, 1992.

Llewelyn, Stephen, ed. *New Documents Illustrating Early Christianity*, Vols. 6–8. Sydney: Macquarie University Press, 1992–1998.

Malherbe, Abraham. *Social Aspects of Early Christianity*. Baton Rouge: University of Louisiana Press, 1977.

————. *Moral Exhortation: A Greco-Roman Sourcebook*. Library of Early Christianity 4. Philadelphia: Westminster Press, 1986.

————. *Paul and the Thessalonians: The Philosophic Tradition of Pastoral Care*. Philadelphia: Fortress, 1987.

————. *Paul and the Popular Philosophers*. Minneapolis: Fortress, 1989.

Marshall, Peter. *Enmity in Corinth: Social Conventions in Paul's Relations with the Corinthians*. Tübingen: J.C.B. Mohr, 1987.

Meeks, Wayne. *The First Urban Christians: The Social World of the Apostle Paul*. New Haven, Conn.: Yale University Press, 1983.

————. *The Moral World of the First Christians*. Library of Early Christianity 6. Philadelphia: Westminster Press, 1986.

Sampley, J. Paul. *Pauline Partnership in Christ: Christian Community and Commitment in Light of Roman Law*. Philadelphia: Fortress, 1980.

————. *Walking Between the Times: Paul's Moral Reasoning*. Philadelphia: Fortress, 1991.

Theissen, Gerd. *The Social Setting of Pauline Christianity*. Edinburgh: T & T Clark, 1990.

Winter, Bruce. *First Century Christians in the Graeco-Roman World*. Vol. 1, *Seek the Welfare of the City: Christians as Benefactors and Citizens*. Exeter: Paternoster; Grand Rapids, Mich.: Eerdmans, 1994.

Studies of the Changing Shape of Evangelicalism

Bellah, Robert, et al., *Habits of the Heart: Individualism and Commitment in America*. Berkeley: University of California Press, 1985.

Durham, Ron, ed. *What Americans Believe: An Annual Survey of Values and Religious Views in the United States*. Ventura, Calif.: Regal, 1992.

Hunter, James Davison. *Evangelicalism: The Coming Generation*. Chicago: University of Chicago Press, 1987.

Kaldor, Peter, et al. *Winds of Change: The Experience of Church in a Changing Australia*. Sydney: Lancer, 1994.

Rawlyk, George. *Is Jesus Your Personal Savior? In Search of Canadian Evangelicalism in the 1990s*. Kingston: Queen's University Press; Montreal: McGill University Press, 1997.

Smith, Christian. *American Evangelicalism: Embattled and Thriving*. Chicago: University of Chicago Press, 1998.

Conservative Accounts of Weakening Evangelical Distinctives

Armstrong, John, ed. *The Coming Evangelical Crisis*. Chicago: Moody Press, 1996.

The Briefing, an Australian publication published by St. Matthias Press and distributed widely in the United States, the United Kingdom and beyond. See <www.matthiasmedia.com.au>.

Erickson, Millard. *The Evangelical Left: Encountering Postconservative Evangelical Theology*. Grand Rapids, Mich.: Baker, 1997.

————. *Postmodernizing the Faith: Evangelical Responses to the Challenge of Postmodernism*. Grand Rapids, Mich.: Baker, 1998.

McGrath, Alister. *Evangelicalism and the Future of Christianity*. Downers Grove, Ill.: InterVarsity Press, 1998.

Rosell, Garth, ed. *The Evangelical Landscape: Essays on the American Evangelical Tradition*. Grand Rapids, Mich.: Baker, 1996.

Wells, David. *No Place for Truth: Or, Whatever Happened to Evangelical Theology?* Grand Rapids, Mich.: Eerdmans, 1993.

————. *God in the Wasteland: The Reality of Truth in a World of Fading Dreams*. Grand Rapids, Mich.: Eerdmans; Leicester: Inter-Varsity Press, 1994.

─────. *The Bleeding of the Evangelical Church.* Edinburgh: Banner of Truth, 1995.

Calls to Reshape Evangelicalism Largely Within Current Structures

Grenz, Stanley. *Revisioning Evangelical Theology: A Fresh Agenda for the 21st Century.* Downers Grove, Ill.: InterVarsity Press, 1993.

─────. *Created for Community: Connecting Christian Belief with Christian Living.* Grand Rapids, Mich.: Baker, 1998.

Hull, Bill. *Can We Save the Evangelical Church?* Grand Rapids, Mich.: Revell, 1993.

Jones, Bryn. *Radical Church.* London: Destiny Image, 1999.

Petersen, Jim. *Church Without Walls.* Colorado Springs: NavPress, 1992.

Pinnock, Clark, and Robert Brow. *Unbounded Love: A Good News Theology for the 21st Century.* Downers Grove, Ill.: InterVarsity Press, 1994.

Webber, Robert. *Ancient-Future Faith: Rethinking Evangelicalism for a Postmodern World.* Grand Rapids, Mich.: Baker, 1999.

Evangelicalism and Postmodernism

Clapp, Rodney. *A Peculiar People: The Church as Culture in a Post-Christian Society.* Downers Grove, Ill.: InterVarsity Press, 1996.

Dockery, David, ed. *The Challenge of Postmodernism.* Wheaton: Victor, 1995.

Grenz, Stanley. *20th Century Theology: God and the World in a Transitional Age.* Downers Grove, Ill.: InterVarsity Press, 1993.

─────. *A Primer on Postmodernism.* Grand Rapids, Mich.: Eerdmans, 1996.

Middleton, Richard, and Brian Walsh. *Truth Is Stranger Than It Used to Be: Biblical Faith in a Postmodern Age.* Downers Grove, Ill.: InterVarsity Press, 1995.

Phillips, Timothy, and Dennis Okholm, eds. *Christian Apologetics in the Postmodern World.* Downers Grove, Ill.: InterVarsity Press, 1995.

Webber, Robert. *Ancient-Future Faith: Rethinking Evangelicalism for a Postmodern World.* Grand Rapids, Mich.: Baker, 1999.

Narrative Accounts of Breakdowns in Evangelical Meaning

Ulstein, Stefan. *Growing Up Fundamentalist: Journeys in Legalism and Grace.* Downers Grove, Ill.: InterVarsity Press, 1995.

─────. *Pastors off the Record.* Downers Grove, Ill.: InterVarsity Press, 1995.

VanVonderen, Jeff. *Tired of Trying to Measure Up.* Minneapolis: Bethany, 1989.

Yancey, Philip. *What's So Amazing About Grace?* Grand Rapids, Mich.: Zondervan, 1997.

─────. *Church: Why Bother?* Grand Rapids, Zondervan, 1998.

See also many of the books in the section below on pastoral-therapeutic responses to abusiveness in churches.

Pastoral-Therapeutic Responses to Abusiveness in Churches

Alsdurf, Joyce. *Battered into Submission: The Tragedy of Wife Abuse in the Christian Home.* Downers Grove, Ill.: InterVarsity Press, 1989.

Beed, Cara. *Cultures of Secrecy and Abuse: A Paradox for Churches.* Melbourne: Beed, 1998.

Blue, Ken. *Healing Spiritual Abuse: How to Break Free from Bad Church Experiences.* Downers Grove, Ill.: InterVarsity Press, 1993.

Born, Marilyn. *"Why Does He Hug Us So Tightly?" Sexual Abuse in Ministerial Relationships.* Melbourne: YWCA, 1996.

Chrnalogar, Mary Alice. *Twisted Scriptures.* Grand Rapids, Mich.: Zondervan, 2000.

Enroth, Ronald. *Churches That Abuse.* Grand Rapids, Mich.: Zondervan, 1992.

─────. *Recovering from Churches That Abuse.* Grand Rapids, Mich.: Zondervan, 1994.

Fortune, Marie. *Is Nothing Sacred? The Story of a Pastor, the Women He Sexually Abused and the Congregation He Nearly Destroyed.* San Francisco: Harper, 1992.

Grenz, Stanley, and Roy Bell. *Betrayal of Trust: Sexual Misconduct in the Pastorate.* Downers Grove, Ill.: InterVarsity Press, 1995.

Horst, Elizabeth. *Recovering the Lost Self: Shame Healing for Victims of Clergy Abuse.* Collegeville, Minn.: Liturgical Press, 1998.

Johnson, Davis, and Jeff VanVonderen. *The Subtle Power of Spiritual Abuse: Recognizing and Escaping Spiritual Manipulation and False Spiritual Authority Within the Church.* Minneapolis: Bethany, 1991.

Models for Reshaping-Discarding Evangelicalism

Andrews, Dave. *Christi-Anarchy.* Oxford: Lion, 1999.

Banks, Robert, and Julia Banks. *The Church Comes Home.* Peabody, Mass.: Hendrickson, 1998.

McLaren, Brian. *Finding Faith: A Self-Discovery Guide for Your Spiritual Quest.* Grand Rapids, Mich.: Zondervan, 1999.

Riddell, Mike. *Threshold of the Future: Reforming the Church in the Post-Christian West.* London: SPCK, 1998.

Riddell, Mike, et al. *The Prodigal Project.* London: SPCK, 2000. (Book and CD Rom)

Rigma, Charles. *Dare to Journey.* Sydney: Albatross, 1992.

Snyder, Howard. *Radical Renewal: The Problem of Wineskins Today.* Touch, 1996.

Tomlinson, David. *The Post Evangelical.* London: Triangle, 1995.

Web Sites

www.ifas.org/wa/index.html	Walk Away—autobiographies by ex-fundamentalists and ex-evangelicals. Most now call themselves atheists.
www.brow.on.ca	why people quit going to church
www.next-wave.org	being a Christian without the normal trappings and its possibilities in the postmodern culture
www.geocities.com/Athens/Cyprus/3743	one person's journey to alternative churches in America, Britain and New Zealand
http://members.tripod.com/nineoclockservice/postevangelicalinks.htm	many links to the growing postmodern-Christian and alternative worship scenes in the United Kingdom and America
www.mailbase.ac.uk/lists-p-t/post-modern-christian	formal and informal articles and discussion groups for postmodern Christians
http://montrosebaptist.com/pages/abuse.shtml	resources dealing with spiritual abuse within mainstream and fringe groups
www.thirdway.org.uk	the modern world through Christian eyes
http://home.onet.co.uk/~andii/newagevangelical.html	the "New Age Evangelical" (read: "evangelicals for a new period")

Index of Ancient Authors

Literary Works

About the Author

Mark Strom lives on a small farm on the rural fringe of Sydney, Australia, with his wife, Susan, and three teenage children, Miriam, Luke and Hannah; border collies Pippin and Abbey; George the horse; and Bird the bird.

Mark likes to think of his life in seasons. First came the chronically ill season (to age fifteen). Then came the "I'd prefer not to remember that period" season stretching into his early twenties. Overlapping somewhat are the various educational seasons. Somewhere in there were the "let's plant a church for people who hate church" season, the "let's start a theological center for people who don't like theological centers" season and the "let's do university ministry differently" season. Overlapping some of these and still continuing is the season of "let's build a business around the need of senior organizational leaders for rigor, integrity and wisdom." Holding all together is the ongoing bliss of being married to Sue and father to three great kids.

Mark believes passionately in the need for wisdom, grace and conversation in all areas of life. He considers himself highly privileged to partner government and business leaders as they wrestle with the personal and organizational implications of wisdom, and to partner Christians from many walks of faith and life as they explore in conversation what it might mean to move from guilt and fear to grace and freedom.

Mark hopes *Reframing Paul* will encourage you in your own conversations. He would be glad to hear from you at <mstrom@hawknet.com.au>.